Michael Bray
Powers of the Mind

Michael Bray is Associate Professor of Philosophy at Southwestern University. His research focuses on populisms and the question of transition.

Michael Bray

Powers of the Mind

Mental and Manual Labor in the Contemporary Political Crisis

[transcript]

Bibliographic information published by the Deutsche Nationalbibliothek

The Deutsche Nationalbibliothek lists this publication in the Deutsche Nationalbibliografie; detailed bibliographic data are available in the Internet at http://dnb.d-nb.de

Cover layout: Kordula Röckenhaus, Bielefeld
Typeset by Francisco Bragança, Bielefeld
Printed by docupoint GmbH, Magdeburg
Print-ISBN 978-3-8376-4147-9
PDF-ISBN 978-3-8394-4147-3
https://doi.org/10.14361/9783839441473

Content

Preface

If there were a single quote epitomizing the kind of thought this book intends to criticize and displace, it might be this reflection, on the occasion of Marx's 200th birthday, in the pages of *The Economist* (May 3, 2018):

Marx's greatest failure [...] was that he underestimated the power of reform—the ability of people to solve the evident problems of capitalism through rational discussion and compromise. He believed history was a chariot thundering to a predetermined end and that the best that the charioteers can do is hang on. Liberal reformers, including his near contemporary William Gladstone, have repeatedly proved him wrong. They have not only saved capitalism from itself by introducing far-reaching reforms but have done so through the power of persuasion. The "superstructure" has triumphed over the "base", "parliamentary cretinism" over the "dictatorship of the proletariat."

Both the blithe dismissal of Marx and the righteous assurance of the liberal reformer (for whom *The Economist* is surely the journal of choice) are underpinned here by a belief in *the powers of the mind*. Rational discussion, compromise, persuasion, are presented as, in and of themselves, powers which can be levelled not only against Marx's supposed "theory of society driven forward by economic forces" but against those economic forces themselves. See capitalism bend to the will of rational persuasion! Through discussion and compromise, workers are enfranchised, "economic concentrations" are broken up in waves of regulatory reform, cycles are smoothed, panics contained. We can learn from Marx about certain faults of capitalism, the author(s) admit, but the proper response to those faults is a new wave of liberal persuasion.

The article ends on a somber note, registering the rise of populist unrest, but it attributes this development to the faults of capitalism, not any intrinsic limit to the project of liberal reform. To the extent reform can be blamed at all, it is in the lack of will of today's would-be reformers, who "are proving sadly inferior to their predecessors in terms of both their grasp of the crisis and their ability to generate solutions." If the super-structure is an apparent shamble, if Parliament seems particularly cre-tinous, time to put on our thinking caps and get to work.

One wonders sometimes at the capacity of the liberal mind to retain its equanimity. Recent years have been difficult, after all, and the supposed powers of the mind have been sorely tested. Those who claim to bear those powers have appeared both overassertive and shell-shocked, supremely confident in the forces of reason yet stunned by the apparent incapacity of the masses to enter into sober discussion and polite compromise. They might come to terms with the resurgence of an atavistic populism amongst the latterly civilized, as in Latin America, but a similar, if more rightward, drift in Europe and the U.S. has been unnerving. If the stern faces of EU officials rejecting any settlement with Syriza and the Greek referendum suggest some other force than compromise at work, the elec-toral victories of Brexit and Trump produced more dispirited responses. On social media and mainstream news, one could watch the "rational" reaction veer into insult: these deplorables, who voted for something they didn't even understand, well, they're going to get what they deserved! The powers of the mind, it seems, could only be undermined by rank stupidity.

The contempt, of course, is mutual. For several decades, there has been a growing resentment of the world of managerial control, credentialed expertise, happiness industries, computerized assessments, financial and professional advice. Amongst wide swathes of the dominated, as well as growing segments of the middle and upper classes (especially those who, by reasons of geography and/or lower-status credentials, are excluded from the most elite circles), the sense that "they think they know better than you" became a political rallying cry. As center-left parties turned decisively towards the interests of suburban professionals and global finance after the 1970s, as meritocracy became a "rare point of consensus" in partisan politics (Hayes 2012: 46; Geismer 2017), the powers of the mind could also come to seem a very real thing amongst those excluded from them. From this angle, every humiliation of expertise might appear to be a blow for freedom, the seizing back of popular sovereignty from an out-of-touch elite remaking the world in their own pretentious image. Meanwhile, increasing numbers register their contempt by simply not voting.

All sides of the contemporary political crisis (save those who abstain) tend to represent themselves as saviors of democracy, conceived either as popular sovereignty (of, perhaps, the "real" people) or an elite mechanism for reasoned compromise. The former has fallen prey to its own forms of elite manipulation, fostering the racist, xenophobic, and patriarchal reactions latent (or not so latent) in the people-nation form of the modern state. The latter presents itself as the last bulwark against regression and pathology, defenders of the norms and niceties of civilization. Or else, in its softer or more desperate moments, it has invoked an empathetic solution: maybe we just need to better understand, speak the language of, the white working class, and then we will be able to see that we all share common interests.

The guiding intuition of this book is that, behind such confrontations, as well as their present incapacity to reach any satisfying denouement, lies a key, and increasingly important, aspect of the historical and political development of capitalist productive relations: the separation of mental from manual labor. That separation, at least in its capitalist form, orig- inates in capital's drive for relative surplus value: ever-increasing incre- ments of "surplus time" in the workday, eked out, primarily, through increases in the efficiency and productivity of labor processes.[1] The management practices and technological fixed capital that facilitate such "improvements" rest, at their base, on a process that Marx anatomized and Frederick Winslow Taylor raised to a "science": the removal of the design and oversight of labor processes from the direct producers them- selves and their operation, through the intermediation of managers, as a transformed, externalized knowledge. What is critical to see, and much of what follows will focus on its multiple implications, is that the generation and monopolization of these new forms of knowledge are not simply a matter of specialization, allowing for greater insight or refinement, but are also a mechanism for wresting *control* of the labor process from laborers themselves. Knowledge and power are linked within the relations of pro-

---

[1] | Which is not to say that the pursuit of absolute surplus value, the lengthening of the working day, has vanished, as the ongoing policing of bathroom breaks or the lines for security checks that tech and retail employees must often wait in prior to and after their paid workday shows.

duction, where mental labor performs the ideological and political *functions*, and borrows the *power*, of capital, not those of some autonomous, empowered mind.

This restructuring of the relations of production, which reached its first peak in the late-19th century era of corporatization and mass production, also radiated out, by way of its political and ideological forms and the material powers of capital, to reshape social and political relations in general. In the early 20th century, the ideology of specialized control functions migrated into the capitalist state under the burgeoning Progressive efforts to reform it. Those efforts intensified representative democracy's presumption of the ignorance of the people, expanding into control over the social reproduction processes of the laboring and unemployed masses, though mediated through the unifying operations of the capitalist state and its legitimating discourse of the "people-nation" (Poulantzas 1978). With that Progressive project, I will argue, began the long-developing roots of today's crisis.

The appeal to the powers of the mind that appears in *The Economist's* analysis represents a failure to understand the roots and the historical evolution of those powers, but also the fact that those powers are, by and large, only borrowed. They must derive ultimately from some other base in social relations: control over resources and products, capacities for organization, or what C.L.R. James called "the always unsuspected power of the mass movement" (cited by Haider 2018: 114). Persuasion only works insofar as it articulates a position that furthers or strengthens an existing power. Compromises always express the balance of forces. The very notion of "the powers of the mind" is ideological in the sense that it articulates specifically capitalist productive relations, legitimating and (re)producing them, rendering them coherent to the very people engaged in them, while also obscuring their roots in class struggle. In this context, the idea of an "objective" knowledge, the practice of a supposedly "rational" politics, function to exclude and control the masses from whom mental labor has been separated.

The political manifestations of that separation are particularly acute today, for the same reason that it is sometimes taken to have disappeared: the disintegration of the industrial working-class as the recognized agent of production and leftist politics. Decimated by waves of automation and global logistics chains, attacked politically by the strike-breaking initiatives and regulatory and legal changes that weakened traditional unions, the working class has not, as some would have it, disappeared but it has disaggregated, atomized, losing much of its sense of a shared identity and common cause (which was always itself partial, leaning on whiteness and maleness). Center-left parties have implicitly identified mental laborers, professional knowledge workers, as the agent to fill that void: a progressivism unbalanced by an organized working class. In the process, those mental laborers have offered themselves up, unwittingly and uncomprehendingly, as a focal point for the resentments that the borrowed power and privileges of mental labor have accrued over the course of the 20th century.

In that sense, contemporary progressives (or liberals)[2] make the same mistake as *The Economist*, as do many of their opponents: imagining that ideas, insights, expertise, are their own source of legitimate power. Insofar as the source of today's increasingly pervasive control-functions is taken to be elite professionals or knowledge workers alone, rather than capital, they become the focal point of a suspicion and resentment that progressives have had difficulty understanding. The tendency to generalize this mistake – to see ideas as (ideally) the only meaningful source of political agency and authority – only exacerbates this failure, making manual labor and class struggle illegible. Here originates the sense of futility in progressives' responses to the contemporary crisis.

Perhaps more troublingly, here also lies the roots of a number of radical or Marxist responses. Many on the left, in other words, have embraced collectivized versions of this perspective, hailing knowledge workers, as a universal figure or avant-garde, a new revolutionary agent. These political utopias of the empowered mind rely, implicitly or explicitly, on an idea of autonomous thought as the ground of social production and transformation, while consigning the majority of the disaggregated working class to political apathy or worse. Though certainly not the only cause, a significant portion of the weakness of the contemporary left (from the center to the radical margins) might be traced to this drift into alignment with elements of the ideological notion of a "knowledge economy." To take advantage of recent stirrings, to resuscitate a mass politics of the left, requires the reversal of this drift, a critical awareness of the effects of the

---

2 | I use these terms more or less interchangeably, while preferring the former for its historical resonances. "Liberal," is also used here in the specifically U.S. sense of center-left, though that center-left is certainly liberal in the old sense as well.

ongoing separation of mental from manual labor, and efforts to begin its dismantling. This book seeks to contribute to that project by offering an initial framing of its terms.

This book was conceived and written quickly (at least by academic standards), a fact that explains some aspects of the approach taken. Its discussions focus primarily on the United States and are traced at a relatively impressionistic level, though informed by social history. More detailed elaborations of specific historical episodes, functions, and conceptions of mental labor would no doubt be of value. So too would a more global perspective on its historical development, allowing for comparative studies between nations and a clearer sense of the combined and uneven development of the separation, in which the functions of mental labor remain, to some degree, monopolized by the overdeveloped countries, while large segments of the populations of underdeveloped ones are cast off into surplus labor armies. At the same time, working through the project led in several unanticipated directions, requiring condensed efforts to familiarize myself with wide and relatively contentious literatures on complex questions. While recognizing the irony of either claiming or disavowing "expertise" in the context of the argument being made here, I also remain responsible for any errors or omissions.

These potential weaknesses have their virtues. Focusing on the U.S. allows the discussion to highlight what would be key and driving developments in any global history as well. The rise of scientific management and of military-funded research into strategic rationalities and information technologies were not unique to this country but reached a particular pitch here (shaped by the unique strengths of its capital and its state in each instance), such that they were recognized by contemporaries as prototypically U.S. phenomena, the basis for widespread processes of "Americanization." Likewise, the broad sweep of the argument makes, I believe, a compelling case for the pervasive effects of the separation of mental from manual labor, its structuring of social and political life as a whole. In the best case, the argument here might prompt more careful, detailed exploration of specific issues, including ones not covered (ecological politics, for example, in light of its own failures at persuasion). At the same time, the hope is that the links traced here to the contemporary political crisis might play some role in informing radical responses to it.

Chapter 1 begins the argument by analyzing the meaning and implications of today's "political utopias of the empowered mind," both those
of (neo)liberal authors who celebrated the potentials of the "knowledge
economy" and those of several contemporary Marxists who strangely echo
that discourse. Chapter 2 provides the theoretical frame for the book,
explaining the meaning and implications of the division of mental and
manual labor for Marx, supplemented by Poulantzas and Gramsci's discussions of its specifically political dimensions.

Chapters 3 and 4 discuss what I identify as the two dominant (and partially opposed) ideological formations of mental labor in the 20th century.
The first, developed out of early managerial discourses, presented knowledge workers as capable of establishing social peace between warring
capital and labor, crystallizing in early 20th century Progressivism. Its
identification of professional expertise with the public good fostered a
belief in the autonomous power of science and rationality, ignoring their
central dependence on the state and the power of capital. Social peace, on
such terms, would always be brokered on terms advantageous to accumulation. In the context of the Cold War, on the other hand, a more aggressive
defense of capitalism's global expansion was identified with the defense
of freedom, as the military apparatus of the state underwrote new forms
of strategic rationality that simultaneously militarized and economized
politics, yielding an ideology of command and control that would be
applied, in the face of economic crisis, to the home front.

Chapters 5 and 6 trace out key effects of these dual ideologies of
mental labor, with a particular focus on locating the growing weakness of
progressive responses. Chapter 5 traces the manner in which race came to
be conceptualized through the frame of the division between mental and
manual labor, first by accounting for racism as an irrational prejudice of
uneducated whites and, then, by realizing "diversity" as a shared identity
of professional knowledge workers. These forms of settlement have proved
extremely volatile today, consigning the majority of racialized population
to surveillance and incarceration, while allowing for racist mobilizations
of resentment over mental labor's control functions. Chapter 6 contex-
tualizes two common analytical and political errors of the contemporary
left – the celebration of information and communications technology as
vehicles for liberation and the dismissal of finance as a mere parasite on
the so-called real economy – as distortions caused by the blindness of

mental labor to its own infrastructural conditions, a blindness to where the power of capital is located.

Chapter 7 attempts to identify an alternative approach to the contemporary political crisis, grounded in a few aspects of Gramsci's "philosophy of praxis." If we cannot overcome the institutionalized separation of mental and manual labor by simple fiat, what avenues are available for projects undertaking the long process of its dismantling? I point here to the renewal of workers' inquiry as a basis for clarifying the changing political and ideological character of the relations of production and identifying modes of resistance within them. At the political level, I point to the resurgence of populism as a site where the project of rendering common sense coherent can begin today. If these dual suggestions appear tentative and even in a certain tension with one another, that is a function not only of the provisional character of this book – which seeks to propose a new frame rather than provide a definitive formulation if it – but also of the tentative character of our political situation, which cannot build on the foundation of a self-conscious working class (or fraction thereof) that Gramsci could presuppose. New experiments are needed in the face of mental labor's expanding control, by way of borrowed powers, over production and politics.

Acknowledgements

Never having felt entirely at home in academia, I am grateful to colleagues and friends who, over the years, have made work within it enjoyable and meaningful. Those, in particular, include Bob Richardson, Amy Wendling, Ella Campi, Bruce Gilbert, Rick Lee, Shannon Winnubst, Molly Jensen, Elaine Craddock, Laura Hobgood, Patrick Hajovsky, and my present philosophy colleagues, Phil Hopkins and Omar Rivera, who have shaped an undergraduate program that avoids most illusions about the powers of the mind. I am also grateful to the many students who approached their education as something much more important than the obtaining of credentials. Their passions and commitments pushed me to understand many things better, and encouraged me to pursue projects, including this book, well removed from my academic training. Those I have learned much from include Marie Draz, Auzimuth Jackson, Steven Powers, Kevin Lentz, Kenny Knowlton and Katie Kelly, who also made the index. The institutional support of Southwestern University has been critical in supporting my often-circuitous path to these projects.

The seed of this book was a paper, "The Limits of Mental Labor: Class & Politics Today," presented at the *Historical Materialism* conference in November 2016. Thanks to Jakob Horstmann, who suggested turning it into a monograph and edited the result; this book would literally not exist without him. An early form of parts of Chapter 5 appeared on the *Historical Materialism* blog as "The White Working Class Does Not Exist: Thinking Through Liberal Postracialism" (Sept. 20, 2017). An early form of one section of Chapter 7 appeared on the *Latinx Spaces* website as "Is There a Left Populism?" (April 3, 2017). I am grateful to both for the opportunity to share work in progress.

Thank you to my parents who, while not always understanding, have never failed to offer unqualified support. And to Luifran, for his growing political engagement and updates on the internecine conflicts of local groupuscules.

This book is for Vanessa, who brooks no high-minded nonsense and yet believes in me, and for Natalia, who says that one day she will read it. May it help you question your own powers, bear, and discover new sources for the ones you will share.

Chapter 1: Political Utopias of the Empowered Mind

> Every economy is a knowledge economy, but not every economy has been called a knowledge economy (JESSOP 2012: 68).

The ideal of autonomous thought has a long philosophical heritage in the West, of which Aristotle's unmoved mover and Kant's vision of enlightenment as the release from self-incurred tutelage are two key signposts. The rational ground that Western philosophy long sought to articulate promised an identification between the forms of knowing and the forms of being that would confirm the priority of thought (Lee 2004). In modernity, the dream of a self-grounded mode of knowledge, shorn of dependence on material or social relations, came to promise not only an escape from the limitations those relations imposed upon us but also a form of instrumental control over them. Autonomous knowledge came to be understood as the condition for empowered minds.

In recent decades, this heritage found a new form. Knowledge, it was supposedly discovered, had become an autonomous *economic* resource. And, in such guise, it could be seen as fulfilling its destiny, becoming the basis for an expansive, accelerating production of ever-new and ever-improving material and social conditions. The economy of today, it is often said, is a "knowledge economy" and, in such an economy, knowledge has been, at last, unleashed, freed from bureaucratic and governmental meddling, a power of its own, harnessed to provide an unparalleled series of innovations and improvements.

This rhyming of reason with economic expansion, however, has generally been structured by series of fuzzy assertions and equations, suggesting nothing so much as efforts to obscure or justify something left largely unstated. What precisely is meant by knowledge, how it functions as a "resource," or what justifies its placement at the center of the economy, have often been left more implied than articulated, in celebratory discourses wherein everyone has (or is about to) become a knowledge worker. To the extent that such rhetoric does cohere, it has often been through a substitution that seems to undermine its central claim. If, in the knowledge economy, knowledge is meant to supplant capital (such that one of its key proselytizers, Peter Drucker [1993], dubbed it a "post-capitalist society"), it does so only by identifying itself with capital, adopting its logic and goals. Knowledge, become an economic resource, falls under the tutelage of economics, articulating a utopic model of contemporary capitalism. Its silent, inverse side, the first section of this chapter will argue, is an increasing subordination and precarity of those excluded from recognized forms of knowledge.

If that is so, then the appropriation of elements of such discourse by the left must appear inherently suspect. In the remainder of the chapter, I trace the extent to which such elements, centered on the roles of knowledge (and its workers) in contemporary production and politics, have come to shape analyses of contemporary political movements, including in two of the most influential theoretical trajectories of contemporary Marxism. Such accounts, I argue, draw on specific notions of "the powers of the mind" (or of mental laborers) for their visions of communist potential and social transformation. In doing so, they also obscure the ongoing impacts of the division between mental and manual labor, consigning their strategic visions to peculiar forms of ephemerality and impotence. Tracing the meaning, history, and contemporary political implications of that division will be the work of the following chapters.

The Struggle for the Knowledge Economy

The idea of the knowledge economy developed in tandem with the process of "deindustrialization" and the supposed disappearance of the working class in the U.S. Knowledge was replacing labor or else labor was becoming knowledge work. Already in 1973, Daniel Bell's account of "post-industrial society" suggested that knowledge had become "a fundamental resource" in economic production (1973: 212). By the 1990s, this idea had become pervasive. Peter Drucker would capture the spirit of the times by hyperbolically surpassing Bell: "knowledge is the only meaningful resource today. The traditional 'factors of production' – land (i.e., natural resources), labor, and capital – have not disappeared, but they have become secondary. They can be obtained, and obtained easily, provided there is knowledge" (1993: 42). More cautious, as befits its institutional responsibilities, the World Bank required a few more years to transition from its 1994 position that knowledge was "a major factor in economic development" to its 2002 view that knowledge was "the most important factor" and that "economic growth is as much a process of knowledge accumulation as capital accumulation" (1994, 2002; cited by Caffentzis 2013: 99).

The only problem was that what such claims meant by "knowledge," how they isolated and identified its leading role in specific industries, remained uncertain. One might think, for example, that pharmaceutical companies produce medicines but, for Drucker, their "actual product" is "knowledge; pill and prescription ointment are no more than packaging for knowledge" (1993: 182). On one level, the meaning here seems clear enough: pharmaceutical production involves large investments in scientific research. But, as George Caffentzis observes, there is an "extraordinary fuzziness" in the terminology such claims employ and the measurements offered to justify them. The growth of "the knowledge-based industry sector" and increasing investments in "knowledge-based intangibles," for example, are two central elements in the World Bank's assessment. Knowledge-based sectors are said to include "high and medium-high technology industries; communications services; finance, insurance, and other business services; and community, social, and personal services." Knowledge-based intangibles point to "training R&D, patents, licensing, design, and marketing" (Caffentzis 2013: 99-100). But the distinctions made to produce these measures seem dubious at best: in what sense do these sectors and intangibles really involve "knowledge" in a manner absent in other sectors or elements of production?

What brings together banks, pornographic film companies, software design and communication corporations, airplane manufacturers under the knowledge-based industry sector rubric that excludes auto companies, real estate firms, restaurants, mines, and farms? Are the former more dependent on knowledge than the latter, do the former create significantly more knowledge than the latter, and/or do the workers in the former create significantly more than those in the latter? (ibid: 100)

There is no clear sense in which that is so. Every enterprise, like every form of work, involves knowledge and learning; almost all capitalist production has, at least since the era of what Marx called "large scale manufacture," involved investments in technologies of production and in certain forms of training and (de)skilling workers. What then motivates the differentiation of some sectors as "knowledge-based," such that their growth is presented as characterizing the entire economy as one defined by "knowledge"? What is knowledge such that it can be said to have increased, such that it can be used to obtain other resources, including labor?

One factor, often implied, would seem to be the quantity, if not of knowledge ("So far, at least, it is not possible to quantify knowledge," Drucker regrets [1993: 185]), then of capital invested in its production. But that would hardly seem to establish the priority of knowledge as such or its replacement of capital. Caffentzis points to the increasing interest of capital in intellectual property as a motivating factor (2013: 106-108).[1] Sectors defined as "knowledge-based" would then be those in which the copywriting of specific productions, methods, algorithms, designs, etc. is largest, both in numbers of copyright sought and in the amount of revenue they yield. Here too, though, a definition of knowledge is circumvented by appeal to a quantity of value. As Caffentizis suggests, an emphasis on intellectual property law allows exponents of the knowledge economy "to speak of intellectual commodities without referring to knowledge or cognition at all" (ibid: 108). But it also tacitly identifies knowledge with capital, as a quantity of value bound for valorization.

In Bell's early account, the emphasis had been on "research and development," science and technology. The "most crucial group in the knowledge society," he insisted, "is scientists" (1973: 216). But two decades later, Drucker is after something more expansive, something commensurate with knowledge's role as *the* central resource of the economy. Knowledge, therefore, is defined as "the means to obtain social and economic results," "information effective in action," "systematic technology" that produces results. Drucker attributes the rise of capitalism itself to the change in knowledge's meaning from "self-knowledge" to this form of technical efficiency (1993: 28-29, 42, 46). And, perhaps most tellingly, he casts *man-*

---

1 | It should be noted that answering this question is not the intention of his essay and he touches on this point only in the context of a broader critique of theorists of "cognitive capitalism," on which, see below.

agement as a kind of meta-knowledge, "the generic organ of the knowledge society," responsible for "making knowledge productive," "supplying knowledge to find out how existing knowledge can be best applied" (ibid: 42-43, 190).

Articulated in this way, however, what is, in fact, novel about the knowledge economy? On Drucker's own account, such instrumentalized knowledge lies at the historical roots of capitalism and, as we will see in Chapter 3, an insistence on "science" as means for increasing economic productivity and efficiency defined the rise of managerialism at the turn of the 20th century. If, as Ernst Mandel argued, Bell's "post-industrial society" is actually *"the period in which all branches of the economy are fully industrialized for the first time"* (1975: 191, original emphasis), Drucker's "post-capitalist society" appears as the complementary image of an era in which managerial forms of organization are extended to all forms of profit-making. Thus, Drucker's justification for the notion of post-capitalism turns on the increasing wealth concentrated in employee pension funds, and the control of pension fund managers over their investment. Such managers, Drucker suggests, "are the only true 'capitalists' in the United States. The 'capitalists' have thus themselves become employees in the post-capitalist knowledge society [...] One implication is that capital now serves the employee, where under capitalism the employee served capital" (ibid: 67). Yet, capital is an odd servant, which imposes its own goal on its purported master. Knowledge, for Drucker, has no goal or meaning distinct from those of capital: productivity, efficiency, accumulation.

If such employees ostensibly supplant capital, they also render non-knowledge workers seemingly irrelevant in Drucker's account. He does not deny that manual labor will persist ("Plenty of people will always be needed who can bring only muscle to the job") but they vanish from his account after a paragraph or two, yielding to the "technicians" who will be "the greatest employment need of the next decades" (ibid: 73). In this sense, his account does appear to differ dramatically from Progressive era programs of managerialism, for which the explicit focus was on the control of manual laborers. But this difference is less than it initially appears, for what the knowledge economy thesis ultimately portends is that all workers should be managed *as if* they were knowledge workers.

Initially, this might appear a good thing, for Drucker insists on the fact that knowledge work requires a certain kind of autonomy, though, tellingly, he does not use that word. What concerns him, after all, is not the liberation of knowledge workers but the increasing efficiency and productivity of their work, once granted the ability to direct and decide their own work-tasks (given goals that are already commensurate with capital's). Freed from niggling oversight, each knowledge worker will do more, but each must also take on more responsibility for the objectives and results of their own work and that of the organization by which they are employed (ibid: 108). This means, in turn, that objectives must become more tightly focused and manageable and that organizations must be transformed in tandem, from the hulking, conglomerated bureaucracies of late-capitalist states and corporations, to streamlined, nimble, outsourcing machines that "will focus on their core tasks. For the rest, they will work with other organizations in a bewildering variety of alliances and partnerships" (ibid: 96). Freed from their tutelage, augmented by computational and informational technologies, knowledge workers become superior instruments of economic expansion. But their power is limited to the range of what they can be assessed as responsible for: flexible firms retain the "power to make decisions about people – whom to hire, whom to fire, whom to promote," as well as the "power to establish the discipline needed to produce results" (ibid: 104).

In this light, the idea of the knowledge economy can be seen for what it most fundamentally is: not the identification of a novel economic form so much as a bid for the transformation of firms and, ultimately, society as a whole, in a manner that will make workers more productive and efficient: focused, flexible, task-oriented, team-based, innovative, collaborative across the public/private divide, distributing responsibility for their fates to individuals (and so without job security, seniority privileges, and so on). The ambiguous measures offered to prove knowledge's central economic role function as justifications for that transformation, for the managerial strategies, governmental policies, and cultural norms now more commonly known as neoliberalism. Firms structured by the ostensible imperatives of knowledge work, firms in which *all* workers were ostensibly knowledge workers, were firms that would no longer recognize the collective protections and securities that labor unions had long fought for, while they also intensified control – by means of assessments of workers' responsibility – over a knowledge consigned to deciding relatively trivial details.

To be a "knowledge worker" in such conditions (outside of the highest positions, which design and implement such models and their assessment, wielding the powers of the firm) was not a piece of luck, but a misfortune, as the ever-increasing inequality in knowledge economies has made clear. If the US economy, for example, grew 230 percent from 1979-2011, riding waves of bubbles and crashes, the income of the bottom 80 percent of its citizens grew only 16 percent. Over that same period, consumer debt soared from $263 billion in 1978 to $3,330 billion in 2015, as working families sought to offset stagnant incomes (Cahill and Konings 2017: 121). One of the "intangibles" of knowledge turned out to be its capacity to design leaner systems of automated production and global logistical systems, allowing for outsourcing and offshoring beyond even Drucker's dreams. As we will see later, the intensified routinization of "knowledge work" was another result.

Since the introduction of this narrative, of course, efforts have been made to articulate some kind of general benefits of this knowledge economy, if often in aspirational, meritocratic form ("opportunities for advancement and recognition" [Drucker 1993: 96]). The speed and availability of information, not its commodification, is stressed (Carlaw et al., 2012). Here too lies the emphasis on the wider availability of education, the increasing ranks of postsecondary students. Yet, once inserted into the vision of *effective* knowledge, education too had to change: "the school will have to commit itself to results. It will have to establish its 'bottom line,' the performance for which it should be held responsible and for which it is being paid" (Drucker 1993: 209). To be effective, education too has to be adaptive, flexible, directed not towards knowledge as an "end in itself" but as a form of instrumentalized autonomy. "Lifelong learning" becomes a model, not of some contemplative "life of the mind, but of a frenzied, anxious quest to become employable, to remain up-to-date in one's "skill set," innovative in one's self-presentation, invested, above all else, in one's "human capital" (Jessop 2012). All this too became part of the responsibility of workers, and an individualizing justification for failure.

Brighter versions of this universalizing story are also told. Richard Florida's celebratory discourse of the "creative economy," for example, saw value in all forms of knowledge and creativity. Even those forms which do not directly obtain economic results are effective in producing the kinds of diverse, artistic, walkable, sustainable, user- and dog-friendly, urban environments to which productive creative workers flock, fostering creative synergy. Economic development and urban renaissance (that is, gentrification) become coextensive. Further, Florida insisted, "[e]very job can and must be *creatified*; every worker must be able to harness his or her own inner entrepreneur" (Florida 2012: 388). Yet, his account of how precisely this might happen remained vague and underdeveloped.[2]

As the gentrification of urban cores and the celebration of innovation and creation have continued apace, the submerged counter-discourse of economic polarization or a "dual economy" has returned with greater force, highlighting the growing differentiation of roughly twenty to thirty percent of the population – highly skilled workers, managers, professionals, with college degrees – from the rest of the workforce.[3] Innovations in and applications of information technology, telematics, and microelectronics have not led to the universalization of empowered knowledge work but to the increasing intensities of labor driven by Toyotism and logistics, to unemployment, underemployment, increased flexibility and precariousness, lower wages, and the spread of colonial and postcolonial forms of "superexploitation" into the global North (Sotelo Valencia 2018).

Even Florida has grown uncertain about the narrative. His most recent book, *The New Urban Crisis* (2017), reads like the chastened musing of a once-utopian reckoning with his vision's failure while still trying to remain cheerful. The "knowledge-based cities" where he had predicted a million creative workers would bloom, have, in fact, extended striated and segregated geographies wherein the "advantaged knowledge workers, professionals, and media and cultural workers [...] were doing fine" but everyone else ("a staggering 66 percent of the population") "ended up worse off" (ibid: xviii). Crushed by the startling realization that the benefits of a "creative economy" might go only to those recognized as creative, that a knowledge economy could bring harm to those cast aside as ignorant, unskilled, or simply superfluous, Florida has little left to offer. He resuscitates a few aspects of his old hopes, now buttressed by a call for statist policies (infrastructure investment, housing subsidies, school reform) he once deemed obsolete and an appeal to capitalists to have a heart (please pay service workers more!). The universality of knowledge work has not

---

2 | Perhaps not surprising, given his earlier co-authored account of "creatified" industrial work, which a more nuanced and critical study has rightly described as a "romanticized caricature of work under lean production" (Rinehart, et al. 1997. See Kenney and Florida 1991).

3 | For sample accounts from two eras, see Burris 1993; Temin 2017.

arrived. It was never intended to. Yet, the story of the knowledge economy lingers on, a denial of the power whose functions it performs.

Utopias of the 99%

In theory, such a situation ought to be advantageous for the left. A growing awareness of persistent inequality, after four long neoliberal decades, increasingly pervades the social landscape, accented by a deepening distrust of traditional political elites. The remarkable U.S. Presidential election of 2016 (both in Trump's ultimate victory and Sander's unexpected strength in the primary) was only the latest in a series of "populist" expressions of discontent and longing for change, beginning at the turn of the century in Venezuela and Bolivia, spreading through much of Latin America and then, unevenly, across Europe and the United States. Syriza and Corbyn, Law and Justice, Fidesz, and Le Pen, at minimum all seem like clear signs that the hegemony of neoliberalism and the knowledge economy is cracking.

Center-right parties have, in their way, been most successful at adapting to this shift, at least so far. Having always been dependent on nationalist and racist elements, they can direct frustration and resentments over the knowledge economy down those paths. Trump's election has proven both that party elites can lose control of that process and that they can learn to live with the products of that failure. The "center-left," meanwhile, has proved unworthy of the moment. Having heavily invested long ago in the vision of a meritocratic, knowledge economy as the way to retain the vestiges of a left identity whilst embracing neoliberal political economies, they have been loath to abandon that vision.

And the radical left? While the rolling wave of social movements, epitomized by the "movements of the squares," has been a promising development, the majority of these movements have been marked by a striking ephemerality. They rise up in response to a crisis or a series of injustices, surge into public awareness and debate, and then seem to vanish in the face of inevitable state-led repression. Partly, as Zeynep Tufekci has recently argued, the character of these movements seems to derive from their substitution of networked communication and social media for the long organizational histories that underpinned prior ones. "Modern networked movements can scale up quickly and take care of all sorts of logistical tasks without building any substantial organizational capacity before the first protest or march" (Tufekci 2017: 70). But they also lack the organizational capacity to actually threaten those in authority. Without capacities for decision-making or consensus building, without even the intention to develop these capacities (given a certain fetishism of horizontality and participation), they suffer from what Tufekci calls a *"tactical freeze."* They struggle to respond to changing situations, to capitalize on apparent victories by pressing forward to other demands or the adoption of new tactics. "[T]he initial tactic that brought people together is used again and again as a means of seeking the same life affirmation and returning to their only moment of true consensus: the initial moment when a slogan or demand or tactic brought them all out in the first place" (ibid: 77).

This freeze, however, is not simply a product of the use of social media or the sudden inflation of protests to movement size. Rather, the initial tactics that brought them together likewise rhyme with the characteristic labor processes of knowledge workers in the knowledge economy, with the kinds of comportment, practices, and expectations into which high-performing students and the children of professional workers are trained or habituated. The flexible, team-based, project-centered autonomy of knowledge work's labor process finds its analogue in the horizontalist, leaderless, consensus-centered model of social movements, and can produce similar results. As Tufekci notes regarding the open, participatory model of "assembly" that Occupy and other movements employed:

Voluntary speaking as a mode of decision making is another impediment to participation because people willing to speak up, especially in a challenging way in public, tend to be from privileged backgrounds, people who already like to wield authority and power, and [...] are mostly men. (ibid: 100)

This is not to say that participatory forms of practice are intrinsically anti-democratic, but without organizations and institutions that facilitate the input and foster the capacities of the dominated, they will privilege those schooled into them based on expectations of their managerial or political roles as knowledge workers. Such forms of organization and decision-making can appear to those practicing them to articulate the maximally democratic forms of political struggle, while foreclosing their ability to involve and inspire the majority of a leftist movement's potential social base. As Tufekci and others have noted, Occupy and other such movements were never actually leaderless but they obscured a clear sense of who their leaders actually were.

The difficulties facing efforts to foster involvement and inspiration today should not be understated. The movements of the squares are symptomatic of a problem rather than culpable for not solving it. As the knowledge economy has done its work, dissolving the traditional bases of class identification, casting off greater numbers into insecure, under-paid, or informal forms of earning their livelihood, incarcerating and placing under penal surveillance many others, encouraging a sense of disenchantment and disinvestment from political institutions and pro-cesses, fostering suspicion of and resentment towards knowledge workers while spreading a shared sense of solely individual responsibility, it has produced a situation in which most visible political struggles and parties, including those of the radical left, are disproportionately composed of knowledge workers. The difficulties of this situation are only compounded by the kinds of discourses that it tacitly encourages: those which foster the notion that knowledge work is, in fact, general, that the knowledge economy (and the practices considered typical of it) are a real basis on which to ground visions of social transformation.

Still, this cannot be reason for attempting to transform those condi-tions, *in theory*, into positive conditions for transformative agency. In the rest of this chapter, I sketch out two perspectives on these movements that betray, at the level of theory, some of the same limitations. Heroizing these struggles against neoliberalism, they simultaneously carry forward key presuppositions of the "knowledge economy." No doubt, the adapta-tion of such presuppositions in these perspectives inverts the direction of Drucker and Florida's accounts in key respects: rather than capital becoming their servant or everyone becoming a knowledge worker, here mental laborers become, implicitly or explicitly, a new collective agent of social transformation. But the end product of such arguments is a simpli-fication of social contradictions and a vision of revolution that reproduces the authority of the mental laborer, weakening its own critical force.

The General Intellect

When Michael Hardt and Antonio Negri's *Empire* appeared in 2000, it was widely received as a theoretical expression of the *altermondialisme* movement that culminated in the 1999 WTO protests in Seattle, an envisioning of its future trajectory. Though the argument of the book encouraged that reading to some extent, it also developed out of (and departed from) a longer theoretical tradition of Autonomist Marxism.[4] Even as the movement itself waned, intellectual and activist interest in that theoretical tradition grew in the U.S. and elsewhere, encouraging a wide range of translations into English, as well as a series of, at last count, four sequels to or extensions of *Empire* by its co-authors (Hardt/Negri 2004, 2009, 2012, 2017). The rise of the movements of the squares has re-centered this tradition, and its contemporary articulations, as an influential model for radical theory.

The specific strength of the Autonomist tradition, itself derived from Italian *operaismo* or "workerism," is its centering of workers' struggles in the evolution of capitalist societies. Rather than a totalizing system that evolves according to its own internal logic, capitalism is understood as a system of domination driven to constantly renewed innovations as a means for responding to and managing resistance. To an extent, *Empire* (and other works inspired by it) maintains this perspective but in a hyperbolic form, generalizing resistance to the "multitude" as a whole, while conceiving that multitude on the model of universalized, networked knowledge work. This expansion is grounded on a core set of analytic terms – "general intellect," "immaterial labor," "cognitive capitalism" – that derive much of their force from a particular reading of a passage in Marx's *Grundrisse* (1973).[5] In that passage, Marx argues that "the "development of fixed capital[6] indicates to what degree general social knowledge

---

4 | Wright 2017 is a useful history of this tradition. It should be noted that George Caffentzis, on whom I drew in the discussion above, also identifies with this tradition, though he, like Sylvia Federici, emphatically criticizes the "post-*operaismo*" trajectory described in this section. Indeed, the quotes in the section above were often directed *against* Negri, et al, precisely for absorbing the perspective of the "knowledge economy" narrative.

5 | See, amongst others, Vercellone 2007, 2009; Boutang 2011. For an early formulation of this approach to the *Grundrisse*, see Negri 1991.

6 | Capital investment in fixed assets: the tools and machinery of production, as well as buildings, etc. This is to be distinguished from "constant capital," which, for Marx, includes all of the means of production, including those, like raw materials, replaced in each production cycle, though the two terms are sometimes used interchangeably.

has become a direct force of production, and to what degree, hence, the conditions of the process of social life itself have come under the control of the general intellect and been transformed in accordance with it" (Marx 1973: 706). From this, proponents of the general intellect thesis derive the idea of knowledge and communication, science, technology and affective interrelations, as a collective production in which all have participated and participate, and which has become the dominant productive agent and source of value in contemporary capitalism.

As a literal interpretation of the text this is problematic, though the text itself (an unedited notebook not intended for publication) is ambiguous. Marx seems to move back and forth in this discussion between an account of what is the case in capitalism and what potentials lie latent in its development, waiting to be unleashed, without clearly delineating the movement from one perspective to the other. Yet, he states clearly enough that the "general knowledge" figured here is not something fully possessed by most. Rather, "[w]hat capital adds is that it increases the surplus labor time of the mass *by all the means of art and science*" (ibid: 708, emphasis added). The "theft of labor time," which lies at the core of capitalist value, counters "the artistic, scientific, etc. development of the individuals," which would require "time set free" (ibid: 705-706).[7]

For proponents of the general intellect as the contemporary source of value, however, Marx seriously underestimated the capacities that capitalism's increasing centering of "immaterial labor" would come to enable (Smith 2013). What Marx took to be a potential of communist society, then, theorists of cognitive capitalism understand as a fracture internal to the current phase of capitalism. The "rise of mass intellectuality" with the postwar expansion of education and training, led to wage laborers becoming a "depository of cognitive competencies that cannot be objectified in machinery," including "the faculty of language, the disposition to learn, memory, the capacity to abstract and relate, and the inclinations

---

7 | Further, Ernst Mandel (1975: 259) offers an entirely different reading of the key passage from the *Grundrisse*: Marx, Mandel suggests, is identifying the "development of fixed capital" as determining and limiting the degree to which social knowledge is integrated into production. "Scientific activity is only a productive force if it is directly incorporated into material production," but whether it is or not is dependent on the prior logic of capital valorization. Science, in other words, *is not* an immediate productive force in capitalism.

toward self-reflexivity" (Vercellone 2007: 6). The general intellect encompasses "the increasingly *social* nature of production," organized "in expansive cooperative networks," taken to follow from this.

Workers are no longer merely instruments that capital uses for transforming nature and producing commodities. Having incorporated the productive tools and knowledges into their own minds and bodies, they are transformed and have the potential to become increasingly foreign to and autonomous from capital. (Hardt and Negri 2017: 115)

Such incorporation ostensibly grounds the multitude's potential for both resistance and "the construction of alternative social relations" (ibid: 78). Communism is already present in the increasing centrality of "cooperation, social and scientific knowledges, care, and the creation of social relationships" (and also "machinic algorithms") in production (ibid: xix, 41).

Thus, while the idea of the general intellect departs from the utopic image of individual knowledge workers animating Drucker and Florida's visions, it often sounds as if it had merely substituted a collective subject for it, leaving the conception of the knowledge economy (or "cognitive capitalism") otherwise intact. It appears, that is, to suggest that the division between mental and manual labor has, in fact, been supplanted, knowledge work *has* been generalized, and so the interests of knowledge workers, their strategies and tactics, are now identical with those of the oppressed and dominated, broadly and diversely conceived. But this ignores Marx's subsequent observation that the products of this general intellect – "all the means of art and science" – become, in the hands of capital, means for increasing exploitation.

Instead, the overwriting of this seperation in the labor process is achieved, theoretically, through a peculiar overwriting of the division between capital and labor (Floyd 2011). The universalization of the general intellect proceeds by way of an ontological subjectivization of fixed capital. The ensemble of productive tools and knowledges that mass intellectuality incorporates – "artificial languages," theorems of formal logic, theories of information and systems, epistemological paradigms, certain segments of the meta- physical tradition, linguistic games, and images of the world" (Read 2003: 131) – are fixed capital, which thus "tends to be constituted and represented within variable capital, in the brains, bodies, and cooperation of productive subjectivity" (Hardt/Negri 2000: 385). "Subjectivity as fixed capital" becomes the grounding condition of "immaterial labor," generating out of these dead forms of communicative production "continual interrelations of communication" (Read 2003: 127).

On one level, this ostensible incorporation of fixed capital seems to signal the total subordination of living labor to capital: "subjectivity as fixed capital would seem to be entirely interior to capital—produced by capital as a functional component" (ibid: 132). But, in a further twist, labor power is also understood as inherently *self-valorizing*: value, which for Marx is the product of "abstract labor" (labor insofar as it is subordinated to the social relations of capitalist production) becomes instead an immediate product of "living labor." Having been wholly subsumed by capital, and the control-functions of mental labor, the subjectivity of labor power becomes simultaneously product *and* producer. "The production of subjectivity ceases to be only an instrument of social control [...] and becomes directly productive, because the goal of our post-industrial society is to construct the consumer/communicator—and to construct it as active" (Lazzarato 1996: 143). The mediated products of capital are depicted as immanent capacities of living labor (Floyd 2011: 73), such that capital can, in turn, be understood as wholly external to labor's (self-)production, violently extracting profit as a form of rent.[8] Only exodus or flight is required (Hardt/Negri 2017: xix).

While these ideas of the generalization and autonomy of "immaterial labor" grant such theories a feeling of "optimism about a new intellect" (Boutang 2011: 3), they do so only by the peculiar conflation of living labor with both mental labor and with capital. Indeed, when reading Hardt and Negri, one can sometimes feel that such optimism has substituted in, by a kind of fiat, for a sober reckoning with the extent to in which a subjectivity produced by the control-functions of mental labor can so simply and emphatically exceed them, turn them productive, despite their forms having been shaped by the imperative of producing abstract (surplus) value. To say that desire always exceeds such forms is one thing; to say

---

8 | "Cooperation, or the association of producers, is posed independently of the organizational capacity of capital[...] Capital becomes merely an apparatus of capture, a phantasm, and an idol. Around it move radically autonomous processes of self-valorization that not only constitute an alternative basis of potential development but also actually represent a new constituent foundation" (Hardt/Negri 2000: 282).

that it submits them wholly to itself, makes them the ground of its own autonomy another. By such a fiat, the difference between the revolutionary "entrepreneurialism of the multitude" can be hard to distinguish from everyday knowledge work: "When we look at young people today who are absorbed in machinic assemblages, we should recognize that their very existence is resistance. Whether they are aware of it or not, they produce in resistance" (Hardt/Negri 2017: 123). Autonomy, once again, seems indistinguishable from its opposite.

Likewise, the argument that all labor today involves immaterial or "cognitive" labor leads to another pervasive ambiguity. While recognizing that such labor is "most visible" in knowledge work (Read 2003: 148), autonomist theories generally point to their inclusion of affective labor, including reproductive or care work, under those categories and/or to the way in which immaterial labor is at work in consumption as well. But these inclusions seem to both undermine the ostensible novelty of "cognitive capitalism" and to obscure divisions within it. If the work of social reproduction is immaterial labor, then what is new about it? "And, equally important, what is gained by assimilating all forms of work – even as a tendency – under one label, except that some kinds of work and the political problematic they generate again disappear?" (Caffentzis/Federici 2009: 130) To the extent that this position mirrors the thesis of a knowledge economy, this theory seems in danger of implicitly affirming its primary effects. To the extent it differs from it, it seems to render itself powerless to confront those effects, dissolving them into an ambience of collective knowledge work that is always already a form of resistance.

The Cognitariat

The notion of a dual economy pointed to above is not intended to deny the increasing economic pressures on many knowledge workers, even those who have done well. Knowledge workers are not capitalists; they do not, generally, have the security or stability that large-scale wealth entails. In that sense, it would be better to speak, as Nick Dyer-Witheford (2015: 75) does, of a *triadic* pattern: "lucrative high-tech capital, professional informational work and grinding proletarian labour." The middle strata of this triad is in constant flux, differentiated by its own internal hierarchies, and parts of it are in real decline or have, indeed, ceased to be part of it. Pressures have become acute on college students and young people who have recently graduated, especially in countries reeling from debt crises and austerity measures. "[I]n education or not, young people are serious candidates for unemployment or casual labor" (Antunes 2013: xviii). But this relative decline in the prospects of *some* prospective knowledge workers must be contextualized within broader socio-economic patterns, especially the continued and even increasing rewards garnered by a still significant portion of professional information work, if accounts of it are not to yield their own utopic figures.

One temptation towards such figures has been that the movements of the squares appeared to some as disproportionately composed of just such "graduates without a future" (Mason 2013), once or would-be knowledge workers, undergoing a form of "proletarianization" (Dean 2016: 17). In that frame, they have come to appear as a new, potentially revolutionary subject. Most famously, perhaps, Paul Mason has argued for a fusion of the unrest of such graduates with the intrinsic potential of information technologies, which he holds to be in fundamental tension with market economies: "information is abundant, not scarce" (2015: 162, cp. Mason 2013). As the product of that fusion, the "new agent of change in history" is "the educated and connected human being," the "networked individuals who have camped in the city squares [...] on the streets of Rio and São Paolo" and who represent "the working class 'sublated' – improved upon and replaced" (Mason 2015: xvii, 212). The "improvement" here appears to turn on education, which Mason equates with a moralized commitment to the common good: "The most highly educated generation in the history of the human race, and the best connected, will not accept a future of high inequality and stagnant growth" (ibid: 29). It is displaced knowledge workers who may deliver on the innovative, egalitarian promise of a networked, knowledge-based world.

Jodi Dean (2014) offers a more compelling argument for the political potential of these graduates (whom she dubs members of the "cognatariat" or "knowledge class"[9]) insofar as she is more attuned to the ambivalence of information technologies. Explicitly rejecting Mason's presumption of their intrinsic conflict with market mechanisms, Dean argues that today, in "communicative capitalism," productivity "derives from its expropriation and exploitation of communicative processes." Having undergone

---

9 | See also the Introduction to Dean 2016, which repeats a number of passages from this article.

real subsumption to capital, "communication does not provide a critical outside" (Dean 2014: 4). Rather, all our interactions – financial transactions, GPS locations, exercise routines, photographs, blog musings, affective engagements with distant or not so distant "friends" – become "raw material for capital." As with the real subsumption of other forms of labor, this transforms the character of communication: there is "a shift from the primacy of a message's use value to the primacy of its exchange value, to its capacity to circulate, to be forwarded and to be counted" (Dean 2014: 6). The quantitative flow of messages, the monetizable "hubs" of the networks they form, eclipses their meaning.

Yet, while stressing the subordination involved in the fixed capital of communication, Dean retains the idea that revolutionary transformation will be modeled on the potentials intrinsic to the forms of knowledge work: "a new common of collective struggle," a struggle over data, knowledge, and affective processes, "the relations we create in common" (Dean 2014: 10, 12). Here, her account overlaps with post-Autonomist ones. If the shift from subordination to resistance is not asserted by fiat , neither is it clearly articulated. At minimum, Dean recognizes the necessity of forms of directly political activity – the seizure of capital and state and so on. Rather than arguing that *everyone* is (already) part of it, the "cognitariat" seems to function as the fusion of a universal class and, in its proletarianized fractions, a vanguard for collective struggle.

It is this direct connection, seemingly taken for granted, between "communicative" workers and the revolutionary potentials embodied in technologies of communication (as collective products) that I want to put into question.[10] After all, if communicative labor is really subsumed by capital, then what reason is there to think that those who perform it might have some unique, intrinsic revolutionary capacity or potential? Edna Brophy (2017) usefully speaks of "abstract communication" as the result of the real subsumption of communicative practices. If there is reason to think that the imposition of such abstraction will foster varying forms of resistance, just as abstract labor in general does, is there also reason to think that such resistance will be made fundamentally new by the communicative character of the labor or the machinery? Put differently, if what is involved is a process of *proletarianization*, why is it also the formation of

---

10 | For a discussion of the technological aspects, see chapter six.

a *new* "knowledge class"? Did prior revolutionary organization not involve cognition or communication?

I do not mean to question the worsening position of many in formerly stable and secure forms of "knowledge work." Stagnant wages, rising student loans, increasing competition for positions enabled by both increased rates of higher education and increasing credentials required for relatively low-skilled work, the automation of office work, the push to render semi-professional work to the same kind of flexibility regimes as low-wage service work, increasingly individualized and isolating forms of assessment, and so on, all put increasing pressures on many who might once have expected a secure post-college career trajectory.[11] Still, a disconnect between the expectations and the reality attached to specific credentials is not wholly new, being a common theme in sociological reflections on the revolts of the 1960s (for example, Bourdieu 1979). More importantly, it is unclear, especially in increasingly individualizing times, that the general response to such a disconnect would tend towards revolutionary transformation. At least equally likely would seem to be efforts by such graduates to "reproduce their own status" (Quart 2018: 109), to demand or to settle for a return to the powers and privileges that their credentials once promised. Many students and graduates who once participated in the struggles of the 1960s, after all, have been willing to make their peace with the "new spirit of capitalism" (Boltanski and Chiapello 2017 [1999]).

In Dean's own discussion, a sign of the utopic construction involved in attributing this revolutionary role to the knowledge class appears in her tendency to simplify the character of the movements she reads as foreshadowing that role.[12] She streamlines her presentations of them in a way that tends to overstate both the centrality of the knowledge class in general and of their "proletarianized" fraction. Thus, she argues "that highly educated young people were over-represented among OWS [Occupy Wall Street] activists and supporters and that many were underemployed, indebted or had recently lost their jobs" (Dean 2014: 2). Yet, while the

---

11 | See Quart 2018 for a particularly effective overview of these pressures and their effects on individuals.

12 | "The protests [...] are protests of those proletarianized under communicative capitalism [...] These revolts make sense as [...] the political struggle of a knowledge class." (Dean 2014: 1)

study of Occupy participants that Dean cites does note that "many of our respondents had substantial debt or had experienced recent job loss," additional observations include that they were "relatively affluent" (more than a third had incomes over $100,000), that 71% had "professional" jobs of some kind, and that immigrants and people of color were significantly under-represented (Milkman/Luce/Lewis 2013: 10-14). Whatever else once can say, this hardly sounds like a movement of the straightforwardly "proletarianized."

Dean's discussion of André Singer's article (2014) on the widespread Brazilian protests in June 2013 makes the problem clearer. She characterizes Singer's account as positing, based on the mismatch between the high-education and low-income levels of those involved, "a new proletariat or precariat taking to the streets" (Dean 2014: 2). But Singer's conclusion is quite different. Rather than endorse the notion of a new "precariat" (a possibility he raises), he suggests that "perhaps the best way to describe the social composition of the demonstrations is to envisage *two relatively equal blocs*. These comprised, on the one hand, middle-class young adults, and on the other, people of the same age but drawn from the lower half of the Brazilian social pyramid" (Singer 2014: 29, emphasis added). The latter are somewhat more educated than one might expect – university enrollments in Brazil doubled between 2001 and 2011 – but this does not, for Singer, produce a singular knowledge class or cognitariat identity.

Instead, Singer argues that there was a "crossover of classes" in the June protests, reflected in their ideologically and politically "multifaceted" character, "in which everyone from the extreme left to the extreme right was to be found," as well as a "latent tension" that occasionally led to violent clashes (ibid: 30, 32, 37). To the limited extent that there was a coalescence of viewpoints and goals, it was shaped, not by the common proletarianization of educated young people from different backgrounds, but by the identification of those from lower classes *with the worldview of the traditional middle class*, a position which "may be a desired goal for those who have begun to move towards it thanks to better educational opportunities" (ibid: 37). That identification was the basis for the ultimate predominance of a "post-materialist" centrism, emphasizing self-expression and quality of life over economic security. This centrism seeks to escape the right/left dilemma "by means of 'greater social participation'—something nobody disagrees with in theory, but which, once it is removed from the realm of distributional conflicts, can only be of interest to those whose material problems have been solved" (ibid: 35-36).

What is critical in Singer's account is how it opens up possibilities for understanding the tensions within these movements, which Dean's account elides, tensions that reflect something of the increasingly polarized character of contemporary societies.[13] For Singer, the libertarian and participatory characteristics of the movement in Brazil appear as a sign of the movement's de-radicalization, its drift into an aspirational identification with the "classless" well-being of the educated middle-class. Others have likewise diagnosed the main horizon of the global occupations as "a better management of the bourgeois state" (Woland/Blaumachen 2014: 12; cited by Dyer-Witheford 2015: 162). From this perspective, the key function of *all* discourses of a knowledge society would be to de-radicalize protest, to guide it towards an aspiration to reinstall the privileges of knowledge work (and, perhaps, someday, to its universalization).

Interestingly, Dean's own theory brings into question the political efficacy of her "new prole." For them, she notes, images take primacy over arguments or demands, individuality over solidarity (Dean 2014: 7), preventing them "from foregrounding our commonality and organizing ourselves politically" (Dean 2017: 4). "New proles often have a strong libertarian bent. They tend to present themselves as post-political or anti-political" (Dean 2014: 9-10). This emphasis on individual insight, development, achievement, creativity, and so on, appears, for her, as an articulation of the increasingly psychotic individualism that capitalism propels us all into, undermining the symbolic authority needed to stabilize its own coherence. In that sense, the revolutionary potential of the "cognitariat" is threatened by the same debilitating individualism that has beset the left since the 70s and which led it to respond

to the attack on the welfare state, collapse of Keynesianism, and emergence of a neoliberal consensus by forfeiting its historical solidarity with workers and the

---

13 | Also, it is difficult to know how, precisely, Dean figures knowledge workers as a *class*. When she defines them as such, she refers to Christian Fuch's account of contemporary class formations. Yet Fuchs does not refer to "knowledge workers" as a class, but as a fraction of a larger formation—"the class of all who are in some sense exploited." (Fuchs 2010: 187)

poor, retreating from the state, and losing the sense that collective solutions to large-scale systemic inequalities are possible are necessary (Dean 2009: 35).

In the place of such collective solutions, the left came (and is this not also a description of an Occupy general assembly or a University faculty meeting?) to reduce "politics to communicative acts, to speaking and saying and exposing and explaining, a reduction key to a democracy conceived of in terms of discussion and deliberation" (ibid: 32).

For Dean, the essential response to this dilemma must be organizational. Much of her recent work (2012, 2014, 2016) is a concerted and powerful effort to argue for the reawakening and re-conception of the question of the party. But, while I agree on the importance of that question, any answer to it must reckon with an implicit aspect of her critique that never comes wholly into focus. To the extent that she, like Hardt and Negri, tacitly identifies the communicative activities of the "knowledge class" as the model for a form of relationality of which we are all equally dispossessed and not as activities themselves shaped by the character of capitalist mental labor, liberation appears tacitly as the realized autonomy of knowledge work, paired with a vague gesture towards its universalization or collectivty. Capitalism's hold on knowledge continues to appear as something external to it. It "seizes and tags" (Dean 2009: 12) knowledge rather than structuring its very forms, practices, and effectivities. The same danger holds then: any party premised on such an approach would inadvertently reproduce the power that knowledge already wields in capitalist social relations of exploitation and appropriation. Political resistance, developed from this perspective, becomes an obstacle to its own ideals.

The Function of Mental Labor

The concept of the knowledge economy is premised on the idea that knowledge as such is a form of (benevolent) power. Ideas can change the world, reform capitalism. Ideas can also be a resource, driving economic expansion or knitting humans together in complex networks of affect and common holdings. It is this latter notion – that knowledge is relational, both collectively produced and productive of collectivity – that distinguishes Negri and Dean's positions from those for whom it represents a kind of apotheosis of entrepreneurial individualism. In this way, knowledge becomes not a means for reform but the substance of revolutionary aspirations. Communist desire is the desire for the freeing of that common production, the overcoming of the external expropriation or dispossession that capital visits upon knowledge from outside.

This last point signals the problems that undermine such aspirations. Placing capital *outside* the relationality of a knowledge and communication really subsumed by capital obscures the relational character of knowledge as it actually exists in contemporary society, specifically the power relations through which knowledge is articulated *and* from which its own power derives. "What capital adds is that it increases the surplus labor time of the mass by all the means of art and science" (Marx 1973: 708). A grounding intuition of this book is that the link between knowledge and the capitalist system of domination should be drawn internally to both, along the lines of the capitalist separation of mental from manual labor as Marx articulated it, not only within society in general, but within labor processes of production and reproduction. At this foundational level, the ideological and political fusion of knowledge and the power of capital, of science and exploitation, is established. A politics that attempts to break free from that fusion without having reckoned with it, that identifies with the positive elements of the knowledge economy without a critique of its (intended) real effects will be undone by them.

At the same time a central difficulty in the development of such a critique must be acknowledged: there is something essential about the assertion that, as Gramsci put it, *everyone* is an intellectual. There is no labor that does not involve conception and preconception, there is no life that is not reflected on, built out of knowledge produced in common. Any political view that does not hold to those claims will itself become a form of meritocracy or technocracy. This is the positively utopic element of Hardt and Negri and Dean's utopias, an image of the end of those control functions which persists in the margins of every liberatory movement. But common sense, the form of knowledge we collectively produce in class societies, is also, as Gramsci argued, a panoply of contradictory and confused ideas, shaped by our own (collective) experiences but also by the dominant ideologies and institutions within which we live and think. The fixed capital we incorporate into our minds and selves is not so easily autonomized.

The difficulty lies in affirming this potential of the common under different social conditions without ignoring or obscuring the relations of power and control that define the social functions of knowledge and the social positions of knowledge workers today. A thought that seeks to become effective must draw its material power from somewhere other than thought. If it does not, reflexively, get a handle on the sources of its own authority and control, if it does not transform the material institutions, the inertial forms, the dependent paths, that give it purchase on the world, through which it moves and draws its meaning, they will overdetermine its meanings and its effects. The dystopia of mental labor is the reproduction of the position of control, authority, and privilege with and from which it already thinks, embodying the forms of power and the forms of blindness they bequeath. The weight of this tradition cannot be overturned simply in or by thought, especially a thought which simply declares that here, now, already, those privileges have been cancelled or exceeded. We should recall the second part of Gramsci's famous decree: "All men are intellectuals, one could therefore say: *but not all men have in society the function of intellectuals*" (Gramsci 1971: 9). The social functions of knowledge workers are not something that can be changed (only) by adopting a "new" form of thought but through the actual transformation of the relations and institutions that shape and determine those functions. A left composed principally of knowledge workers cannot, any more than capitalism, simply be *persuaded* to change; it must itself be transformed by a collective power that rivals its own. The question is if and how we might enable such a transformation.

The division between mental and manual labor produces strange political effects. As we will see, this is partly because its political effects do not map in any direct or simple manner onto class position. While the "manual" working class largely consists of people without college degrees, for example, there are a large number of people – 17 million small business owners (or "petite bourgeoisie"), – who do not have a college degree and are not part of that working class. Two-thirds of small-business owners in general describe themselves as conservative, 86 percent are white, 92% say they vote regularly in national elections, and their average salary is $112,000. "There are also 1.8 million managers, 8.8 million supervisors, and 1.6 million cops whose jobs don't require a college degree" (Moody 2017: 176). Even if the numbers for those without a college degree skewed somewhat lower in these categories, they would still stand well-apart from the averages for those without a college education, almost half of whom do not vote and who tend to be to the left on issues of economy and the role of government. Evidence suggests that the support for right-wing populisms also comes disproportionately from this field of relatively well-off, quasi-independent people without a college education, likely motivated, in part, by imbalances of power between them and their more properly credentialed peers.

My contention will not be that a leftist politics oriented by the division between mental and manual labor would convert such people to its cause. At best, it might weaken some of their resolve. More important would be its impact on those do not vote, who find political processes as they exist without meaning, who generally have little access to institutions or organizations that foster their own political capacities and perspectives. The democratization of knowledge, politics and production is not an ideal that can be either presupposed as given nor put off until some far-off point when the people have been properly educated and moralized. It must begin now, in a process as critical of the powers of mental labor as those of capital. In what follows, I attempt to further that critique by sketching key episodes and tensions in the historically evolving social functions of mental labor across the 20th century, the ways in which they inform the contemporary political crisis, and, most tentatively, the avenues by which transformation might begin.

Chapter 2: The Division in Theory

> The knowledge in play [...] is in no way proper to all
> individuals; it is separate knowledge, a moment in
> the metamorphosis of capital, obeying it as much
> as it governs it at the same time.
> LYOTARD, quoted in TIQQUN 2001: 31

The division between mental and manual labor has not played a central role in the historical tradition of Marxist theory in the global North, despite the organization of *The German Ideology* around it[1] and Marx's claim, in his critique of the Gotha Program, that its disappearance is a defining feature of "the highest stage of Communism." If reflections on that division have not been entirely absent from the tradition, they have been mostly present on the margins, acquiring a certain centrality only at exceptional moments, such as the *Prison Notebooks* of Antonio Gramsci, work produced in the orbit of the inter- and post-war Frankfurt School (especially that of Adorno and the fifty-years gestating monograph of Alfred Sohn-Rethel),[2] and work produced under the influence of Maoism

---

1 | See Balibar 1983, as well as the next section.

2 | For this tradition, the division between mental and manual labor is explained principally in reference to the abstract form of exchange. As will become clear, I follow the alternative tradition that focuses on relations of production. For reasons of space, I do not take up a direct comparison of these traditions. On Adorno and this division, see Read 2005. The preface to Sohn-Rethel 1978 is a short "thought-biography," sketching an account of why the work took fifty years "to mature," as well as its/his relationship to Adorno. For critiques of Sohn-Rethel's approach, see Jappe 2013 and Postone 1993: 171-179. Poulantzas 1978 also contains several arguments for analytically prioritizing productive relations over the form of exchange. See, for example, pp. 49-53, 54-55, 63-65.

and the Chinese Cultural Revolution, especially in France, by thinkers like Étienne Balibar, Charles Bettelheim, and Nicos Poulantzas. The roughly contemporaneous work of Harry Braverman is a somewhat singular exception in English-language traditions. In contemporary Marxist theory, that division has been almost entirely marginalized.

This contemporary marginalization is clearly influenced by the milieu sketched in the previous chapter: in a knowledge society or cognitive capitalism, whatever importance the separation of mental from manual labor may once have held is often taken to have been eclipsed by the rise of "immaterial labor" or some general "intellectualization" of computerized labor processes. If industrial work now often involves as much tending and monitoring computerized machinery as direct, physical labor, if service work, mobilizing a set of communicative and affective capacities, has quantitatively eclipsed industrial labor, and if the "intermediate" strata of managers, professionals, software engineers, etc., has grown substantively over the course of the twentieth century, then it has seemed to many that the division between mental and manual labor is no longer of much importance.

A first step in reasserting its importance is simply to emphasize that the division itself does not turn directly on the character of the work involved. "In reality, this should not be at all conceived as an empirical or natural split between those who work with their hands and those who work with their head: instead, it directly refers to the political-ideological relations prevailing within particular relations of production" (Poulantzas 1978: 55). Here, Braverman's emphasis on *the separation of conception from execution* is particularly useful (Braverman 1998: 79). Braverman, in fact, substitutes this division for that of "mental and manual labor" precisely to avoid the misleading empirical implication, in an era when "work done primarily in the brain" was also becoming subject to procedures of rationalization. "The functions of thought and planning became concentrated in an ever-smaller group within the office, and for the mass of those employed there the office became as much a site of manual labor as the factory floor" (ibid: 218). Further, Braverman argues that the division between "brain" work and manual labor had existed in every known human society as part of the social division of labor, whereas that between conception and execution, which involves, fundamentally, *control* over the labor process, was proper only to capitalism. Those focused on the analysis of capitalism, he suggests, should thus favor the specificity of "the separation of conception from execution."

The focus of this book is on the social and political relations that are involved in and shaped by the separation of conception from execution. Why, then, have I not followed Braverman in using those terms exclusively? The answer lies in the first sentence of this paragraph: I am concerned not only with the relations of production but also with social and political relations not directly part of capitalist processes of production, yet shaped by them. I am concerned, in Poulantzas's terms, with the political-ideological conceptions that are intrinsic to those productive relations and which radiate outward into society as a whole. The separation of conception and execution must not only be conceived and executed, it must also be explained, legitimated, and enforced. And the terms of that defense take the form of asserting, "demonstrating," persuading others of the empirical or natural difference between those who conceive and those who execute – there are "body-men" and there are "men without bodies" (Balibar/Wallerstein 1991: 211). These differentiations become available in turn for use in explaining and legitimating new organizations of power and authority in relations more or less removed from any immediate relations to production processes, across the divide between the "economic" and the "political" that capitalism also articulates. The separation between conception and execution becomes adjunct to the organization and legitimation of hierarchically structured institutions and practices of education, the design of state strategies for increasing the well-being of its population, or the political posture of knowledge workers who view the masses as "stupid" or uneducated.

Put differently, Braverman's substitution too easily removes the other dilemma that has played a role in marginalizing the division between mental and manual labor: its liminal status between the anthropological and the historical, seeming to be both an intrinsic differentiation of human nature (if shifting in its specific expressions) and a division proper only to the capitalist mode of production (Balibar 1983; Read 2005). This division within the conception of the division is central to its political-ideological force, to its capacity to legitimate elements of capitalist social relations in terms of an ostensibly natural division of human nature (drawing, as well, on naturalized racial and gender divisions). It also explains the tendency of the division between mental and manual labor to produce strange political effects, ones that seem not only divorced from class divisions, but obscuring of them. "Unique to capitalism is its combining in one single social structure the *two* forms of the division between mental and manual labor, the historical origins of which are entirely different" (Balibar 1983: 115, my translation). In the unity of this difference lies both its elusiveness and importance.

In this chapter, I map out the coordinates of the division itself, in its specific capitalist unity, while also tracing how it migrates across the division between the economic and the political (and back), shaping the character of both productive relations and the state. The critical question remains, as it was for Braverman and Poulantzas, that of control.

The Original Class Relation

Marx's initial discussion of the division of mental and manual labor articulates this difference-in-unity, as he moves between broad views of history and detailed analyses of the capitalist mode of production. In *The German Ideology*, an unpublished effort by Marx and Engels "to settle accounts with our erstwhile philosophical conscience" (Marx/Engels 1976a: 146), it appears as simultaneously central and marginal. Central, because their critical attack on the "Young Hegelians" turns on the idealist faith invested in conceptual struggles. The Young Hegelians produce their own utopias of empowered minds: "Since [they] consider conceptions, thoughts, ideas, in fact all the products of consciousness, to which they attribute an independent existence, as the real chains of men (just as the Old Hegelians declared them the true bonds of human society) it is evident that the Young Hegelians have to fight only against the illusions of the consciousness." Demanding a different *interpretation* of the world, they "are only fighting against '*phrases*,'" not "the real existing world" (ibid: 149).

In sketching out an understanding of history grounded in "real individuals" and their relations, then, Marx and Engels must explain how it is possible that – in a world comprised of those individuals, their production of life, the material conditions for that production, and the social relations they compose – such an idealism is possible. How is it that consciousness, "from the very beginning a social product" (ibid: 158), can come to think of itself not only as self-determining but as determining, in turn, the character of struggles within the social-material world? Their answer lies in the emergence of the separation of mental from manual labor: consciousness can understand itself as autonomous to the degree that individuals involved in mental labor become separate from direct involvement in the production of material subsistence. This separation initiates the long process of alienation in which workers are divorced from "the real intellectual wealth of the individual" which "depends entirely on the wealth of his real connections" (ibid: 163). It is not that these connections no longer exist – the individual has not become autonomous, any more than her consciousness – but they become powers outside of her control and understanding. The control mental laborers exercise masks the extent to which their power derives from others, the products of their labor, and the institutionalized relations the mental laborer has to them.

From this moment onwards consciousness can really flatter itself that it is something other than consciousness of existing practice, that it *really* represents something without representing something real; from now on consciousness is in a position to emancipate itself from the world and to proceed to the formulation of 'pure' theory, theology, philosophy, ethics, etc. It is also at this moment that the division of labor "becomes truly such." (ibid: 159)

The importance of this last point has perhaps not been emphasized enough. It identifies the separation of mental from manual labor with the beginning of exploitation, and so of class struggle. Consciousness can flatter itself that it is something other than consciousness of existing practice only once there are mental laborers who live off of the labor of others and so do not participate directly in the manual work required for the reproduction of the community. Inversely, the sustained reproduction of exploitative social relations requires a political-ideological production of justifications and enforcement mechanisms for those relations, as well as a set of institutions (and staff for them) that embody and reproduce those political-ideological relations. There is "civilization" (the subject matter of "written history") only if there are

at least some members of the community who have enough *leisure* – in the technical sense of being released from directly producing the material necessities of life – for governing and organising and administering a complex society; for defending it against outsiders, with whatever weapons may be needed; for educating the next generation and training them in all the necessary skills, over a period of perhaps ten to twenty years; for the arts and sciences [...]; and for the other requirements of civilized life (de Ste. Croix 1981: 36).

Conversely, of course, there is only leisure for some insofar as there is exploitation of many and an organization of social relations towards producing and controlling the surplus. Thus, the division between mental and manual labor and class struggle have a common and reciprocal historical development.

This is not to claim that the division between mental and manual labor caused exploitation. Clearly, it developed in a process of co-evolution: the slow development of leadership or governing functions, the control over land and agricultural resources and their distribution, centralized demands for more complex forms of conception and planning, and encouraged ideological justifications for that centralization.[3] But what this co-evolution makes clear is that the "flattery" consciousness bestows upon itself is not separable from real forms of power and control that those who (claim to) embody it exercise over the productive activities of others. "Pure" theory, theology, philosophy, ethics, etc., are made possible by the leisure that exploitation creates. Their "power" is parasitic off that of the class power that derives from and enforces social relations.

Yet, despite this apparent centrality, the division between mental and manual labor makes only two further explicit returns in *The German Ideology*: first, it is identified as a division of labor that splits the ruling class (its "conceptive ideologists" are opposed to its "active members" [Marx/Engels 1976a: 173]) and, second, "the greatest division of material and mental labor" is identified with the separation of town and country (ibid: 176). Both of these points suggest complications concerning the relationship between mental labor and exploitation. First, having tacitly connected them – exploitation develops in tandem with the division between mental and manual labor – Marx and Engels also partially distinguish them. "Active" exploiters are generally not "the thinkers of the class," those who provide "illusions and ideas." Second, mental labor is simultaneously identified with the exploitative position of the ruling class and with the existence of a political realm at least potentially separate from such economic activity. "The existence of the town implies, at the same time, the necessity of administration, police, taxes, etc., in short, of the municipality, and thus of politics in general" (ibid: 176). As if hesitating about such a separation, Marx and Engels tend here towards a reductive identification of politics and state with the direct interest of the ruling

---

3 | For one account of this evolution, see Flannery/Marcus 2012.

class, disguised by an "illusory" set of forms,[4] despite their suggestion that "ideologists" can enter into "a certain opposition and hostility" to the class's "active membership." But what is clear at this stage is that the power, simultaneously illusory and real, accumulating around mental labor cuts across both production/exploitation and politics/domination.

This originary and expansive role of the division between mental and manual labor in the initiation of "civilization" goes some way towards explaining its central yet liminal status in Marx and Engel's early sketch of social history. The division appears as the very ether in which (written) history moves, the original split or lack that makes it possible, established at its beginning, indexed by certain enduring divisions, like town and country, and engaged at the level of broad theoretical questions concerning consciousness and social relations, but not otherwise traced in its concrete development and contradictions over the course of history (compare, for example, their more detailed sketch of the evolving forms of property). There is something here of the "anthropological," as Etienne Balibar (2012, 2017) has suggested, a division that precedes capitalism and appears somehow linked (albeit in variable forms) to natural or "given" differences that are also mediated socially.

Marx and Engels show little interest in mapping out any such anthropology. Rather in *The German Ideology*, the division, as a frame for synopsizing all of human history, seems to facilitate headlong rushes across historical epochs to arrive in the course of a page or two at reflections on the character of capitalism that punctuate and disorder anything approaching the materialist account of human history that the first part of the text at times seems to be proposing. Marx, in other words, is not concerned so much with the priests and clan leaders of ancient communities; rather, he wants us to grasp how the products of our own activity have come to take the form of a fateful power to which we must submit and how our ideologues are not so much challengers as accessories to that power. What we find in the *German Ideology* is something like a set of historical vignettes or synopses intended to illuminate (through their similarities

---

4 | "[A]ll struggles within the State, the struggle between democracy, aristocracy, and monarchy, the struggle for the franchise, etc., etc., are merely the illusory forms in which the real struggles of the different classes are fought out among one another." (Marx/Engels 1976a: 160-161)

and differences) specifically capitalist forms of consciousness, ones that characterize even its would-be radical critics like the Young Hegelians.

Marx and Engel's approach here articulates what we might now call, following Freud, a logic of "deferred action" (*Nachträglichkeit*): "experiences, impressions and memory-traces may be revised at a later date to fit in with fresh experiences or with the attainment of a new stage of development" (Laplanche/Pontalis 1973: 111). The meaning of the division between mental and manual labor, while traced back to the very beginnings of human civilization, is constantly being (re)articulated in terms that can only hold, properly, within capitalism itself. The invocation of "politics in general" is a key instance of this approach, insofar as the division between economic and politics is only proper to capitalist societies (Wood 1981).

By the time of the composition of the *Grundrisse* in 1857-1858, Marx had become wholly conscious of this approach to understanding historical societies, articulating it directly in reference to the abstract, apparently transhistorical concept of "labor." Such a concept, Marx argues, comes into focus only when labor itself has become really abstract, when it has "become the means of creating wealth in general, and has ceased to be organically linked with particular individuals in any specific form" (1973: 104). More generally, "the simplest abstraction [...] which modern economics places at the head of its discussions, and which expresses an immeasurably ancient relation valid in all forms of society, nevertheless achieves practical truth only as a category of the most modern society" (ibid: 105). Understanding processes of historical development, then, is only possible through the use of concepts produced by and in relation to modern society. But such understanding likewise requires a recognition that other forms of society "contain" the forms of bourgeois society "always with an essential difference" (ibid). For Marx, this means that earlier forms of society are not steps leading teleologically towards modern forms. To understand them as such was to understand them in a one-sided fashion, an index of the extent to which capitalist society had not yet become self-critical, the extent, in other words, to which it saw itself as the natural unfolding of intrinsic human desires or capacities.

Marx's relatively brief engagements with the separation of mental from manual labor follow this approach: that division, which attains its more or less complete form only in "the most modern society,"[5] is identifiable in every form of written history. Yet, there is an essential difference: in all societies prior to or distinct from capitalist society, this division is articulated through specific positions in the social division of labor, i.e., the distribution of community members into specific fields of production, both general (agriculture, manufacture, merchant) and particular (wheat farming or ranching, pin- or soap-making, dry goods or hardware sales). The priest or philosopher occupies a specific social position as well, albeit one that appears as labor only retrospectively, from the standpoint of modern society. Only with the actualization of "abstract labor" does the division between mental and manual *labor* itself become thinkable (Balibar 1983: 108). In capitalism and only in capitalism, arises the division of labor in manufacture, the breaking down of a single production process into a series of steps assigned to distinct individuals, none of whom participate in, nor need to understand, the process of production as a whole. This latter form, which yields increasingly abstract labor, represents "the conscious, methodical and systematic form of capitalist production" (Marx 1976: 485).

Classical political economy, Marx suggests, had read the social division of labor in terms of the division in manufacture, "i.e., as a means of producing more commodities with a given quantity of labour, and consequently of cheapening commodities and accelerating the accumulation of capital." This too was a form of retrospective understanding but one that missed the essential difference. Their error can be glimpsed by comparison with writers from antiquity, who were "exclusively concerned with quality and use value": separate branches of production allowed individuals to cultivate their inclinations and talents in a process wherein "both product and producer are improved" (ibid: 486-487). Exactly the opposite is the case for the division of labor in manufacture, which is characterized by the fact that "the specialized worker produces no commodities." Instead of producing a specific kind of good, the worker performs a specific act or set of acts in the production of some good. She makes the head of a pin or she enters discrete items of data into software that pro-

---

5 | "The separation of the intellectual faculties of the production process from manual labour, and the transformation of those faculties into powers exercised over labour, is [...] finally completed by large-scale industry erected on the foundation of machinery." (Marx 1976: 548-549)

cesses it. Whereas the division of labor in society is mediated through the purchase and sale of the products of different branches, in manufacture it is mediated "through the sale of the labour-power of several workers to one capitalist, who applies it as combined labour power." From this follow a set of further differences: the concentration of the means of production in a small set of hands vs. their dispersal amongst numerous producers; *a priori* planning of the process of production vs. an *a posteriori* necessity imposed by exchange upon the unregulated caprice and contingency of independent production; the undisputed authority of the owner of capital vs. competition between autonomous agents (ibid: 476). All of this is driven by capital's pursuit of greater productivity and efficiency, a drive to perpetually increase the amount of (relative) surplus value produced and to intensify capitalism's control over the labor process.

This essential difference of the capitalist division of mental and manual labor signals both a continuation of the pre-capitalist form and a fundamental transformation of it. It sets mind above matter, but it no longer conceives of mind as something potentially pure or properly contemplative. Knowledge, as we saw Drucker argue in the last chapter, becomes effective. This produces an important inversion of the split within the dominant class sketched in *The German Ideology*: the active component of that class is now linked to a specific form of knowledge. The "functioning" capitalist is the one that oversees the labor process and exploitation, the one that takes a direct interest in knowledge of the labor process. The "lending capitalist," representing capital as property, has no direct need for the knowledge involved in such functions. Here too, there is a unity of differences: "In the reproduction process, the functioning capitalist represents capital against the wage-labourers as the property of others, and the money capitalist participates in the exploitation of labour as represented by the functioning capitalist" (Marx 1981: 503). This division could also be materialized in the form of machine technologies (and those who designed and developed them) and the functions designed into their forms. Large-scale industry "makes science a potentiality for production which is distinct from labour and presses it into the service of capital" (ibid: 482).

Finally, with the rise of joint-stock companies, the "functioning cap-italist" can cease to be a *capitalist* at all, as the "function of managerial work" is separated "more and more from the possession of capital," del-egated to a new form of worker. The power of capital is wielded by such workers, while money capital becomes increasingly concentrated in banks (or shareholders), until "there remains only the functionary, and the capitalist vanishes from the production process as someone superfluous" (ibid: 512). In the discussion of this shift in the draft text published by Engels as volume 3 of *Capital*, Marx focuses on the latent potential in this division between capital and its functions: the joint stock company is, as Marx famously puts it "the abolition of capital as private property within the confines of the capitalist mode of production itself," anticipating the "cooperative factory" in which "the opposition between capital and labor is abolished" (ibid: 567, 571). But in the manuscript of volume 1, published after the composition of that draft, Marx focuses on the powers exercised by management. Rather than merely a group of workers paid "wages for skilled labor" (ibid: 510), supervisory staff are portrayed here as an officer corps: "officers (managers) and N.C.O.s (foremen, overseers), who command the labor process in the name of capital" (1976: 450). And the function they are delegated is an avowedly "despotic" one, which transforms the interrelation between various labors into what appears as "a plan drawn up by a capitalist, and, in practice, as his authority, as the powerful will of a being outside them, who subjects their activity to his purpose" (450). Even in the draft of volume 3, Marx notes the extent to which the co-evolution of credit with joint-stock companies *increases* the power of this will, allowing the individual capitalist "an absolute command over the capital and property of others, and, through this, command over other people's labour. It is disposal over social capital, rather than his own, that gives him command over social labour" (1981: 570). As in the *Grundrisse*, Marx's accounts waver between the immanent promise of a labor process loosed from capital's control and the recognition of new, delegated forms of intensifying control, but the tendency of his thought appears to be towards the recognition that, whatever their latent potentials, these new forms of organization push control ever more deeply into the labor process itself.

The detachment of conception from execution increases the rate of production, lessens the value of labor-power, and increases the amount of surplus value extracted. Knowledge becomes abstracted from an increasingly abstract labor. "The possibility of an intelligent direction of production expands in one direction, because it vanishes in many others. What is lost by the specialized worker is concentrated in the capital which confronts them," as "the intellectual potentialities of the material process of production" come to appear "as a power which rules over him" (Marx 1976: 482). In Marx, the punctuated history of the division between mental and manual labor is a history that illuminates this power, bringing its crippling force into relief against the essential differences that define its prehistory. And it is that power, expanded by credit's command over social capital, that stands behind the supervising officer who acts on capital's behalf, according to its goals. If that power is wielded by the mental laborer, it does not derive from her, but from her position as a functionary or representative of capital.

Capital, in other words, increasingly realizes its own innate tendencies through the labors of knowledge workers. This speaks to another likely reason for the relative lack of attention to the division between mental and manual labor in Marxist theory: such theory's focus on general tendencies within the social totality. As Marx's *Capital* suggests, demonstrating the intrinsic contradictions of capital accumulation requires a critique that operates, initially, at a level as abstract as the capitalist forms of time, labor, and value. The increasingly global character of capitalism also means that even more concrete analyses must often appeal to the level of statistical aggregates. The division between mental and manual labor tends to vanish at such levels of analyses precisely because such abstract forms or aggregate measures presuppose its effects: that a capitalist society tends to mirror the tendencies and contradictions that Marxist theories have analyzed is, in no small part, a function of the ongoing work of managers, engineers, scientists, educators, lawyers, social workers, health care professionals, and so on. The very concept of "relative surplus value" denotes a process of increasing productivity and efficiency that came, very quickly, to require the "scientific," superintendence for which Frederick Taylor established an enduring model. The reproduction of labor power has required enormous investments, often, though not solely, at a state level, in the production of "knowledges" to manage. The legitimacy of the system itself has done the same. When mental labor is performing its functions, it tends to vanish into the "natural" laws of capital.

Tendencies of the Division

Marx's analysis offers a preliminary but prescient account of the division between mental and manual labor as it would develop in joint-stock corporations and in the development of management as a specific form of ostensibly scientific knowledge.[6] Its prescience derives from the structural logic that Marx identifies at work in both the rise of specific managerial functions and the centralization of capital: the pursuit of relative surplus value. If the most direct way to increase surplus value is simply for capital to employ wage laborers for increasing amounts of "surplus time" beyond that in which they produce value equivalent to their wage, this approach has intrinsic limits, both because of the bio-physical limits of workers who require nourishment and sleep and because of workers' resistance, which, for a long time, centered precisely on the question of the length of the workday.[7] The successes of those struggles helped to motivate capital's focus on decreasing the amount of "necessary labor time" required in a day, rather than increasing the length of the workday itself. This could (and can) be done by direct interventions in the social reproduction forms of workers, reducing the level of "subsistence" wages– by forcing a switch from wheat to potatoes as staple food, for example (Bhattacharya 2017: 84-85; Thompson 1963: 347) – but it can also be done within the labor process itself, by increasing the productivity of those sectors selling the goods of subsistence. Potatoes or shoes that require less labor time to produce require a wage equivalent to less labor time to buy, thus lowering the value of labor power as a commodity. In this relationship, as Marx put it, we have "the solution to the following riddle: Why does the capitalist, whose sole concern is to produce exchange-value, continually strive to bring down the exchange-value of commodities?" (Marx 1976: 437)

There is also, of course, a more direct and individualized motive for capitalists to increase productivity (and Marx suggests it is from such motives, in the context of coercive competitions, that the "immanent laws of capitalist production" are manifested [ibid: 433]): the surplus profit each capitalist can gain over their competitive rivals in the market. The capitalist that decreases the time of production first, through refined divisions of labor or, increasingly, the introduction or improvement of machinery as the driving element of production, is able to "squeeze an extra surplus-value" out of them (until such a time as their competitors adopt the new methods) by selling their commodities at a price above the labor-time expressed in them, yet below that of their rivals (ibid: 433). "The technical

---

6 | See the next chapter for a fuller discussion of this point.

7 | Detailed, of course, in Marx's lengthy discussion of those struggles in industrial Britain (Marx 1976: 340-426).

and social conditions of the process and consequently the mode of production itself must be revolutionized before the productivity of labour can be increased" (ibid: 433).

Such revolutions in labor processes require planning that presuppose a separation of conception from execution, the removal of knowledge and control from the direct producers. The ongoing cycles of competitive reproduction of capital, the continuing quest to further increase productivity and surplus profit, thus drive an increasing contribution of knowledge workers to the functions of capital. At moments, Marx appears to clearly recognize the expansive growth of "knowledge workers" that the pursuit of relative surplus value portends. Criticizing Ricardo in *Theories of Surplus Value*, for example, Marx notes that "what he forgets to emphasise is the growing number of the middle classes, those who stand between the workman on the one hand and the capitalist and landlord on the other. The middle classes [...] are a burden weighing heavily on the working base and they increase the social security and power of the upper Ten Thousand" (cited in de Ste. Croix 1981: 29).

What was most important to Marx, at least in the context of *Capital*, was the form that this "burden" took, the effect that the transformed production process had on the workers subsumed to it. Most immediately, the very character of work becomes increasingly debilitating. Repetitive in quality, conforming in demand, accelerated to whatever pace the machinery (and, to a lesser extent, the human body) can maintain, "factory work exhausts the nervous system to the uttermost; at the same time, it does away with the many-sided play of the muscles, and confiscates every atom of freedom, both in bodily and intellectual activity." Even in cases where the work becomes less physically demanding (the machine and its prime mover now bringing their own force to bear[8]) this too is "an instrument of torture, since the machine does not free the worker from work, but rather deprives the work itself of all content" (Marx 1976: 548). Intensified, emptied of content, "abstract labor" becomes an oppressive reality.

---

8 | It should also be kept in mind here, though I shall not have space to give it much attention, that this force is that of *carbon*. The real subsumption of labor is enabled only by the mobilization of coal, and then oil, with all the increasingly clear destructive effects that brings, as Andreas Malm (2016) has masterfully argued.

Resistance to those effects, Marx suggests, tends to be overwhelmed by the "general law of capital accumulation." As capital investment in machinery increases, as the labour-power of each individual worker becomes immensely more productive and the portion of her working day dedicated to generating surplus value for the capitalist increases, and as the amount of products produced by each hour of labor grows, the demand for labor, relative to the extent of the total capital, tendentially decreases. More capital employs fewer laborers, as the evolution of the auto industry can suggest in shorthand. "Modern industry's whole form of motion there-fore depends on the constant transformation of a part of the working pop-ulation into unemployed or semi-employed 'hands'" (ibid: 786), leading to the growth of a "reserve labour army" that can be thrown suddenly into new spheres of production, while also acting as a permanent threat to workers already employed, lowering their wages and lessening their bargaining power.

The key result of these tendencies is the increasing *precarity* of workers: "the higher the productivity of labour, the greater is the pressure of the workers on the means of employment, the more precarious there-fore becomes the condition for their existence" (ibid: 798). It is not widely appreciated, perhaps especially under the continuing ideological impact of the post-war "golden age," that this precarity and not the general impov-erishment of workers was Marx's central critique of capitalism's impact on the working-class. Certainly, there would be increasingly large "sections of the working class" that were "pauperized," as some, having been resigned to the reserve labor army, would never emerge out of it, becoming "unem-ployable," succumbing to despair or rage, finding other avenues, criminal or otherwise, to stay alive. The increasing contributions of technology and machinery produce accelerating cycles of the absorption and expulsion of labor. Even in periods where the majority of workers receive a somewhat larger portion of their ever-increasing surplus-product, the relative luxuries obtained "no more abolish the exploitation of the wage-labourer, and his situation of dependence, than do better clothing, food and treatment, and a larger *peculium*, in the case of the slave" (ibid: 769).

Such periods will, inevitably, cease (as one did in the 1970s), as the con-tradictory tendencies of capital, including the falling rate of profit, produce downturns in which the precarity of the worker becomes manifest. The point is that workers are subject to a system of production, designed by mental laborers, that serves profit and not their own well-being. Whatever consumption that subjection enables, in production and in the exchange of labour-power for money, it necessarily entails the degradation of workers, the emptying of labor's content, alienation from "the intellectual potentialities of the labour process," submission to the dictatorship of the factory, and the transformation of "life-time into working-time." "It follows therefore that in proportion as capital accumulates, the situation of the worker, *be his payment high or low*, must grow worse" (ibid: 799; emphasis added). The detailed division of the labor process, premised on the division of mental and manual labor, is the driving logic directing these effects.

Marx is clear, as well, that such fundamental transformations in the division of labor in the process of production have equally transformative effects on the division of labor in society. "It is machines that abolish the role of the handicraftsman as the regulating principle of social production," creating a "simple division of the workers into skilled and unskilled," combining them "into a single mechanism" (ibid: 491, 486, 489). The division between mental and manual labor, in other words, becomes increasingly central, polarized, and pervasive. No longer does it merely denote a small group of "governors" and ideologists, positioned (albeit at the top) amongst a diversity of different forms of labor (the vast majority agricultural producers) that still combine conception and execution. Rather, it increasingly divides the entire social field, as the majority of workers have the conception and control of their labor processes stripped from them, while a growing but still-minority fraction of laborers monopolizes those powers, performing the functions of capital. Thus is inaugurated the triadic pattern of social divisions which has become increasingly pervasive (and globalized) up to the present day (Dyer-Witheford 2015). The critical point is that the accumulation of social and scientific knowledge, as well as the institutionalized forms of their practice, are driven by capital, shaped by the essential difference that links them to control. If the joint-stock corporation announces the possibility of capital's removal from productive relations altogether, it also forecloses that possibility through the borrowed power and goals of mental labor.

The Political-Ideological Character of the Division

Another way of grasping the unity-in-difference of Marx's conception of the division between mental and manual labor is to see it as a key instance or, perhaps better, the central conductor, of what Balibar calls the "short-circuit" in Marx's work, "an immediate relationship, a correlation which develops historically through economic and political mediations between the form of the labor process and the state" (Balibar 1994: 136). It is in a similar vein that Poulantzas insisted on the *political-ideological* character of the relations of production:

The relations of production and the relationships which comprise them (economic ownership/possession) are expressed in the forms of powers which derive from them, in other words class powers; these powers are constitutively tied to the political and ideological relations which sanction and legitimize them. These relations are not simply added on to relations of production that are 'already there,' but are present themselves, in the form specific to each mode of production, in the constitution of the relations of production. (Poulantzas 1975: 21)

Capitalism involves what Ellen Wood (1981) called a "privatization" of certain aspects of the political that preceded it: the absolute right to private property defines the relationship between capital and labor as a matter of private contract, securing the functional control of capital or its representatives over the labor process ("the dictatorship of the factory"). But the political character of those relations has effects well beyond that "private" domain, providing a kind of nucleus shaping the forms and relations of power, as well as the discourses articulating and legitimating them, in society as a whole.

The political realm, the capitalist state, does have a certain separation and autonomy from productive relations, deriving from the fundamental separation of laborers from the means of production. The general, systematic compulsion this yields, in which each laborer must sell their labor power to *some* capitalist, though not to any specific one, frees the relation of exploitation from any direct, personal authority outside the labor process. Conversely, it frees the state from the regular enforcement of such personalized forms of domination, allowing it to become "an assemblage of impersonal, anonymous functions whose form is distinct from that of economic power" (Poulantzas 1975: 54). Rather than protecting and enforcing each specific relation in a pyramid of politico-economic powers, the capitalist state can focus on the reproduction of the system as a whole, while formally occupying a (transcendent) position above the fray.

The state is nevertheless shaped by the powers that order (and disorder) that society and the discourses that sanction them, precisely because it derives its power, ultimately, from capital. The "autonomy" of the capitalist state is derived from the separation of mental from manual labor and is increasingly modeled on its form in the relations of production. "Separated from the relations of production, the State takes up position alongside an intellectual labor that has itself been divorced from manual labor: it is the corollary and the product of this division, and at the same time plays a specific role in its constitution and reproduction" (Poulantzas 1978: 56). The latter role is of particular importance because of the contradictions it can introduce into the development of capitalist social relations: as the general arbiter of order and consent in the system as a whole, yet dependent (most evidently and directly for its revenues) on powers derived from ownership over the means of production and control over production processes, the state appeals to and reinforces "the practical supremacy of a knowledge and discourse" (ibid: 56). Yet, whatever powers of "persuasion" its agents have must derive ultimately from their capacity to articulate forms of knowledge (science, strategic rationality, etc.) that further the strategic goals of a predominance of fractions of capital in the balance of forces the state crystallizes. They "have been constituted as a specialized professional corps through their reduction to functionaries or mercenaries of the modern state" (ibid: 57).

There is no ideal knowledge, then, from which the best political order can be autonomously derived, any more than there is a stable division between mental and manual labor by which the state can be self-evidently legitimated. Whatever transcendence is involved is wholly negative:

> We could thus say that every form of work that takes the form of knowledge from which the direct producers are excluded, falls on the mental labour side of the capitalist production process, irrespective of its empirical/natural content, and that this is so whether the direct producers actually do know how to perform this work but do not do so (again not by chance), or whether they in fact do not know how to perform it (since they are systematically kept away from it) or whether again there is simply nothing that needs to be known. (Poulantzas 1975: 238)

What distinguishes mental from manual labor is not its character or content but its functions of domination and command (enabled by independent access to the means of production), the exclusion of the masses from some knowledge, a "secret," that may not exist, that may not even be secret but is experienced as un-usable, irrelevant, "not for people like us," and so on. What matters is the separation inserted between the form of knowledge and the (potential) power of the people separated, the way in which that knowledge becomes a property to which they have no valid claim, a vehicle for control over them or their activities, and for the legitimation of that control. This separation tendentially shapes the character and content of forms of knowledge as well, structuring the forms of machinery, scientific research, state policies, decision-making processes, etc. in ways that presuppose and reproduce that separation. It likewise divides positions of mental labor themselves into an ascending bureaucratic hierarchy of increasingly secret, "need-to-know," knowledges.

In capitalist production processes, then, "the labourer is brought face to face with the intellectual potencies of the material process of production, as the property of another, and as a ruling power" (ibid: 235). The same is true in relation to the apparatuses of representative democracy, established – forthrightly in the debates over ratifying the U.S. Constitution – as a mechanism for keeping the masses at a distance from any direct exercise of power, such power being ceded to the "wise" citizens they elect. Unlike in the workplace, the vote here provides a justificatory structure to the ruling power; "it has *legitimately eliminated* the possibility that the 'sovereign nation' could govern itself" (Balibar 2015: 42). In this way, as Balibar argues, the formal constitutionalism of liberal-democratic representation turns on the combination of

the performative declaration of the universality of rights with a new principle of the separation of governors from the governed, which [...] Catherine Colliot-Thélène has provocatively called the principle of the 'ignorance of the people.' We could also say, on an institutional level, the 'incompetence in principle' of the people, of which the capacity of representation is the contradictory product (Balibar, 2014: 10).

As the incarnation of mental labor's separation from manual, the state excludes the governed from any direct concentration of a power of their own internal to its apparatuses (Poulantzas 1978: 56, 142). The state too appears as the property of another, a ruling power, sustained by variegated discourses of wisdom, merit, and expertise. Mental labor simultaneously delineates and divides the class position of workers in productive relations while (re)producing the masses as the isolated subjects of political exclusion and representation.

The declaration of the universality of rights (at least for citizens) is not without effects, reflecting more generally the legitimation burdens of the capitalist state, which, to keep alive the contractual pretense of "liberty, equality, and Bentham," must win some degree of consent (buttressed by apolitical resignation before "secret" knowledges) from those it represents. The state cannot depend solely on the abstract compulsion of separation from the means of production but must actively produce forms of more or less active consent to the orders and divisions of capitalist society, while also coercively policing violations of them. As representative of the "people-nation," the state is traversed by popular struggles, as well as by the struggles of the dominant class, which it unifies, to maintain the subordinate position of those it excludes from its secrets. Because there is no single or stable way to produce and police this consensus, the effects of such struggles also divide the powers that comprise and support the state. "Contradictions between the power bloc and the dominated classes directly enter into contradictions within the power bloc" (Poulantzas 1978: 143).

They also enter into the forms of knowledge, producing a fundamental tension internal to the forms and practices of "mental labor" that the state incarnates. In broad terms, this tension can be seen as analogous to the distinction Pierre Bourdieu (2000) drew, late in his life, between the "right hand" and the "left hand" of the state. On the one hand, in their role in securing the reproduction of capital accumulation, apparatuses of the state draw on and produce discourses closely linked to "dictatorship of the factory," stressing the need for (rational) control, efficiency, productivity, scientific progress, economic growth, "law and order," and so on. On the other hand, in their role of representing the people-nation (and producer of a more or less unified interest of "capital-as-a-whole"), apparatuses will emphasize the public good, the national interest, juridical fairness, the amelioration of economic downturns, support for and oversight of social reproduction processes, a "safety net," workplace safety, environmental well-being, and so on. These discursive tendencies are neither wholly contradictory, nor internally stable. They articulate historically variable ensembles of concepts and practices mapping out responses to, forms of managing, the intrinsic contradictions of the capitalist state, which must secure and further capital accumulation, unify the fractions of the capitalist class, and legitimate the social and political orders to the popular classes. No long-term strategy of the state could wholly exclude either pole, lest the state fall into crisis. Likewise, each generally acquiesces to a third, interrelated discourse, of military/policing/security that constitutes the "borders" of the state's concerns, the racialized identity of its "nation" (Singh 2017; Balibar/Wallerstein 1983).

Mental Labor as Process and Struggle

In debates over the "new class" in the 1970s, efforts to account for the social position of knowledge workers or intellectuals often became bogged down in what can now seem rather sterile debates about this group's class position. Dogmatic assertions that "there is only one working class!" were often countered by simultaneously finicky and ambiguous categories. Important questions regarding political strategies were waylaid by more or less formalistic debates over the proper boundaries between social classes. Was the new class (however named) a class? If so, what made it one? If not, why not and what, instead, was it? A fraction, a stratum, something else? The abstract and often belabored formalism of these discussions (one hopes never to read Poulantzas on productive and unproductive labor again) leaves an aftertaste of disappointment: despite frequent moments of insight, no specific definition of the class position of this grouping, even a "contradictory" one, ever appeared wholly convincing, no critique of those definitions ever seemed to arrive at a wholly satisfying alternative. One arrives at the feeling that the wrong question was being asked and answered.

The sterility of that debate, I think, derived from the shared confidence on most of its sides that some definitive boundaries could be arrived at, that class analysis was "primarily a means of *categorizing* people." But to speak of class, as Charles Umney has recently emphasized, is "a means of explaining the processes and pressures that define capitalist societies." To speak of two fundamental classes, as Marxism does, is "not to claim that these categories are exhaustive, nor that they explain the life conditions of everyone who fits into either of these broad groups [...] But they do offer a way of categorizing the kinds of pressures and conflicts that characterize all capitalist societies" (2018: 23-24). Even more importantly, they offer a way of conceptualizing the contradictory historical development of capitalist societies. The concept of political class formation, or class composition, is central here, insofar as it emphasizes that the changing and variegated social relations that are articulated through such pressures and struggles do not spontaneously produce clearly defined collective identities. Rather, class composition requires active and ongoing "hegemonic" work around shared similar and overlapping experiences, including, centrally, the shared experience of collective struggles, to produce common understandings and motivations. Such a focus on process does not obscure the heterogeneity of class formations but, rather, allows those heterogeneities to be understood as articulations of the contradictions internal to the processes of capital expropriation, accumulation and reproduction.

What comprises the commonalities of knowledge workers, as well as the broad tensions between them which we will trace in the next two chapters, is not their location within a *category* as such but their evolving position(s) within the historical and political development of the division between mental and manual labor, as an ongoing articulation of the contradictory character of capitalist productive relations (the need for increasing control over the labor process and laborers in the pursuit of relative surplus value) and the evolving unity-in-contradiction of those social relations and the reproductive, unifying, and legitimating functions of the state. Because this division is defined by (and defining of) the political-ideological character of relations of production, the position of mental labor itself is over-determined by the legitimating form that its self-understanding, paired with the delegation to it of the control functions of capital, offers. Outside of some explicit effort to question the meritocratic ideological structure of a separated mental labor and to align with some alternative social power to that of capital, the position, experience, and institutional forms of mental labor will align it with capital (which ultimately condones – and funds – its ideas, or does not).

In his well-known discussion of intellectuals, Gramsci also focuses neither on the question of whether intellectuals are a class, nor on "the intrinsic nature of intellectual activities," but on "the ensemble of the system of relations in which these activities (and therefore the intellectual groups who personify them) have their place within the general complex of social relations" (Gramsci 1971: 8). There are, as Gramsci puts it, "historically formed specialized categories for the exercise of the intellectual function. They are formed in connection with all social groups, but especially in connection with the dominant social group" (ibid: 10). Intellectuals (or knowledge workers), then, have no fundamental social substance of their own, at least not *as* intellectuals.

There is, however, a set of corporeal practices and developed capacities that defines the intellectual:

The critical elaboration of the intellectual activity that exists in everyone at a certain degree of development, modifying its relationship with the muscular-nervous effort towards a new equilibrium, and ensuring that the muscular-nervous effort itself, in so far as it is an element of a general practical activity, which is perpetually innovating the physical and social world, becomes the foundation of a new and integral conception of the world. (ibid: 9)

One must learn to control and organize one's own muscular-nervous activities as the precursor of developing the intellectual capacities to organize oneself and others with ideas (hence Gramsci's pedagogical emphasis on early learning-by-rote[9]). But the power or influence of ideas comes not from the ideas themselves but from their capacity to illuminate, render coherent, the positional experiences and the developed common sense of those to whom one speaks. For Gramsci, *"being-in-history* is already immanent to thought [...] and, even more importantly [...] *theory itself* is a particular mode of historical being, or a *practice*, which [...] remains immanent to and not transcendent of such historical experience" (Thomas 2009: 358).

The link between intellectuals and class, on Gramsci's account, appears as a question of the sociohistorical perspective which they strive to render coherent. The social background of the intellectual herself informs but does not determine the perspective she adopts (since she can be assimilated to other classes). This does not mean intellectual activity is autonomous: its categories are formed *especially* in connection with the dominant social group, which controls the state, schools, mass media, and so on. The effectiveness or power of such categories lies not in the intellectual act as such but in its representation and reception by "an entire social group conceived in movement and thus seen not only in its current and immediate interests, but also in its future and mediated interests" (Gramsci 1995: 353). Another way to make this point is to recall Gramsci's

---

9 | "In education one is dealing with children in whom one has to inculcate certain habits of diligence, precision, poise (even physical poise), ability to concentrate on specific subjects, which cannot be acquired without the mechanical repetition of disciplined and methodical actions." (Gramsci 1971: 37)

account of hegemony as "a combination of force and consent" (Gramsci 1971: 80): ideas produce broad social consent only insofar as some power that backs them has the power to compel assent or to make such compulsion seem likely. To gain authority ideas have to *prevail*.

Gramsci's insight remains critical and provides a thread through the next two chapters: neither ideas, nor intellectuals, are intrinsically productive or empowered. Their force derives from the social group, the class, whose interests they articulate and cohere. If "[t]he beginning of critical elaboration is the consciousness of that which really is, that is, a 'know thyself' as a product of the historical process which has left behind an infinity of traces without an inventory" (ibid: 342), then what follows is an effort to begin compiling an inventory for the critical elaboration of the contemporary politics of mental laborers. We start with "progressives."

Chapter 3: The Labors of Progressivism

> The Progressive movement was born of discontent with the division and dispersion of power in the American system [...] Their alternative was to concentrate power while anchoring its exercise in [...] the authority of experts (SKOWRONEK/ENGEL 2016: 6, 9).

This chapter and the next trace the historical evolution of the tensions within the social position of mental labor, between mental laborers, and between mental and manual laborers, over two key transitions in the 20th century. As the productive relations and the balance of forces in U.S. society changed, the dominant ideological forms and functions of mental labor also shifted, along with the form and functions of the state. These shifts were not foregone conclusions, nor deterministic expressions of economic forces, but political and ideological articulations of developing balances of forces, intended to provide resolutions for contradictions emergent in the social relations of their times. The rise of a specific ideology to dominance was dependent on its capacity to give more or less coherent form to the shifting interests of capital, while also providing some degree of legitimation in the eyes of dominated groups. Thus, as I argued in the first chapter, the rise of "knowledge economy" discourse – the articulation of mental labor as centered on the management of knowledge work - was much less a symptom of a new role for knowledge as an economic resource, than it was the articulation of a specific vision of reconfigured firms (and states) that would cement the decline of organized labor, in the workplace and in the political sphere, and restart accumulation.

The triumph of that discourse and the productive and political relations it helped install – as well as the broader triumph of the forms of strategic rationality I will discuss in the next chapter – have often generated nostalgia for the forms of mental labor that they supplanted. To many, Barack Obama's election as President appeared to promise of a renewal of "the progressives' century," a mantle he explicitly donned (Kloppenberg 2016). In the face of growing partisanship, inequality, and individualism, Obama spoke in terms of the public good, a purer politics of reasoned deliberation, under the measured guidance of science and expertise. The goal of this chapter is to trace this progressive[1] articulation of knowledge's functions, which remains, in somewhat altered form, the credo of most "suburban liberals" (Geismer 2015) and their academic counterparts, back to the historical context of its emergence in the late 19th and early 20th century. In that context, such nostalgia will seem largely unwarranted.

What Progressivism represented, in effect, was the founding legitimating discourse for the new cadres of managers and administrators that emerged in tandem with the rise of corporations and the bureaucratization of the state in the late 19th and early 20th centuries. Developing initially in struggles over the relations of production, as a discourse legitimating enlightened managerialism, progressive thought came to identify itself with the state precisely because it shared, while helping to redefine, a central goal of that state: the production of "social peace" between classes that had entered into a condition bordering on open war in the last quarter of the 19th century. This pacifying goal, including the need to assuage the demands of increasingly mobilized dominated classes (farmers, artisans, industrial workers), produced a form of conception that disavowed any direct link to capital's interests, forwarding the value of scientific expertise as its own authority. In this way, it offered knowledge, supposedly linked intrinsically to the public good, as a means for the apolitical resolution to political conflict.

In reality, however, the successes of that discourse, like the state it came increasingly to define, were commensurate with its capacity to secure the ongoing accumulation of capital. Thus, alongside the legitimating discourse and material bases for consent it developed, it also articulated a newly pervasive system of control over the popular classes: their subordina-

---

1 | In what follows, I capitalize "Progressive" when referring to the specific movement of the late 19th and early 20th century, while leaving it uncapitalized when referring to the general set of ideas, the logic of mental labor, which that movement inaugurated. See Skowronek/Engel 2016 for a similar usage, as well as the concept of the "progressives' century."

tion to forms of expertise through which capital came to expand its control over the social reproduction of labor power in exchange for the amelioration of some of its conditions. The condition of this expansion was an intensification of the political separation of mental labor from the people. Rather than a live alternative to the contemporary political crisis, then, the progressive project is, in key respects, its font and its ongoing source.

Hegemony Born in the Factory

Although the U.S. was a relative latecomer to industrialization, a number of factors contributed to its early adoption of a model of "mass production." [2] The relative absence of pre-capitalist social relations, the relatively decentralized character of its state, the increasing strength of capital in relation to a largely immigrant working class, and the increasing infrastructural and consumer demands of a quickly growing population dispersed over an enormous territory, all served as incentives towards a greater concentration of capital and a relatively unique focus on the "scientific" reshaping of productive processes. As factories grew larger and more complex, the direct supervision by owners and traditional forms of managing workers came to seem deeply inadequate (Freeman 2018: 106).

Frederick Winslow Taylor's "scientific management" was emblematic of the kind of answers developed to this problem. His proposal for "task-based" control of the labor process – specifying the precise steps to be followed, the precise movements by and time allotments in which they should be performed – turned explicitly on managers assuming the "burden" of "gathering together of the traditional knowledge which in the past has been possessed by the workmen and then of classifying, tabulating and reducing this knowledge to rules, laws, and formulae" (Taylor 1998: 15). This burden, Taylor argued, would bring an end to the "soldiering" of workers (performing the minimum possible amount of work) by granting managers control over production by way of their monopolization of, now scientific, knowledge of the labor process. Yet, it would also generate "maximum prosperity," increasing production to such an extent that workers' wages would rise even as owners' profits increased, and so

---

2 | These forms, a central aspect of "Americanization," would ultimately reshape European productive relations as well, especially in processes of postwar rebuilding (see Nye 2013, ch. 4).

offering the wages of a "high-priced man" as recompense for increasingly regimented forms of labor. A similar logic would come to underpin Henry Ford's introduction of the assembly line.[3]

Taylor thus brought to pointed expression a bid for social authority that the newly developing corps of corporate managers had been developing over the previous decades: scientific knowledge of the elements of the labor process would not only increase productivity (and profits) but also yield social peace between labor and capital (Shenhav 2002; Khurana 2007). The late 19th century rise of both corporatization and managerialism was driven by a dramatic cycle of unprecedented financial panics and depressions, punctuated by the rise of the Knights of Labor, the Populist movement, and widescale labor unrest, which yielded what Steve Fraser describes as a "revulsion" amongst the bourgeoisie against the unregulated market (2015: 37). If the reformed legal charters that allowed for widescale corporatization no longer included the requirement of serving a specifically defined public good,[4] the developing discourse of managerialism stressed its capacity, if giving the functions of corporate control, to correct for inefficiencies of markets and assuage workers' unrest. Maximum prosperity could be the basis for a new model of the public good and the national interest.

Gramsci glimpsed something of this process, arguing that, in Fordist America, hegemony "is born in the factory and requires for its exercise only a minute quantity of professional political and ideological intermediaries" (1971: 285). But that hegemony turned, as he noted, not solely on rationalizing the labor process and increasing wages but also on the provision of "various social benefits" (ibid) and a concern with workers' physical and moral well-being. Gramsci's focus was on the moral oversight of workers' private lives embodied by Ford's "Sociological Department,"[5] but that effort was of a piece with a general trend of U.S. firms

---

3 | After the introduction of the assembly line in Ford's factory, "[f]ifty-two thousand men were hired to fill thirteen thousand jobs in 1913." In the face of this annual turnover of 400%, Ford introduced the five-dollar day (Nelson 1995: 162), his own version of "maximum prosperity."

4 | On legal aspects of corporatization, see Sklar 1988; Barkan 2013.

5 | "'Puritanical' initiatives simply have the purpose of preserving, outside of work, a certain psycho-physical equilibrium which prevents the physiological collapse of the worker, exhausted by the new method of production" (Gramsci

(especially large ones) towards "welfare work," increasingly systematized efforts to "improve the lot of their workers" with the idea that doing so "encouraged self-betterment, loyalty, and cooperation – that they inspired the employee to become a better person and a better worker" (Nelson 1995: 99). The origin of these efforts appears to lie in company towns' offerings of social, educational, and recreational facilities and activities to lure workers to their rural settings. In urban milieus, they centered on improvements to factory conditions (cleanliness, lighting, ventilation, dressing or "rest" rooms), relief associations, annual outings, etc., and were especially common in workplaces that employed a large number of women. More systemic forms generally involved the hiring of a "welfare secretary," usually women who had been nurses or teachers with experience in philanthropic work, and whose variegated duties centered on "improv[ing] the general morale" of the workforce (ibid: 105).

Thus, in the U.S. at least, early aspects of "the welfare state" had their origins not in the state but in large firms, where they were explicitly intended to offset and ameliorate discontent and harms that newly rationalized labor processes might foster.[6] Over time, this complex of functions and services tended to split. There was a trajectory internal to the factory, from the "welfare secretary" to "human resources" departments as we currently know them – constructing a series of "rituals of knowledge" concerning hiring, firing and the mediation of workplace conflicts, while also overseeing systems of health insurance and retirement savings that, in the U.S., remain largely privatized products of firm-specific union victories. Other functions, especially those tied to the general social reproduction of labor power, would be taken up by and expanded through the Progressive movement's focus on charitable work and government reform. These

---

1971: 303). Ford's Sociology Department was forthright about this intent. "Its principal responsibility was to ensure, through investigations of the workers' homes and family life, that they shared their employer's middle-class values and warranted the five-dollar day" (Nelson 1995: 162-163).

6 | As opposed, for example, to the earlier case of Germany, where Bismarck's "passive revolution" sought to absorb workers' discontent into identification with the state through the provision of health, accident, old-age, and disability insurance. The German welfare state would, of course, become a key inspiration for Progressive politics – the tour of Germany was often a defining experience for progressives of the era (Rodgers 1998).

efforts included housing and community-improvement work (epitomized by the settlement house movement), the regulation of workplace conditions, and the expansion of public education. In the process, Progressives extended the subjects of such concern beyond industrial workers, identifying the reserve labor army (albeit not under that name) as a central object of concern, while pursuing projects that amalgamated social work, moral uplift, and the amelioration of class conflict.

One sign of the continuing influence of the factory origins of these projects is the extent to which Progressives retained scientific management's discourse of efficiency as the basis of social peace, often more so than the businessmen Taylor had struggled to convince (Haber 1964: 17). The idea of objective science came to encapsulate this fusion of truths that were simultaneously productive and collective, useful, yet unswayed by particular interests, and so in service of a common or moral good (Khurana 2007: 51-64). It also articulated a form of knowledge proper only to a select, educated few. Consolidating authority in their hands, it was argued, would be a means to overcome the partisan divisions and public pressures that kept the state from achieving meaningful reforms, just as scientific management ostensibly solved the conflict at the core of production. "Progressive reform took the corporate model of organization from the economy and transferred it to the polity, thus making political centralization concomitant to the centralization of economic production" (Larson 2017 [1977]:143) but also, ostensibly, to the realization of representative democracy's promise: "The regulation by the power of the state of these industrial and other social relations existing among men is an essential condition of freedom" (Ely 2006 [1903]: 57).[7]

In the process, the population became the object of something akin to scientific management, expanding knowledge worker's proclaimed expertise from control over the production process to control, potentially, over the entire ambit of the labor force's social reproduction. Unlike what Gramsci believed concerning hegemony in the factory, however, this process would come to require a much greater quantity of professional political and ideological intermediaries. The discourse and practices of "professionalism"

---

7 | Gramsci also recognized this possibility: "Though these tendencies are still only 'private' or only latent, they could become, at a certain point, state ideology" (1971: 304).

came to provide the means for identifying a set of agents ostensibly worthy of wielding science in the name of the public good.

The Professional, Ascendant

Prior to the 19th century, the place of "professions" in the social division of labor in both Europe and the U.S. was relatively restricted, mainly confined to divinity (and its offshoot, university teaching), law, and medicine, and ensconced in more or less intimate relations with aristocratic and church elites (Larson 2017 [1977]: 4-5). Such positions were based more on social position than any verifiable claim to objective competence and, while there were, for example, village or town doctors who tended to peasants or craftspeople, "'common' and 'learned' practitioners inhabited different social worlds. Even though they practiced in related fields, the rigidity of the stratification system prevented the constitution of unified areas within the social division of labor" (ibid: 3). Such quasi-professionals were also distinct from the competence-ensuring systems of guild craftsman-ship, which operated outside the university system and usually had more popular backgrounds and clientele. The guild system was linked to the rise of urban markets; the professions remained apart from them much longer.

Indeed, the initial growth of markets, rather than enhancing the position of professions, tended to disrupt it. Claims to medical competence had to compete with a rush of patent medicines and homeopathic cures, pressing those committed to an ostensibly genuine medical knowledge to create a specifically medical market that could materialize a measure for their competence. "The various professional services, therefore, had to be *standardized* in order to clearly differentiate their identity and connect them, in the minds of consumers, with stable criteria of evaluation" (ibid: 14). That need led to the formation of professional societies that monop-olized systems of validation and accreditation, grounded in a university education as the now increasingly required path to accreditation. Such societies were also "bound to solicit state protection and state-enforced penalties against unlicensed competitors – that is to say, those producers of services whose training and entry into the market they had not controlled" (ibid).[8] The ideal of science, the university, and the state were combined to secure monopolies over specific forms of knowledge.

Professionals appeared initially in their "pure" form in those spheres, especially medicine and law, where specific roles for mental laborers in the social division of labor had pre-existed the onset of capitalism. This history crystallized in the fact that, at least for a while, such professionals operated at a relative distance from the conglomeration of industrial and state bureaucracies (though not from the market), thereby epitomizing the independence that science was taken to require and serving as a model for the host of newly professionalized natural and social sciences that defined themselves as professions in the Progressive era. "Almost every group within the new class experienced its formative growth toward self-consciousness in roughly the ten years from 1895 to 1905" (Weibe 1967: 127).

As professionalism expanded, however, its market-based independence became even more tenuous. This was especially so for professional fields in more direct relation to corporations and their intensifying division between mental and manual labor. Engineers adopted models of professionalization and accreditation, while remaining dependent on the firms that would (or would not) hire them. Some, like Veblen (1921), would see engineers' professionalization as the sign of a nascent social planning divorced entirely from the interests of an increasingly absent share-owning capital. But, ultimately, either through personal identification or the threat of unemployment, engineers' politics would tend to identify with that of owners (Layton, Jr. 1971). Taylor, an early member of the American Society of Mechanical Engineers, would serve as its president from 1906 to 1907. But he also helped inaugurate the differentiation of managerial from engineering functions that led to a push for the design of university-based business schools in turn (Khurana 2007).

If engineers and managers worked to model their collective position on norms of professionalization, their efforts to do so were limited by their "permanent subordination to organized and increasingly complex economic enterprises" (Larson 2017: 26). At stake here was the notion of a commitment to the "public good" which connected traditional professions

---

8 | This trend took longer to establish a secure foothold in the United States, interrupted by the Jacksonian backlash that led to the collapse of nascent credentializing systems, but the spread of the ideal of science would reinvigorate it in the last quarter of the nineteenth century (Khurana 2007: 64-71).

to the states that authorized them, but which firm-based professionals tended to replace with a formation centered on status, "which exalted the *expertise* of this dependent professional and made it the base of a grandiose social role" (ibid: 30). Over the course of the century, many of the new professionalized positions, and even traditional ones like medicine, would find themselves in increasingly analogous positions as meritocracy became its own justification.

For many decades, however, this peculiar social position of professionals – a monopolized market position over knowledge – underpinned the ideological forms of Progressive politics, as waves of sociologists, social workers, architects, urban planners, etc., developed and advocated for new visions of a "social politics." That this independence, in fact, involved dependence upon state and educational institutions could be (re) articulated as a measure of their merit, the official recognition that legitimated their authority. Fantasies of a prosperous, orderly world run entirely by professional expertise would become standard narratives of the progressive century, from H.G. Wells to Michael Young.

Class Powers and the Political Project of Progressivism

Progressive politics was comprised, essentially, of efforts to realize, or at least asymptotically approach, that fantasy. "It developed the notion of social control into a program of planning and placed the professional expert near the top" (Haber 1964: xii). The Progressives of the early twentieth century sought to reform both state and economy in the image of this expertise, establishing a more rational and less divisive polity, less subject to class and partisan conflict, more orderly and well-designed. They sought, in short, a world ruled according to a tacit identification of managerialism, science, and the practices and habits of middle-class professionals: efficient, productive, objective, wholesome, steering towards the common good. To the extent that other groups failing to embody these ideals, Progressives were "radical in their conviction that other social classes must be transformed" (McGerr 2003: 79, xv). Yet, at the same time, the contradictions internal to their ideals, as to their social position, left Progressives subject to social forces for which they could not fully account, lest they undermine the supposed authority of their expertise or reveal the weakness of its power. In this section, I sketch key elements of progressive politics, focusing on its contradictory relations with three social groups: professionals themselves, capital, and the proletariat.[9]

The unique social position of professional knowledge workers shaped the contradictory character of their political project from its beginning. The process of professionalization involves an explicit, yet ambiguous, fusion of the individual and the collective: market monopolies over specific forms of knowledge could only be established through a combination of collective organization and state support. Setting up professional associations, designing university curriculums, and establishing rules for accreditation, educating the public and/or industry regarding the proper qualifications for certain forms of knowledge work, required collective identification with other professionals of one's sort and, more distantly, with professionals as a whole. And yet, such actions yielded primarily individualized benefits – "income security and social respectability" (Larson 2017: 81) – accrued in competitive markets. The collective character of the project was thus defined in reference to the knowledge such workers accrued, not to shared struggles or shared rewards. The common good Progressivism invoked turned on a vague vision of the national spirit, paired with a more specific image of comfortable, middle-class domesticity as the rewards of merit. Even at that level, its collectivity was inherently exclusionary: the point was to monopolize access to and control over knowledges, while providing (or incentivizing) analogous, if lesser, forms of comfort to others.

A weak collective serving individual ends required links to the state, precisely because individual "experts" needed a source of power and authority stronger than such a collective could develop if their knowledge was to become socially effective. Even in the limited ambit of a professional career, the state's exclusion of non-credentialized claimants was critical to success. The tendency of progressive politics across its century has been to leverage such bids to embody and define state authority, aided by a shared educational and cultural background with state and party elites (and, to a lesser extent, owners of capital), in order to exercise an outsize influence on policy (cp. Geismer 2015: 12-13). Known for their efforts to end political corruption, Progressives sought to temper democratization as well, precisely because it threatened to undermine the special powers delegated to

---

9 | I use this term here in the way Dyer-Witheford suggests: to include both "wage laborers" and "the unemployed and paupers" (2015: 13).

the knowledge workers. The principal form through which Progressives sought to institutionalize those powers was, appropriately, that of independent regulatory commissions or executive agencies, which represented "a higher form of social effort" precisely because they invested authority in expertise (Ely 2006 [1903]): 55). Yet, in practice, they proved broadly ineffective, beset by and dependent on powers internal and external to the state, compromised in their supposed independence, and exacerbating conflicts they were intended to resolve (Grisinger 2016: 360, 377).

A similar contradictory logic defined Progressives' ambiguous political relation to the bearers of capital. Certainly, as some historians have emphasized, an explicit disgust with the wealthy animated core aspects of the Progressive movement, especially its successful push, under Woodrow Wilson, for graduated income and estate taxes (McGerr 2003, 2016). More generally, the indifference of the wealthy to the plight of workers and the poor was seen as a key cause of social unrest. Criticism of the wealthy thus centered on their egoism and amorality, their willingness to disregard the common good in pursuit of their own excessive pleasures. But, as such, it was a critique launched though an identification with values of efficiency, hard work, and (self-)control that had their roots in the capitalist labor process, while also linked to efforts to obtain credentials. If Progressives viewed markets, like firms, as requiring the regulatory supplement of scientific expertise in order to ensure some minimal level of fairness, safety, and social cohesion, they shared this suspicion of *laissez faire* with many of the titans of corporate monopolies.

Indeed, unless we grasp this overlap (forecast by managerialism) between the Progressive critique and the evolving position of the most advanced and centralized fractions of capital, it can be difficult to understand how so many Progressive reforms could have been implemented or why the culture of expertise should ultimately have become so pervasive. Accounts of Progressivism are often vague about how "middle class radicals" could come to be so influential when, by even the most generous reckoning, "knowledge workers in the first decades of the twentieth century comprised no more than 1/5 of the population, far smaller than the agrarian producers at the base of Populism in previous decades (McGerr

2003: 43, 30).[10] If not explicitly attributed to the persuasive power of true ideas, the tendency is still to credit the autonomous efforts of knowledge workers. Michael McGerr, for example, argues that Progressive achievements occurred in an interregnum when the contesting classes were too weak to triumph over one another: "Progressivism unleashed a powerful reforming dynamic across America, just at the time when farmers, workers, and the upper class were all too weak or divided to command the nation" (ibid: 53).

But this is likely to take the Progressive's developing view of themselves too much to heart, leaving undetermined precisely why such views would come to shape the coming century, from the New Deal to the "suburban liberals" of the contemporary Democratic Party, so deeply. It seems questionable to argue that the upper class was weak and divided at the very moment when it had consolidated, in the form of railroad companies, corporations, and banks, institutions of unprecedented political-economic power. If, by 1890, "51 percent of all property was held by the top 1 percent, and 88 percent of the population controlled just 14 percent of the wealth" (Rana 2016: 45), it seems difficult to argue that the upper class was "too weak or divided to command the nation" (McGerr 2003: 153). Certainly, financial crises, labor turmoil, scandals over meatpacking processes, and so on, presented challenges to the security of ongoing profits, but the conditions argue more for a relatively centralized power with looming problems to solve, rather than a power too weak to command social labor. As revisionist accounts have argued for some time, Progressive reforms largely served to foster the long-term interests of "big" capital, rather than presenting a fundamental challenge to them. "It is business control over politics [...] rather than political regulation of the economy that is the significant phenomenon of the Progressive Era" (Kolko 1963: 3). The Progressives sought to extend to the state the managerial model initiated in factories, not to challenge the new orders of business.[11]

---

10 | McGerr includes in his count all sales and clerical workers, in addition to professionals, managers, etc., as well as their family members, to arrive at this figure.

11 | "In fact, the major corporations tended to move somewhat ahead of the reformers in attempts to extend the range and continuity of their power through bureaucratic means." (Wiebe 1967: 181)

At the same time, the idea of "business control over politics" should not be overstated. If the reforms and regulations that Progressivism instituted were in the broad interest of business, they were also regulations that businesses could not maintain on their own. Competition between individual firms, contradictions between different fractions of capital, and the broad distrust of business in an era of labor unrest, agrarian protest, the reconfiguration of labor processes, and so on, meant that the intervention of the state, as representative of the "people-nation" and unifier of the dominant class was a requisite of systemic reforms. But this also meant that, in the experience of Progressives as of many businessmen, the relationship between the two groups appeared as (and in certain cases, in relation to certain firms or fractions, actually was) deeply contradictory. Operative in these conflicts was precisely the notion of the "public good" on which Progressivism insisted and which it would mobilize against recalcitrance. To save the system would require overturning private interests not yet in line with the new spirit of the times. A new form of professionalized public service articulated a viewpoint that could render these disordering pressures legible to at least those capitals concentrated enough to cover the costs of reforms without a significant loss in profits.

At issue here, in other words, were early but definitive stages in the general shift that Poulantzas analyzed in monopoly capitalism: "the displacement of dominance within the CMP [capitalist mode of production] from the economic to the political, i.e., to the state," as the state becomes involved in "the actual process of the extended reproduction of capital as a social relation" (Poulantzas 1975: 100-101). It is this transformation that the political agency of mental laborers helped inaugurate, in coalitions with "big capital." "These coalitions offered the intellectuals political strength beyond their meager numbers and promised the interest groups improved services through bureaucratic organization," while "institutionalizing the place of the 'bureaucratic and professional elements'" (Skowronek 1982: 45). This was the kind of bargain early knowledge workers were more than willing to make. The general rise in economic growth and productivity, as well as an increase in the average standard of living, provided "decisive affirmation of science as the predominant and undisputable system of cognitive and ideological validation. Expressed in the emergence of scientific management ideologies and in the notion of a transpolitical state, the shift in dominant ideology legitimized the status of the expert and exalted his role" (Larson 2017: 200).

Conflicts over moral reforms or the speed and character of specific policy changes were real but could generally be resolved through evolving procedures of bureaucratized state decision-making. The unities-in-division fashioned between these competing interests and the applications of policy science by newly minted professionals were acts of reconstruction of the state, generally serving the efficient expansion of the economy as a whole (while, no doubt, leaning on the specific interests of the newly minted institutional forms of big capital which were, after all, "the future" of that economy).[12] The ability to develop and enforce such policies would require an increase in the administrative power of the state relative to individual private firms (and relative to the powers of the legislative branch) but the power itself still ultimately derived from capital. Imposing that power indirectly, by strengthening the legitimacy and authority of professional expertise and state institutions, allowed capital to both resolve many of the problems it was confronting and to accrue greater social legitimacy. The state could only be an "objective," scientific appraiser of regulatory schemas, after all, if its administrative associations were removed from the direct influence of the electorate. The key was to make that removal appear like a part of the same "fair dealing" that progressives claimed regulation would serve: "The bitter resentment of corporate power would be diffused and absorbed by a commission dedicated to the promotion of business confidence, industrial efficiency, and fair dealing in its reconciliation of disputes" (Skowronek 1982: 146). In the long run, these transformations would allow a shifting of blame for economic failures and tensions from business to state elites. In the meantime, Progressive reforms would allow firms to free themselves from the direct costs of "welfare work," while granting mental labor at the state-level a greater legitimacy as representing (or as concerned with) the "people-nation."

In this manner, another layer of separation between governors and the governed was added to the state's representative structure, in the name of correcting the worst excesses of capitalist social relations and producing social peace. Typically, progressives feared what they saw as the ignorance of the masses even more than the anarchic competition of free markets or the egoism of the wealthy, a fear that would only grow after the Russian

---

12 | See, for example, the discussion of early railroad regulation in the US in Skowronek 1982 or of anti-trust policy and judicial oversight in Sklar 1988. Also, Kolko 1963.

Revolution. The masses in ascendance were too indiscriminate to recognize the proper rewards of merit that professionals had worked so hard to receive. Their political project was an extension of this achievement, which they did not intend to relinquish. "Science" simply demanded that the bearers of capital, in their productive and consumptive roles, live up to the morality that, in the factory, brought them their profits.

At the same time, we need neither understate nor wholly instrumentalize the moral character of progressive appeals, their shock at urban conditions, their attacks on child labor and the evils of drink. Such empathic impulses could (and can still) be a motivating force for knowledge workers, especially insofar as the reforms they drive do not require changes from mental laborers themselves. Rather, the world is to be made over in their own image. Increased regulatory oversight and social interventions produce increased opportunities for state-funded knowledge work. Thus, in most forms of progressivism, the idealist tendencies of mental labor coalesce into a kind of moral idealism, a more or less radical intent to make the world better without fundamentally changing what it already is, at least in relation to oneself.

This was not a vision of the working-class winning its own rights but of the application of expertise to social problems and to persons who, left to their own in competitive markets, would suffer some form of demoralizing, de-individualizing harm (just as professional expertise, left to the open market, would suffer from the competitive appeals of charlatans and quacks). "[R]eformers most wanted workers and the upper ten to become different people, the sort who would not pursue their own interests exclusively" (McGerr 2003: 134). And this meant, for many Progressives, a distrust of labor unions' class-based organization, even if they could support union actions in cases where capitalists' egoism was too excessive (Croly 2006b [1914]). While empathetic to workers' suffering, progressives tended to view that suffering (and the conditions that produced it) as rendering workers unable to help themselves: "it was up to compassionate outsiders to remake the working class" (McGerr 2003: 134). This view also shaped their particular focus on children and education. If it was too late for working-class adults to take on the values of professionals (or, at least, become "dutiful, hardworking loyal citizens"), it was not so for their children. "Our problem," as Woodrow Wilson once suggested, "is to make them as unlike their fathers as we can" (ibid: 100, 110-111).

As history would show, there was an essential ambiguity in such conceptions regarding whether the poor were to be held responsible for the lack which expertise filled, or whether that lack was a product of social conditions that could be ameliorated. Progressives differed on the answer to that question, but they could also largely avoid it, insofar as either answer solicited the same cure: scientific education and moral reconstruction. The vision of that cure shaped the increasing role of the state (and of middle class reformers) in the social reproduction of the working class. Under Progressive influence, the state first undertook a direct concern with "family management" or "the scientific management of domestic work," an enterprise that centered on the reformation of education and training of women in "the basics of modern domestic efficiency" (Dalla Costa 2015: 7-12). Yet, because so much of their work simultaneously involved drawing children out of the home, remaking them in a more responsible image under guides more responsible than their parents, this was a vision of reproduction as reconfiguration. Social peace would come by producing workers who thought and lived like knowledge workers, but more cheaply and without credentials.

Finally, Progressives sought to further dilute the structures of representation, especially as they related to the working class. Power was to be centralized because "the average American individual is morally and intellectually inadequate to a serious and consistent conception of his responsibilities as a democrat" (Croly: 2006a [1909]: 23). Adopting the electoral elements of the Populist program (direct elections of senators, referenda, etc.), Progressives paired them with an assault on the supposedly corrupt mass party "machines" that had brought the masses into active engagement in democratic life. Insisting on secret ballots, while reducing the number of elected positions and the frequency of elections, transformed the act of voting into that of the isolated individual as bearer of professional political knowledge, sapping it of the collective character which, for all their problems, party machines had granted it. "Democratic" reforms, Progressives demonstrated, could be paired with massive declines in democratic participation and enthusiasm (Kornbluh 2000; Haber 1965).

Premised on a separation of mental from manual labor, of political governance from the governed, progressive politics could not fundamentally question structures of domination, nor wholly countenance any independent struggle or institutions of the working class. The vision of shared national interests that its knowledge served could, thus, never essentially improve on Taylor's: the expansion of production and consumption and the quasi-universalization of, or at least subordination to, professional values. Even in the handful of cases where progressives leaned towards "socialism," their conception of it involved state ownership, expert management, and increasing efficiency and productivity, not workers' control over the labor process or a reconfiguration of their exclusion in principle from political rule.

Still, as labor unions continued to strengthen over the first half of the twentieth century, progressives had to come to terms with them, often pressing union leaderships to model themselves on professional bureaucracies, yet also, of political necessity, incorporating some of their substantive goals into a coalitional politics. The Democratic Party, like other center-left parties of the mid-twentieth century, became the bearer of this coalition. A full development of this historical trajectory would need to carry forward into the New Deal and Keynesianism (Dalla Costa 2015; Mann 2017). For our purposes here, it is enough to observe that the project of state control over the social reproduction of labor power, as well as the material incentives provided for consent, broadened and deepened across this period, in response to the pressures of mass movements, depression, world war, anticolonial, and civil rights struggles. What also endured was the peculiar political fusion by which mental laborers, viewing themselves as autonomous, motivated only by a concern for the common good, could draw on and direct the power of capital as a whole towards the social peace it needed for ongoing accumulation.

By way of this fusion, progressive intellectuals could view themselves as the bulwark of social order, its high-minded guarantors and protectors. "*Civilization*," as Keynes put it in 1938, "is a thin and precarious crust, erected by the personality and will of a very few, and only maintained by rules and conventions skillfully put across and guilefully preserved" (cited by Mann 2017: 9). It was only with the crises of the 1970s, capital's determined quest to restore the falling rate of profit, and the ascension of a novel, less peaceful, conception of mental labor, that the coalition that defined the progressives' century would begin to collapse. The weakening of labor and the shifting discourse of political economy enabled the ascension of a new cohort of professional progressives to almost complete control of the Democratic and other center left parties.[13] In the process, they would also betray their fundamental weakness.

Perceptions of the Governed

As Barack Obama donned the mantle of Progressivism, seeking to reinvigorate its vision of a shared national purpose (Kloppenberg 2016), the Tea Party popularized a long-gestating conservative critique of Progressivism as a malicious conspiracy against American values and the Constitution, premised on the idea that "the governing elite knows best" (Teles 2016: 453). In the confrontation between the two, progressivism was projected into the center of the contemporary political crisis, as both its solution and its cause. If it is, in actuality, neither, the discussion above points to the ways in which the latter is closer to the truth.

A fuller sense of the specific "neoliberal" turn given to mental labor (and progressives' acceptance of much of it), as well as the perverse dynamics of racial liberalism, developed in subsequent chapters, will help clarify some of the complexities of this confrontation. Here, I want only to point to this battle over the meaning of the progressive tradition and its political sequels – Obama's inability to achieve much of what he attempted (especially that shared sense of national purpose), the surprising support for Bernie Sanders in the 2016 Democratic primary, and the even more surprising general election victory of Donald Trump – as symptoms of the dead-end of that tradition, and the centrality of the division between mental and manual labor to the ongoing crisis. Two central determinants of that crisis, in other words, are a long-gestating resentment of the privileges and ostensible powers of mental labor and the incapacity of contemporary progressives to meaningfully respond to it.

For all the powers of control it is granted in its separation from manual labor, mental labor also suffers, as Marx and Engels suggested, from the terms of that deliverance. It tends towards reverie or rigidity, to an idealism that functions as a form of wish-fulfillment, resorting to denial (often via a wall of statistics) when reality does not match up with its "scientific"

---

13 | "Marking a trend that began with McGovern's candidacy, in 1988 a majority of professionals supported Dukakis in the presidential election [...] [B]y 2012, Barack Obama earned the support of an overwhelming number of knowledge workers, particularly those with a postcollege education." (Geismer 2015: 2)

predictions, forced into reckoning only by falling profits or recalcitrant workers. The cluelessness of management is a cliché amongst workers for good reason, as is the rank stupidity of the routinized vision of work tasks and personalities contained in managerial and human resource grids, assessment mechanisms, and morale boosters. The archetype here too is Taylor and the "curious blindness" at work in his "consuming search for exactitude" in the time-study of specific work tasks. This "keystone" of his system

was in fact shot through with guesswork, although he disguised this by inventing seemingly precise percentage formulas to account for unexpected circumstances and by equipping his time-study men with carefully constructed record blanks, which were nevertheless of little help in fulfilling the perplexing burden Taylor imposed on them to separate the 'necessary' from the useless motions (Rodgers 1978: 54-55).

For capital, this blindness of mental labor is not (only) a weakness. It is also a means for placing blame, when profits fall or workers become recalcitrant, onto mental labor itself: the problem is not capitalist relations of production but a regrettable error that can be corrected by replacing management staff, hiring new consultants, or adopting a new managerial regime ostensibly more in tune with workers' concerns.

At the same time, this idealism operates, in its borrowing of power from capital and state, with a real and pervasive force. If the rationalized labor process is distanced from the experiences of the workers submitted to it, if it is run through by inefficiencies, irrationalities, or an overarching cruel indifference, workers must nevertheless submit to it if they wish to draw their wage. Those who design and manage such systems – whatever their apparent stupidities – have behind their authority an entire system of pedagogical sorting, assessing, and credentialing, recognized and endorsed by capital. As an ideological construction materialized in social relations, the division between mental and manual labor operates as (if) real, defining social relations, producing core elements of common sense and of subjectivities. The more pervasive this ideology becomes, the more those defined as "manual" (or unskilled) laborers suffer from it.

At the same time, we must avoid adopting this ideological perspective in our understanding of manual laborers themselves: they are not mere dupes or objects of an imposed system of thought. They think, see through the ideology, bear witness to the cluelessness of managers and "liberal elites," struggle to solve the dilemmas of their own social conditions, to render their own experience coherent. To the extent that they fail in these tasks, they are not any different from the mental laborers on whose follies this book is principally focused.

It is worth recalling that, in the period just before Progressivism, its precursors in managerialism and fiscal governance elicited waves of resistance to the rule of mental labor, claims to the rights – and to the wholeness – of labor itself, which, at least for many skilled, craft workers and small farmers, was still something that could be summoned in recent experience. In the 1870s, the Knights of Labor could argue that *"workers' inventiveness* was the source of social and economic progress" and that this recognition justified not only the full citizenship of workers but also the democratization of the workplace itself (Voss 1993: 82). Likewise, the Farmers' Alliance sought to assert their rights and capacities to rule on their own behalf, incorporating the newest findings of agrarian science into their farming practices, while designing new models for the state's role in the economy that would support yeomen farmers against the incursion of railroad profiteers, mortgage banks, and industrialized agriculture (Pollack 1990; Postel 2009). But the Knights and the Populists were decimated by the consolidated powers of capital, which would find the Progressives more amenable.

Across the twentieth century, in a history yet to be traced in full, workers experienced and resisted the intensifying function of capital, the control that knowledge workers exercised, in the labor process, in the educational system, in culture, and in the state. In the 1980s, a quantitative survey of workers would reveal just how central this element had become in their experience: "For both men and women the mental-manual class division is the single most important determinant of class perception" (Vanneman/Cannon 1987: 81). But the lack of consistent and coherent theorization of this division and its effects has also left uncertainty about the implications of such perceptions. The occasional efforts to address that uncertainty are haunted by the same separation they seek to analyze.

In the 1970s, for example, Richard Sennett and Jonathan Cobb diagnosed the complex affective character of workers' absorption of the meritocratic discourse of "ability" as the legitimation for authority over them. On Sennett and Cobb's account, that discourse postulates that "everyone in this society, rich and poor, plumber and professor, is subject to a scheme of values that tells him he must validate the self in order to win others' respect and his own" (Sennett/ Cobb 1972: 75). Based on their interviews with manual laborers, they argued that this discourse of ability failed at an abstract level yet succeeded at a personal one. When the "ability" of "educated men" is "considered in essence rather than in relation to his personal background and memories," then the worker finds it "a sham, and repugnant." And yet, "the power of the educated to judge him, and more generally, to rule, he does not dispute. He accepts as legitimate what he believes is undignified in himself." This, Sennett and Cobb suggest, is what explains that workers, despite their fundamental resentment of mental laborers' authority, do not rebel more actively against it. Workers "are not rebellious in the ordinary sense of the word; they are both angry and ambivalent about their right to be angry" (ibid: 78-79). They feel cheated unfairly of the freedom to develop themselves that mental laborers are presumed to have had, yet have trouble repudiating the right of such "developed" individuals to hold positions of authority. They suspect that to challenge the limits on their freedom "they must *first* become legitimate, must achieve dignity on a class society's terms, in order to have the right to challenge the terms themselves" (ibid: 153).

In some respects, this analysis complements one from two decades earlier, which reads the effects of the mental/manual division principally through the confrontation between political conceptions of freedom and individuality and "a mechanized way of life at work, mechanized forms of living, a mechanized totality which from morning till night, week after week, day after day, crushed the very individuality which tradition nourishes and the abundance of mass-produced goods encourages" (James 1993: 116). This tension, C.L.R. James argues in his analysis of U.S. society in the 1950s, produces a "sleepless antagonism between the workers and the supervising personnel, from which arises an abnormal tension, continuous disruption of production and an atmosphere which periodically explodes in labor conflicts of great violence over apparently secondary questions" (ibid: 108). James traces the expressions of that antagonism in mass culture, in the filmed exploits of gangsters and private detectives, where, for workers, the "bitterness, the violence, the brutality, the sadism, the desire to revenge themselves with their own hands, to get some release from what society has done to them since 1929," finds temporary solace in the image of an individual who goes out and does the job himself. This, for James, explains the divergence between the "vulgarity" of mass culture and the refined *ennui* of high culture: "Intellectuals are bored. The masses are not. They have no freedom and they resent it" (ibid: 121).

Yet, there is also a divergence between these accounts in their readings of workers' personal experience. In Sennett and Cobb's account, the manual worker grasps the "sham" of ability abstractly but, at the individual level, doubts the validity of his own judgment. This account seems to capture something important about the manner in which the separation of mental from manual labor embodied in institutions of education, work, and politics becomes so fundamental that it is transformed into self-doubt. It is not that workers cannot understand, cannot know. As Poulantzas said, it might not even be that there is anything to know. It is that they do not feel the right (do not have the habit) of speaking in certain ways, about certain things, from which they have been excluded, about which no one listens to what they have to say. To know the manager is blind is different from feeling entitled to speak like a manager, which is different again from inventing how to work and think together without a manager.

Yet, where Sennett and Cobb see workers as ambivalent about their anger in immediate and personal situations, James find them animated, in their daily work, by a revolutionary immediacy:

the political ideas of workers are one thing, the deep responses to their work, the thing by which they live is something else [...] [O]ver and over again, the same workers who express as far as general politics are concerned conservative and even reactionary sentiments, will immediately turn around and express with regard to their daily work sentiments with the most revolutionary implications conceivable (ibid: 167).

This combination of a vast rage and local knowledge informed James's conviction that "in two years, or five, in ten, that does not matter," there would be a radical new political party in the United States, comprising many millions of members, advocating workers' control and management of industry, along with "complete technical education" for everyone (ibid: 274-275).

If our first thought might be that the difference here is one of historical situation, it is worth remembering that the 1970s were actually a period of widescale workers' mobilization, wildcat strikes, and demands for revisions of labor processes (Windham 2018). Did Sennett and Cobb miss something? Was James overly optimistic? Perhaps both. Perhaps workers are not only ambivalent about their anger but also angry, in turn, about that ambivalence. To be brought face to face with one's own self-doubt can be enraging.

Still, what both analyses overlook, I want to suggest, is the extent to which the transition to *political* questions, or to questions of work and exploitation posed in a political register, inserts a second layer of separation between workers and expression or action. This second separation was the very product of the Progressive project, of their adaptation of the discourse of management to the political sphere. Politics has its own discourses, styles, and institutions, its own elites, its own secrets and doubts, while carrying out the same reduction of individual feelings, interests, and needs to irrelevance before the objective, scientific knowledge of experts. This is what people tacitly recognize when they say that they are "not interested in politics," that what one feels about one's daily work of production or reproduction is inadmissible in such a sphere, despite the fact that it would seem to be about nothing else. Ambivalence and anger might travel the short circuit from economics to politics (the former expressed, most often, by a simple withdrawal from politics altogether) but, without some reciprocal, critical, and collective articulation of them, the very things that the Progressive reduction of politics to isolated acts voting and expert commissions meant to exclude, they will not find a voice recognized as legitimate.

Inversely, the more or less definitive political separation over the last four decades between progressive professionals and workers has produced (or, rather, exacerbated) a form of political stupidity in progressives that mirrors and extends that of management. Set free from any substantive internal counter-powers, these parties of professionals have more or less wholeheartedly embraced ideals of "hard work, intelligence, and skill elevated meritocratic individualism" as their guideposts, pursuing policies marked by a diffuse "class-blindness," benefitting themselves, yet fortifying structures of economic and racial inequality (Geismer 2015: 8-10). It is not entirely mental laborers' fault: their work is well paid but rare and the meritocracy they subscribe to makes incessant demands on their responsibility. "They and their work are effectively bound up in one anxious embrace. Managers, scientists, lobbyists, researchers, programmers, developers, consultants, and engineers, literally *never* stop working" (The Invisible Committee 2009: 47). Not to mention that the world they work to control becomes fiendishly complex: just-in-time production, global logistical structures needing constant rerouting, automated programs and machines breeding new bugs with every update, sprawling urban complexes with digital infrastructure, financial trades by the millisecond, endless committees and subcommittees and reports and self-assessments. It is not entirely surprising the professional groups turn inward upon themselves, turn workspaces into quasi-communities. Increasingly, knowledge work knows only itself, which makes it all the easier to believe it is the only kind of work.

No longer is there even much pretense of improving conditions for manual workers. As wages remain stagnant, as inequality yawns ever wider, as everyone becomes subject to cycles of debt and risk assessment, as racial divisions spring back fresh and raw into public expression, progressives seem paralyzed in the face of the anger and frustration that will not, ultimately, be left out of politics, that does not take political forms they recognize as legitimate, and that is generally directed against them. Like Obama, they summon us to recommit to a form of national unity that the Progressives imagined at the start of the twentieth century. But the one thing conservatives are right about is that such a unity, on such terms, is no longer imaginable. It was so only for those who could imagine themselves as supervising a new, progressive tide of history, sweeping forward into enduring social peace.

Confronting novel social forces, summoning novel hopes, early twentieth century Progressivism put itself forward as the calm hand (and scientific mind) that could unify them, give order to them, harness them towards an obscure but materially substantive progress. In the ruins of those visions, today's progressives see primarily a world haunted by atavistic forces of ignorance and prejudice they thought had been banished over the course of their century. They summon visions of unity more as an exorcism of those specters and the disorder they augur, than as a plausible promise of a better future. Even on its own terms, that is not particularly inspiring.[14] Increasingly, it seems that progressives are the only ones who believe in their once ordained role. They explain their failures through a ghoul's list of specters from the past: the white working class, Russians,

---

14 | Though in a figure like Obama, it could temporarily be, insofar as his election seemed to symbolize a substantive reckoning with racial history. That it would not, in fact, be that had everything to do with Obama's progressive politics.

socialists who don't care about race or gender. Only these atavistic ghosts keep progressives from their rightful task of ruling the world as experts.

No one else knows how the world can hold together today without fundamentally changing: either the migrants must go or fossil capitalism must, but liberals are unlikely to get rid of either. Too empathetic to do nothing but too beholden to capital (which needs cheap labor and fossil energy) to enact fundamental change, progressives dither, couching their "moderation" in the language of high principle and objective science. The children must be let out of cages but ICE will remain. Carbon might be taxed but the infrastructure of the fossil economy will stay in place. Inequality must be addressed but professionals are part of the 99% too and will make sure that nothing too dramatic happens. Again, there is the implicit refrain: if everyone just thought and acted like professional knowledge workers, none of this would be happening. But without a counter power to press it into some substantive action, the makers of the knowledge economy turn in upon themselves, finding solace in the transformations that information science might yet bring about, the new energy source that science might yet uncover, and the optimism that a few more suburban liberals in the right districts might swing the next election their way.

Chapter 4: Mental Labor Declares War

> The first rational actor was the thermonucle-
> ar-armed national security state.
> (AMADAE 2016: 287)

At first glance, the neoliberal era can appear a fundamentally "anti-intel-lectual" one. The fostering of resentments ("They think they know better than you!") against traditional professionals in the social state, as well as professors and leftist students, the dismantling of many of the traditional safeguards of academic security and intellectual freedom, the expansion of intellectual property, the general insistence on the economic utility of programs of study and curricula, the rise of political leaders who disavow all the most basic trappings of intellectual insight, have led to a sense, for many intellectuals on the left, of being under siege, a feeling that the entire basis of a certain kind of intellectual autonomy, which material-ized in university accreditation and the public recognition of professional expertise, is being systematically dismantled, submitted to the cold logic of accumulation.

Much of this is, in an important sense, true but the paradox is that this attack on intellectuals and knowledge work has itself been devel-oped and fostered by distinct fractions of knowledge workers and a trans-formed ideology of mental labor. This chapter develops a sketch of the specific character of this transformed ideology by tracing the origins of their rising hegemony back to the peculiar hothouse of "military-indus-trial-academic technocracy" (Turner 2006) that came into being during World War II and intensified over the course of the Cold War. It is now, of course, commonplace to observe that neoliberal theory did not spring into existence *ex nihilo* on some cold, oil-deprived day in the 1970s but was the product of a long march through institutions and think-tanks undertaken by intellectuals discontented with the progressive/Keynesian common sense of the long 20th century. In its best-known form, this story centers on the continuing influence of the Austrian émigré, Friedrich Hayek, his theoretical conception of the market as an autonomous information-processing, price-finding machine, and his central role in founding the Mont Pèlerin Society (Mirowski 2013; Mirowski and Plehwe 2009; Dardot and Laval 2013).

Yet, in key respects, this story goes too far back in time to wholly clarify either why neoliberal theory was able to triumph during a crisis occurring some 40 years after the first meeting in Mont Pèlerin or what exactly defined the conception of knowledge work that ultimately triumphed, reshaping in the process much of our collective understandings of social relations, political systems, and economic goals. Hayek's influence no doubt remains important, but he often serves, as we will see, as a kind of legitimating icon for a conception of knowledge and knowledge-practices divergent from his own and having distinct socio-political origins.

Other historical accounts of neoliberalism have emphasized the "businessmen's crusade," in which corporate executives, seeking to roll back labor's gains and counter the waves of anti-capitalist social movements, entered more concertedly than before into practices of political fundraising, lobbying, campaigning, strategizing, and the coercive use of municipal debt (Phillips-Fein 2009, 2017). On their own terms, these histories seem unassailable, offering critical articulations of the specific political pathways by which power consolidated behind a shift in the character of capitalist political-economy.

My question here is somewhat different. I want to trace the origins not of the political movement's victory but of the specific epistemological, or political-ideological, conception of mental labor, of the form that knowledge should take and the effects it should have, that arose in the postwar period and that, combined with the power of capital, directed neoliberal transformations of economy and politics. Those practices were defined by new forms of "strategic rationality," epitomized by game theory, that emerged and rose to increasing dominance in the Cold War crucible.

If, at the turn of the 19th century, the developing model of corporate management informed the recasting of the U.S. state in Progressive bureaucracy, at the mid-point of the 20th century, it was the state that led the way towards a new ideological articulation of mental labor. In the dynamics of the Cold War, where the global defense and expansion of capitalism as a socioeconomic system could be presented as a defense against the forces of evil, the U.S. state could, at least for a time, square the contradictions between its national vocation and the global advancement of the (relatively unified) capitalist class, enforcing a compromise with the (relatively empowered and organized) dominated classes at home while violently suppressed them abroad. In this context, state apparatuses, especially the military, were driven to develop new forms and practices of mental labor adequate to increasingly complex problems of control and direction. In the process, the conception of mental labor's intrinsic *telos* shifted from one of producing social peace premised on the public good, to one of winning wars, thermonuclear and insurgent, and imposing order, a difference that indexes the specific social relations and forms of crisis operative in the historical epochs of their respective hegemonies.

The broad influence of this project, which expanded outward along the axes of both governance and private capital, bespeaks the intertwined interests of large firms, economic policy makers, and Cold War races to arm, surveil, and intervene in third world countries, focused on an intensification and acceleration of technological innovation and linked to a need for ever more exact planning within firms, military programs, and, to the extent possible, in the macroeconomy. At its base, this trajectory of developed capitalist societies, epitomized by the U.S., turned on the dwindling of sources of surplus profit other than technological innovation and the acceleration of the turn-over time of fixed capital (Mandel 1975: 192, 222). The large-scale investments of capital required for both research and the development and constant upgrading of fixed capital assets, as well as the increasing complexity of the processes of production, drove a need for a tighter and more exact control over the components of those processes, including, of course, labor. The fall of the rate of profit that begin to set in in the 1960s – in part, precisely because of growing investments in fixed capital – would only intensify that quest for control. Increasingly, as Ernst Mandel argues, capital was inherently constrained *"to increase systematic control over all elements of the processes of production, circulation, and reproduction, a systematic control which is impossible without regimentation of the economic and social life as a whole"* (1975: 241). The strategic rationality produced by the Cold War technocracy, conceived on the model of military "command and control," would be brought to bear on the task. Its bearers would become organic intellectuals of capital, no longer identifying mental labor with the state's embodiment of a national interest potentially opposed to individual capitals and intent on incorporating workers, but, instead, more openly identifying with power, articulating a shared capital-state project of revivifying capital accumulation and fragmenting worker resistance.

At stake in the growing conflict between the progressive conception of knowledge's social role and that of strategic rationality were the contradictions that the political separation of mental labor had produced and the emergent tensions between it and the needs of capital in crisis. The struggle to generalize neoliberal rationality, to achieve hegemony for it, had to move, at least initially, by way of popular appeals grounded in long-simmering resentments and distrust. Ironically, the rise of the knowledge economy and its supporting political structures, were facilitated by a manipulation of the growing anger against professional knowledge workers. What lays siege to progressive intellectuals today is, in a sense, a monster of their own making, which is why it has proved so difficult for them to resist and why so many have so easily accommodated themselves to it.

The Rationality of (Cold) War

In search of new imperialist forms in a newly divided and contentious world, the U.S. state, taking advantage of the post-war situation into which it had emerged as the only undiminished industrial power, developed "soft" forms of power meant to pacify racialized antagonisms and persuade third-world nations to opt for the promises of capitalist development.[1] However, as the Soviet Union demonstrated its capacity to launch satellites, build nuclear weapons, and challenge the dominance of liberal democratic capitalism in Eastern Europe and beyond, the U.S. state also undertook massive investments in scientific research and development, intended to ward off the threat of Soviet dominance in technology. R&D spending by the federal state grew an average of 10% in constant dollars every year between 1960 and 1967 (when total funding reached $16.5 billion). 91% of those funds went to defense, space, and atomic energy research (Bell 1976: 259).

One central component of this research was the development of new models of "strategic rationality" meant to guide the increasingly global

---

[1] | See the following chapter for more on this progressive side of post-war state projects.

interests of U.S. capital through the perils of mutually assured destruction and guerilla insurgency. Unprecedented threats appeared to require new forms and practices of knowledge. If one traces the development of the key discourses of contemporary neoliberal political economy – game theory, public and rational choice theories, law and economics – they all have interlinked roots in this military program of research, which brought together knowledge workers from a variety of academic disciplines and business sectors and created novel forms of public-private partnerships. Collectively, they answered to a felt need for new forms of decision-making and computation to address complex tasks requiring quick decision times, running from the aiming of anti-aircraft armaments to the organizing of supply distribution to thermonuclear war (Edwards 1996, Erickson et al. 2013, Franklin 2015, Mirowski 2002, Amadae 2003, 2015, Davies 2017, MacLean 2017).

The RAND corporation, initially a joint venture of the Douglas Aircraft Company and the U.S. Army Air Force (with deep links to the Ford Foundation), was a central nexus of these developments. Conceived as a quasi-independent vehicle for the evaluation of military hardware problems and development, the intellectuals employed by RAND quickly took on broader aspirations, developing models of rational systems analysis, that were first applied to the question of the relative nuclear capacities of the United States and the Soviet Union, before being adopted by Robert McNamara as a model for running the Pentagon and ultimately extended by Lyndon Johnson to all apparatuses of the government, including his Great Society programs. Privileging "claims of scientific rigor and objective calculation" as the proper principle of authority, this model of analysis usurped traditional sites, from the "experience and judgment of seasoned military officers" to the *demos* (Amadae 2003).

The prospect of thermonuclear war was an ideal horizon for the apotheosis of an abstracted model of mental labor: there were literally no experiences that could inform strategic approaches to it. "The unknown proportions of thermonuclear war opened a window for conquering uncertainty with pure intellect" (Amadae 2015: 76). Rational decisions in such unprecedented conditions would need to be made quickly and could not be informed by historical precedents. Similar constraints were taken to hold in relation to guerilla conflicts, where insurgent and counterinsurgent forces faced off in a struggle ultimately determined by the ability of each to sway the neutral majority of the local population, necessitating (for the counterinsurgents at least) precise, overwhelming attacks that would undermine the insurgency's support (Harcourt 2018). Mental labor came to be envisioned as a totalizing form of abstract, yet effective modelling, the embodiment of military command and control functions in uncharted territories.

The proposed models for this approach were, ultimately, algorithmic. Game theory, perhaps the most influential of such models, promised nothing less than "a set of rules for each participant which tell him how to behave in every situation which may conceivably arise" (Neumann and Morgenstern 2004: 31). But it could provide such rules (even for the limited cases of two-party, zero-sum games, which it had some success at mathematically modeling) only by operationalizing a number of abstract assumptions as given conditions for decision-making: "only outcomes factor into choice, value is fungible and precedes social context, individuals act independently despite others, and gratuitous generosity is counter to instrumental rationality" (Amadae 2003: 288). The rational choice, according to the "expected utility" that classical game theory provided models for calculating, was therefore that which maximized one's own potential outcomes. Applied more broadly to social and political relations in general, these assumptions fostered a view of agency that was not only hyper-individualistic and defensive of the status quo but also counseled "defaulting" on any collective terms of agreement, no matter what other agents do, as the only means for maintaining "strategic rationality," even (or especially) in a case as extreme as nuclear war (Amadae 2015).

Counterbalancing the relative simplicity of the rules that strategic rationality claimed to derive – and which would ostensibly allow for their quick and consistent use in war-time decisions – were the massive amounts of data that would be required to apply them to complex situations, and which, like expected utilities, would need to be rendered into a quantitative, calculable form. The application of such rules required a vast expansion of surveillance and data-gathering operations, and the demands of processing that data helped drive the design of increasingly powerful computers. Emblematic here was the SAGE continental air defense system, undertaken around 1950, and envisioned as providing a wholly computerized system for identifying and neutralizing a Soviet missile launch against North America. While it drove innovations in computer, network, and interface technologies, SAGE was obsolete before it became operational and it never achieved the automated control its designers had envisioned. In the face of the "unruly complexities" real life tests involved, the abstract, formal procedures of the system programming always faltered, requiring work-arounds by the system's human operators (Edwards 1996: 108). Despite this failure, SAGE articulated an aspirational model that would define what Paul Edwards calls the "closed world" model of such rationality: "enclosed and insulated, containing a world represented abstractly on a screen, rendered manageable, coherent, and rational through digital calculation and control" (ibid: 104).[2]

Internal to their abstractions, however, the rules of strategic calculation retained a substantive orientation derived from their combination of economic, military, and political elements. Game theory was shaped by a set of presuppositions drawn directly from neoclassical economics: the individual as calculating, rationally-choosing, self-interested, self-maximizing, her desires quantitatively ranked. Yet it brought those presuppositions to bear on scenarios of conflict and domination, zero-sum games between competitors with neither mutual trust nor (verifiable) shared interests. The result of this peculiar "short circuit" between the economic and the political was a fundamental departure from core precepts of traditional liberalism, in which the market was understood as the site of *reciprocal* exchanges serving the general interest and the political realm rested on a capacity for mutual forbearance, an "individual's self-incurred responsibility to avoid harming others," trusting that others would do the same. Subordinating politics to the individualizing, competitive logic of market transactions, while casting economic activity within a zero-sum conception of Cold War rivalry removed external, moral limits on the strategic calculations of individual minds, simplifying the elements strategic thinking had to calculate (Amadae 2016: 39).[3] There was no room for a common good in such calculations, only self-interest, simple rules, and an abundance of good data. Applied to economic and political questions (as

---

2 | For more on the implications of this shift and the role of computer technology, see Chapter 6.

3 | This difference can be overstated, of course. Amade tends, I think, to take classical liberalism too much at its word. Her account presents the difference between liberalism and neoliberalism as one of fundamental (ethical) commitments, whereas I conceive it as a difference between *ideological* systems of justification of capitalist political relations, each with their own internal contradictions.

well as psychological and evolutionary ones), strategic rationality carried over this militarized reframing of economic assumptions. The context of its application is always presumed to be akin to war. The pursuit of individual interests is always a game carried out in hostile territory, proscribing collaboration or solidarity. What matters is the outcome, not the means by which it is arrived at.

To the Victor, the Spoils

The alignment of this rationality with neoliberal political economy required a transition away from a fundamental tenet of pre-war neoliberal theory, including that of Hayek and the German ordoliberals. For them, the competitive, price-determining market was to be the central "decision process" by which the production and distribution of goods was guided. It could perform that function only insofar as a specific "economic constitution" was in place, a set of fundamental rights maintaining a consistent juridical frame for real and meaningful competition between individuals, "prevent[ing] monopolistic and cooperative practices from subverting or circumventing the price system" (Davies 2017: 83).

The Chicago School's "Law and Economics" movement, under the influence of R.H. Coase's seminal 1960 paper, "The Problem of Social Costs," abandoned this vision of an economic constitution underpinning pure market competition and market-determined prices.[4] In brief, Coase had argued that, if the costs of all economic activity, including regulation, were taken into account, then "industrial strategies which undermine competition could be efficient, relative to the other alternatives (especially when those alternatives included costly regulatory interventions)" (ibid: 84). Because market transactions have costs, market exchanges may not always provide the best means for achieving the efficiency-maximizing goal of competitiveness. This conception allowed neoliberal political economy to make peace with corporations and quasi-monopolies. If corporate forms of internal planning yielded efficiencies that offset the impact

---

4 | This is not to say that later neoliberal thought abandoned all ideas of a "economic constitution." Quite the contrary. But the constitutionalism it embraces is one that, rather than protecting the rights of individual economic agents, requires governments to enact specific fiscal, trade, or other economic policies informed by the competitiveness evaluations of economists.

of market dominance on prices, and if, in principle, future competition was possible, should prices scale too high, then strategic management of a firm could be competitively superior to open market competition.

Two effects this shift had are critical. First, the strict application of Coase's cost-evaluation transforms the character of law and rights along the lines forecast by game theory: it is only outcomes that matter and the only outcome that matters is one that can be quantitatively measured, i.e., economic growth and wealth maximization. Law itself has no normative character from such a perspective, rather its "basic function [...] is to alter incentives," to shift the costs according to which rational actors calculate the course of action that is in their interests (Posner 1981: 75; cited by Davies 2017: 88). "Rights are no longer intrinsically meaningful or defensible; instead, they exist and are justified as means to effectively generate wealth." If the progressives had sought to establish a common interest in "efficiency" as the means for a just peace between labor and capital, for neoliberals "'efficiency' became a proxy for 'justice'" (Davies 2017: 87) or justice became equivalent to "wealth maximization" (Amadae 2003: 206-207).

Second, the shift from normative legal principles to the analysis of relative efficiencies (competitiveness) as the basis for sound markets likewise shifts the site of "decision processes" from market agents to economists and administrators who carry out cost analyses (including, increasingly, as a part of juridical procedures). A peculiar form of objectivity is attributed to neo-classical economic analysis, "elevating [it] to an unprecedented authority in determining the optimal institutional and legal arrangements [...] The economist's vocational and epistemological distance from moral reasoning is the crucial ingredient in neoliberal legal authority" (Davies 2017: 101). The abstraction at the core of strategic rationality becomes equated with the "objective" distance required for sound political judgment.

At the same time, this intrinsic valuation of abstraction and mathematical forms of reasoning means that the strategic effectiveness of such models was never subjected to traditional scientific trials intended to prove their validity. Even failures, like that of SAGE, seemed to leave the vision of strategic rationality untarnished. "[R]ational decision technologies gained legitimacy not on paper or in intellectual debate, but *because* they became institutionalized in practice [in key agencies of the state] and played the role of transferring authority, rationalizing ponderous decisions, and shaping the material reality of people's lives" (Amadae 2003: 72).[5] Once directly backed by the powers of state and capital, the logic of mental labor could ostensibly be deduced from mental labor alone.

Rather than being adopted by the state through the persuasive appeals of intellectuals linked to it by the mediating function of university accreditation, the chain of influence now moved from *de facto* legitimacy within state apparatuses towards a broader acceptance by academic and social institutions. This transition was not taken for granted, precisely because the established hegemony of progressive intellectuals within the elite university system and in the "left hand" of the state made substantial assistance from those quarters unlikely. Rather, business interests launched a strategy, modeled on the history of the revolutionary left, of constructing an alternative institutional base for its own cadre of mental laborers, ones less tied to the fetish of professional "autonomy." "'We can learn a lot from Lenin and the Leninists,' suggested Murray Rothbard, the Manhattan-based talent scout for the Volker Fund," primarily "the 'advancement of the "hard core" of libertarian thought and libertarian thinkers' from which all else would flow in time" (cited by MacLean 2017: 84).

Expanding on the base of ideas and intellectuals cultivated by the military apparatuses, private capital, under stress, increasingly financed the diffusion of a rationality that validated and directed profit-maximization, laying aside the terms of the social peace that progressivism had brokered. Large scale donations to universities underwrote the hiring of department heads with free rein to stock their programs with ideological compatriots, elevating programs at previously marginal institutions, as with James Buchanan at the University of Virginia (hired in 1956) and then at Virginia Polytechnic Institute (1969) ([MacLean 2017: 109] or William H. Rikers at the University of Rochester [1960] (Amadae 2003: 167-171).[6] An explosion of business-friendly, business-funded, and sometimes CEO staffed policy institutes or "think tanks" took place over the course of the 1960s and 1970s. "Older organizations like the American Enterprise Institute (established in 1938) underwent revivals [...] while new outfits like

---

5 | MacLean also observes how James Buchanan's arguments concerning the self-interested reasoning of public officials were never supported by the analysis of specific cases (MacLean 2017:98).

6 | The "Navy's RAND-style think tank, the Office for Naval Analysis," was also housed there from 1967 through the 1970s.

the Heritage Foundation, the Cato Institute, and the American Legislative Exchange Council all burst onto the scene" (Waterhouse 2014: 7).

This development of counter-institutions outside the state offered to neoliberal radicals the same benefits it had for Leninists: a distance from the contradictions between different state apparatuses that ground ideas down into unifying, centrist compromises in "the national interest," allowing for the articulation of "pure" ideals and fighting strategies. Yet, if the dilemma of the Leninist party was its relation to a mass movement, whose force it drew upon and strove to direct, these think tanks drew their power (and these knowledge workers their salaries) directly from capital. In its early years, for example, Cato was wholly dependent on Charles Koch, who had helped conceive it. The capacity to inject enormous amounts of cash into small, previously marginalized intellectual circles, gave capitalist donors enormous influence, producing what one participant in Cato called "this bizarre gravitational shifting as Planet Koch adjusted everyone's orbits" (quoted in MacLean 2017: 142).

From such realigned planets emerged a host of graduates and acolytes that spread across the academic, think tank, and public policy worlds, over time converting prestigious business, economics, and political science departments, accruing legislative influence, and being appointed to judicial and administrative positions in federal and state governments. In the course of two to three decades, capital created a new cadre with direct ties to private capital's power and a presence in a widening number of state apparatuses, supplanting progressive state intellectuals.[7] The balance of forces in the state was fundamentally altered, as was the function of mental labor within it. In this respect, at least, the strategy of war has been an unalloyed success.

---

7 | The Reagan administration already employed "more than two hundred members of conservative think tanks": "Hoover (55), Heritage (36) and AEI (34) were particularly large sources of personnel" (Chernomas/Hudson 2017: 32). Mahler 2018 details the enormous sway that Heritage has had over administrative appointments in the Trump administration.

The Legitimacy of War

For some analysts of this success, its self-funding, self-authorizing, self-accrediting circle of influence, has allowed it to supersede the traditional legitimacy crises of the state (Brown 2015). But this is to overstate the difference between the progressive state form and the neoliberal one. Progressive experts did not, any more than neoliberal ones, seek legitimation from the public for their expertise; rather, both sought to insulate decision-making commissions and administrative branches from such influence. The *ethos* and the institutions that accredit such experts has undergone a fundamental shift but that does not necessarily undermine the state's legitimation requirements.

As Poulantzas (1978: 32-33) argues, the capitalist state has always employed "several discourses" or, rather, "a discourse that is broken into segments and fragments according to lines intersecting the strategy of power." One of those segments, that which addresses, while constituting, the "nation-people," serves a legitimating role in relation to the dominated. Another "concerns [the state's] strictly *organizational* role vis-à-vis the dominant class, including that of *formulating and openly expressing the tactics required to reproduce its power.*" This second segment is not hidden. The state has little need for conspiracy. "The truth of power often escapes the popular masses. But the State does not intentionally conceal it from everyone: rather, for infinitely more complex reasons, the masses do not manage to hear the state discourse directed to the dominant classes" (ibid). The separation of mental labor, as embodied in the state, from the political masses allows the strategies of the dominant to be articulated openly, albeit in forums and in forms that are not attended or read or experienced as relevant to those excluded from contributing to the decision procedures in question.

Still, the shift in the substantive values orienting these new forms – the maximization of wealth above all – does open the possibility of legitimacy challenges from those without access to such wealth. It is in relation to such potential challenges, in the legitimating segment of state discourse, that Hayek's thought continues to have wide influence, insofar as it provides a novel, populist strategy for it. Emphasizing both the liberating, equalizing character of market agency *and* the necessary or fate-like character of market processes, Hayek articulated them as reciprocal expressions of a single, spontaneous, market order. Since only the market can provide meaningful information, in the form of prices, regarding changes in the complex of market relations, all would-be experts are equally ignorant. Each agent can bring to bear only that "knowledge of particular circumstances of time and place" (2014: 95) that he has as a function of his unique circumstances and each is equally free to use his particular knowledge as he judges best. No one is inherently wiser than anyone else because no one has a substantially more comprehensive or totalizing insight of "society." Yet, at the same time, the price of this constitutive ignorance is that the verdicts of the market cannot be challenged and should not be altered. Some will lose, through no fault of their own, but to attempt to redress those losses would be to bring disorder to the machinic, market intelligence that directs the distribution of resources and the constant lowering of prices.

Drawing on Hayek allows the legitimating segment of neoliberal state discourse to occlude its organizational segment's emphasis on the state's role in imposing competitive logics and on experts' role in calculating competitiveness. Instead, it focuses attention on the agency of traditional, progressive knowledge workers and their interventions into the social order in the name of the public good or "social justice." The political defense of market freedoms is identified with a war waged on those experts, bureaucrats, and ideologues that have distorted the market order, producing losses which might otherwise be attributed to the market.[8] Resentment against mental labor, in other words, is channeled into a reordering of the state in the service of greater exploitation. Legitimacy is purchased by the perpetual fostering of anxiety and resentment towards the state that the progressives made. This ingenious legitimation strategy grants to neoliberal discourse its tincture of enduring exceptionality: there is always some vestige of the welfare state yet to be dismantled, always some self-serving, "progressive" bureaucrat yet to be revealed as the self-maximizing actor she pretends not to be. The ideal, normal condition of a wholly reconfigured state never arrives. Rather, this utopic segment of neoliberal discourse legitimates the political maneuvers by which a new breed of mental laborers organizes and maintains its own power and implements its strat-

---

8 | Cp. Mirowski 2013: 82, who notes that neoliberalism "seems at first to be a radical leveling philosophy, denigrating expertise and elite pretensions to hard-won knowledge, instead praising the 'wisdom of crowds.'"

egies for the expansion of capital accumulation. Unending war against progressives is a means to perpetually mobilize its troops.

The seamlessness of these new discourses and practices of mental labor should not be overstated. The ongoing redirection of resentment against progressive professionals and the welfare state is not merely a strategy but also a symptom of the resentments that neoliberal control of economic and political orders perpetually invokes. Because capital accumulation is riven by contradictions that can never be wholly resolved, this control over ever more complex competitive structures of distribution and production, more intensive waves of automation and outsourcing, is always breaking down, along with the ostensibly self-regulating operations of the market. Insofar as it can only resolve these crises through appeals to certain progressive methods (as in the financial bailout), the attack on them can also never end.

This segmented discourse has tended to confound its progressive critics. Every effort to reveal the hidden secrets of neoliberalism's organizational discourse gets caught up in its rhetorical exercise of expertise, its claim to know better than the dupes who have fallen for the trick. Each high-minded invocation of the public good or national interest can be stripped bare and revealed to be a defense of the positional interests of suburban liberals or young urban professionals, an assertion of their right to continuing sipping lattes while other people suffer. For the progressive who cannot reckon with their own social position, neoliberal discourse appears to have laid the perfect trap: it may be impossible to criticize it without a critique of the division between mental and manual labor.

The Coercive Supplement to Social Reproduction

As the rate of profit continued to fall across the 1970s and labor proved recalcitrant to efforts to raise it, the deepening symptoms of stagflation, the end of Bretton Woods, and the apparent strategic weakness of a governing elite fallen prey to OPEC and Iranian hostage takers, shaped the occasion for the emergence of neoliberal hegemony. The businessmen's crusade (Phillips-Fein 2009) pressed for a political complement to the management process commonly known as "deindustrialization": the shifting of production sites to lower wage regions, certainly, but, even more importantly, a round of intensive reconstruction and automation of labor processes (Moody 2018). The conjuncture facilitated both firms' retrenchment against aggressive unions and a bid to take over the state by a new breed of politicians and intellectuals, for whom strategic rationality would be the guiding model in this new battle to liberate capital from constraints.

In the process, the political implications of strategic rationality's abstractness were made manifest: its simple rules, its grounding presuppositions, can be brought to bear effectively on social reality only to the extent that reality is constrained to match those abstractions. Only by omitting much of the contingency of meaning and value that characterizes any concrete situation, the constitutive character of interelationality and uncertainty, can such reasoning be applied to them. Whatever does not conform to the premise of self-interested self-maximization comes to appear as a failure to achieve that goal. This explains the peculiar, highly specific, flexibility of its applications, shifting effortlessly from the staunchest defense of "established facts" to the most intensive skepticism of "scientific consensus," all depending on the extent to which such truths further the economic and political outcomes that such rationality presupposes and serves.[9] The inverse side of skepticism is the force used to subsume the world under a rationality identical to the maximization of self-interest.

Coercive force, in other words, is intrinsic to strategic rationality's applications, reshaping the field of choices through the threat of punitive sanctions, constraining an opponent's available options to the limited, quantitatively ranked outcomes on which strategy's implementation depends, maximizing one's own gains by demonstrating a willingness to "defect" from the game (Amadae 2016: 56). Rather than a natural logic, strategic rationality depends on the *making real* of its own assumptions. "We're an empire now," as an aide to George W. Bush once famously remarked, "and when we act, we create our own reality. And while you're studying that reality [...] we'll act again, creating other new realities" (Suskind 2004). Command and control become understood as the generalized imperative of all agency. All "humanistic" values or principles, from progressive invocations of some common good to radical critiques of exploitative social

---

9 | Cp. Stengers 2018: 17: "Scientists then discover, sometimes to their astonishment, that their traditional allies can be relied upon only when the 'facts' help 'increase productivity' – when that isn't the case, they are open to being transformed into promoters of relentless skepticism."

relations, become so much ambiguity to be sliced through by the clear lines of individualized, quantifiable strategies.

One can find this coercive logic at work everywhere today: in the view of competitiveness as something imposed by a strong state; in visions of new military forces so mobile and flexible that they can set conditions on the ground in response to a continuous flow of surveillance data; in the pedagogy of game theory itself, whose students "learn to limit their horizons regarding legitimate action as they conform to the tacit assumptions underlying strategic rationality" (Amadae 2015: 27); in the imposition of logics of "risk" onto (indebted) individuals and states to enforce their compliance with logics of capital accumulation; in the racializing practices of policing and incarceration; in the transformation of welfare into "workfare." Here, I want to focus briefly on this last example, precisely because it was central to establishing the hegemony of neoliberal rationality. If the anti-welfare campaign, "more than any other single thing, ushered in the neoliberal moment" (Briggs 2017: 13), it did so by bringing to bear both a coercive reordering of the field of choices for social reproduction and a populist attack on progressive elites.

The welfare state that progressives built had, of course, never been without its own elements of coercion. Its premise was an intellectual suspicion regarding those unable to care for themselves without state assistance (as of those unable to become "middle class" in general). But the generally rising demand for wage labor in the post-war era, as well as the moralized imperative to maintain social peace for the sake of efficiency, meant that, as long as someone proved to be "deserving" (a term that enclosed of course its own racialized, sexual, and other exclusions), they could generally expect some degree of state support, lest the predations of individual capitalists exhaust labor power's capacity to reproduce itself or tip the balance of social peace towards conflict.

Within this progressive frame, it ultimately proved possible to articulate welfare as a *right*, thereby recognizing the legitimacy of poor women's reproductive labor and its contributions to society. That, at least, was the premise and the promise of the welfare rights movement of the 1960s and 1970s. Backed by the threat of social unrest and a newly electorally empowered Black population, increasingly central to the Democrats' electoral coalition, that struggle was initially successful, at least in part. Welfare benefits and the population to whom they were available both increased substantially over the latter part of the 1960s. Progressive courts likewise appeared increasingly sympathetic to this juridical construction of state aid.

As economic conditions became more precarious, however, the racially motivated backlash to this movement – energized by the portrayal of urban uprisings by racialized surplus populations as the chaotic denouement of the Civil Rights struggle – became a central plank of a populist attack on progressive elites. That attack gave a particularly concrete, affective purchase to the discourses of public choice and market freedoms now favored by capital, yoking together resentment against the increasing control of knowledge workers over productive and reproductive relations with racialized divisions and suspicions central to US history as a settler colony. State assistance was presented as "the self-serving creation of a liberal 'intelligentsia' that used big government to shower public benefits on the poor—at the expense of workers' checkbooks and most cherished values" (Soss/Fording/Schram 2011: 33). Tax cuts became the material substratum of consent for the suburban middle class, while struggles to "remake welfare as we know it" provided a trial-run for the rationalizing of non-market spheres under market-like logics. A certain safety net would still be provided (albeit in smaller dollar amounts) but in a revocable form, subject to a range of sanctions requiring recipients to adapt themselves to the demands of the low-wage labor market in order to receive temporary aid.

On one level, the logic of this transformation merely extended the conception of the "deserving poor." Yet, by intervening directly in the processes of social reproduction rather than judging their results, by making welfare payments a kind of wage for the proper comportment of oneself, one's family, and one's childrearing (and birthing) practices, it revealed the ambition of neoliberal political economy to remake social reproduction itself into a domain subject to competitiveness and strategic rationalities. No longer could deserving recipients be left to negotiate the balance of wages and reproductive labor within the terms of their own judgment. Rather, the receipt itself coercively enforced a choice of work reduced to the range of jobs and wages capital was willing to offer. The progressive moral pedagogy of the welfare state gave way to an imposed imitation of "the pressures and incentives of low-wage markets [...] The adults who participate in welfare programs today are not positioned outside the market; they are actively pressed into accepting the worst jobs at the worst wages" (ibid: 7). Pushed to the margins, the growing intermittent labor force is forced to take responsibility for itself, to develop what modest forms of "human capital" it can attain, or to accept consignment to the informal margins of a political economy that increasingly lacks a place for them. Either way, the state will renounce all responsibility for aiding them after a handful of years.

The social worker is the (often unwilling) representative face of new "authorities" imposing this structure onto the choices of those below them (Soss/Fording/Schram 2011: 48-49), "a new breed of expert" whose knowledge work is "devoid of the traditional moral baggage of professionalism, and rooted instead in a dispassionate ability to measure, rank, compare, categorize, and diagnose, apparently uncluttered by moral, philosophical or social concerns" (Davies 2017: 147). Subjecting the lowest fractions of the proletariat to endless surveillance, review, and judgment (when not passing over into direct incarceration), the workfare state lays bare the coercive control that underpins the reduced set of choices we are all compelled to make, while serving as a warning to those not (yet) subject to its review. For that majority suspended in an increasingly confused, fragmented "middle" – neither part of the upper fractions of mental labor nor the lowest, surplus rungs of the working class – the balance between the experience of empowering choices and coercive reduction varies, across different individuals and across an individual life, but a sense of anxiety and frustration, of being held responsible for something over which one has little control, becomes increasingly pervasive.

Happiness as a Wartime Industry

Disciplining the poor only scratches the surface of the potential value of such experts and the forms of (self-)control they have developed. So it should not be surprising that, in recent years, in the face of increasing rates of exhaustion, depression, aimlessness, and uncertainty amongst employees at all levels, an entire industry of intensifying efforts to define and quantify "happiness" has sprung up, offering a variety of mechanisms for (self-)surveilling, (self-)assessing, and (self-)directing individuals' pursuit of that elusive goal. The private/public fusion of responsibilities that neoliberal governance prefers links the privatization of responsibility (as well as costs and profits) with a paternalistic advisory and regulatory regime that oversees and directs behavior, affect, and general "well-being" (Davies 2017).

In this form, companies have discovered a new form of "welfare work," addressed initially to their executive and knowledge workers but open to expansion beyond them. These programs are also available for individual purchase as well, and amenable to state administration in certain circumstances. As each sphere of human life is opened up to competitiveness, programs appear to assist us in maximizing our performance. Depression, sadness, isolation, and so on, appear not as social or relational problems but failures at self-maximization. Strategic rationality become the basis for a kind of rationalized, human-capital developing, competition-ready, form of "self-help," reshaping management into a form of therapy, "propping up the well-being of individuals, in order to keep their enthusiasm for service-based jobs as high as possible" (ibid: 127; see also Illouz 2008; Silva 2013). Well-being becomes a form of human capital, "an input to certain strategies and projects, a resource to be drawn upon, which will yield more money in return" (Davies 2017: 114). To be unhappy in a world where so much money is invested in your happiness is to be culpable at best, unemployable at worst. In this way, the controlling designs of mental labor (for all of the schemas, assessment tools, plans, programs, aids, etc., have been designed by and in the image of knowledge workers) penetrate further into the lived experience of all: "we are now witnessing the discreet return of the 'scientific management' style of Frederick Winslow Taylor, only now with even greater scientific scrutiny of bodies, movement and performance" (ibid: 136-137).

What might initially appear surprising, however, is that it should be this industry, and analogous forms of "empowering" the choices of those without much choice, that have come to represent the contemporary face of progressivism. But this adaptation of progressives to the conditions of neoliberal hegemony is perhaps not so confounding. The pragmatic, adaptive aspect of progressivism always aligned itself with what was "possible," meaning what capital and politicians were willing to accept, fund, and empower. Securing the ongoing (if now more tenuous) position of professionals in the contemporary political economy, while seeking to maintain some form social peace, remains the core of the progressive project. It is just that the terms of the peace to be established look less like a compromise between warring classes and more like providing comfort (or cover) to the casualties of strategic rationality's wars.

Once the application of that rationality, the imposition of competitive logics to the social order, became the accepted requirement for ongoing capital accumulation under new conditions, progressives were unlikely to oppose it. Rather, they came to position themselves as what Jamie Peck calls the "roll-out" face of neoliberalism, offering to ameliorate and reregulate market forces in ways that would correct for specific market failures that the initial phase of "roll-back" neoliberalism brought in its wake (2010: 22-24). Such amelioration often took, and continues to take, the form of further interventions in the choices and incentives offered to individuals as market-agents, only this time ostensibly for the common good, meaning to encourage (or "nudge") individuals into choices enabling their well-being. This drift of "progressive" policy was epitomized by Obama's hiring of the Chicago law professor, Cass Sunstein – one of the authors of *Nudge*, a popularizing account of "behavorial economics" (Thaler/Sunstein 2008) – to oversee the Office of Information and Regulatory Affairs.

While behavioral economics, at least in this instantiation, is grounded on a certain critique of the rationalizing assumptions of neoclassical economic and game theory, that critique centers on the incapacities of *individuals*, their inability to embody the pure strategic reasoner required for competitive success. Its goal is not to redeem substantive social relations or collective agency, but to offer the equivalent of tricks to correct for such individualized defects, using "the cognitive biases revealed by behavioral economics to justify expert manipulations of 'choice architecture'" (Soss/Fording/Schram 2011: 51). Already implicated in the coercive structure of welfare reform, contemporary progressivism has sought to import "softer" forms of imposed guidance into tax codes, regulatory policies, and so on (Mettler 2011), while insurance firms, technology companies, and others have worked to embed it into the personal-device infrastructure of our lives (often with government encouragement or support). In this way, progressive neoliberalism increasingly becomes the face of the explicit extension of neoliberalism's coercive logic into the ostensibly "private" realm of social reproduction, opening itself to new rounds of populist attack. Another perverse irony of neoliberalism is that, the more the progressive project accommodates itself to strategic rationality, the more transparently it becomes precisely what the public discourse of neoliberalism accuses it of being.

This in turn allows the proponents of a purer strategic rationality to not only mask their own interventions but to legitimate new applications of coercive force. A controlling elite that can never quite be banished becomes today a justification for more extreme measures. The tension between the simultaneous derision and intensification of mental labor's design and control functions across labor, politics, and social reproduction, between populist rage and a competitive, meritocratic pursuit of individual advantage, increases over time. The only thing that links these two aspects of neoliberal discourse is the *ethos* of (cold) warfare: in trials of steel and silicon the old powers are to be done away with and new powers will arise through feats of entrepreneurial daring. As the tension increases, as the neoliberal era yields more not less inequality, this *ethos* comes front and center in increasingly bellicose form, at once more populist and more authoritarian.

This performative contradiction in the new ideology of mental labor, like the segmented discourse of the state, has never been hidden. The liberal knowledge worker who triumphantly points out that Trump, having talked a populist game, now appoints financial elites to his cabinet has not unmasked a secret hypocrisy (demonstrating, once again, her superior insight), any more than the one who, forty years earlier, made the same devastating *bon mot* concerning Reagan. Rather, what underpins the functioning of this contradiction – the fact that it can continue to play a certain legitimating (and electoral) function – is, in large part, the social position of progressives themselves and the trap it lays for them. Progressives' highlighting of neoliberalism's contradiction is neutralized precisely because of the way they (tacitly or explicitly) resolve it: they do not want to do away with its meritocratic elitism. A similar logic plays out in Supreme Court politics, where progressives' embrace of juridical wisdom as a site for political change has fallen prey to the rise of Law and Economics alumni. Such forms of elitism were, as neoliberals know, a core element of progressives' efforts to broker a managed peace between labor and capital and it is why left-center parties have managed to accommodate themselves so well to neoliberal times – it has come with such lucrative market positions for professionals who accommodate themselves to its logic.

It is only that the progressive knowledge worker wants peace, not war; competition, yes, but with a somewhat greater degree of empathy (and oversight) for those subdued by it. More job training, perhaps; a few more safety nets; some legislation that "nudges" the masses along more rational lines rather than simply abandoning them to their fate. We should not understate the benefits of this "softer" form of neoliberalism, the extent to which it can make life more livable for many people and groups, as the early years of Trump's presidency have made clear. But having absorbed so much of neoliberal rationality, progressives' defense of those lives becomes increasingly threadbare, thrown back on warnings about the supposed pathology and ignorance of populist others.

The problem for progressives is that the populist moment in the segmented neoliberal state discourse is actually the moment of truth in it: as seen at the end of the previous chapter, the resentment against, even rage over, the control that mental labor exercises over one's work and life has been the most direct and animating experience of class antagonisms amongst "manual" laborers since at least the 1950s. To attack *that* moment, then, is to fall once again into the trap that neoliberalism lays for the "liberal elite," to prove it right or to prove, at least, that there is no alternative to it. The relatively small number of white manual laborers, employed and unemployed, who voted for Trump, and the many more who did not vote, likely knew or suspected that he would not carry out much of what he seemed to promise. But at least he had said something of the truth, at least he had made those other elites *look* as stupid as we knew they were. If the "leftism" of knowledge workers appears more hypocritical than the neoliberal project, it must be time to seek a different form of leftism.

The only apparent way to constructively oppose neoliberal logic would be to take up the attack on the power and privileges of mental labor that animates its populist side and render it coherent, turning it against neoliberalist meritocracy, its experts and apologists but also against the regnant forms of progressivism that seek to hold on to a distinction between themselves and roll out neoliberals. By replacing Hayek's invocations of a quasi-divine market and his distrust of monopolies with the assessments of neoclassical economists and the celebration of corporate efficiencies, actually existing neoliberalism has potentially left itself open to such an attack, especially in light of the failures of such experts that the financial crisis revealed. This may be all the more so to the extent the effects of austerity programs cannot be limited to those broadly judged to "deserve" them. But any effort to capitalize on those contradictions would need to be part of a serious and programmatic attempt to dismantle the division between mental and manual labor, in economy and polity. The lack of direction or purpose of progressives in the long aftermath of the financial crisis and the halting emergence of contradictory forms of left populism might both be taken as confirmations of that claim.

Chapter 5: The Final Progressive Settlement
Racial Liberalism and Its Discontents

> I hate the white good conscience. I curse it. It sits on the Right's left, at the heart of social democracy. (BOUTELDJA 2017: 27)

Central to the defeat of progressivism by new, neoliberal "state mercenaries," untroubled by visions of a common good, was the mobilization of a racism that liberalism had, with moderate success, repressed but with which it had never fully reckoned. In "racial liberalism" (Singh 2004; Melamed 2011), racism came to be conceived of as a kind of pathology, an atavism of the uneducated, that placed it, *a priori*, outside the ambit of the knowledge worker. Racial liberalism, that is, comprehended racial politics through the prism of the separation of mental from manual labor, establishing the framework for a "professionalization" of race that would ultimately allow it to diversify the personnel of knowledge work, while consigning the vast majority of traditionally racialized persons to more trenchant, because disavowed, modes of racialization, backed by meritocratic principles and the carceral state. At the same time, this conception handed over resentments regarding the borrowed power of mental labor to the articulations of racist theories, which would triumph, in part, by "revealing" (again and again) unholy alliances between progressive elites and a racialized underclass. These trends, which have culminated in Trump's White House and progressive confusion in the face of it, need to be situated in a longer history that explains the affective link between the resentment of mental labor's control functions and the racialized structuring of poverty and class.

The grounds for that link were established by the terms of the Cold War civil rights settlement, a key element in the "soft" side of the U.S. state's new imperialist strategies. Racial liberalism had never intended the direct empowerment of poor women and families that the welfare rights movement, at least at its most radical, articulated; rather, it had imagined a specific management of race and racism, as well as racist and racialized populations, that would transform, without undermining, the forms of expression and practice proper to the racial state and elite white supremacy. Both racism and its effects on the racialized became individualized instances of pathology to be overcome by education and a social engineering administered by the state and its knowledge workers.

Situating the neoliberal counterattack and its ongoing aftermath within this history of this confluence between mental labor and racial politics opens up new perspectives on those politics over the last four decades. Flummoxed by the backlash against this pedagogical beneficence, racial liberals continue to prove unable to reckon with the revaluation of their own terms that neoliberalism undertook, an incapacity their ongoing fixation on the ignorance and pathology of "the white working class" echoes. It also makes clear that any effective anti-racist politics today would need to involve criticism of the control functions of mental labor, not to prove the truth of the unholy alliance that the counterattack named but to transcend the racism that still structures racial liberalism.

My intention in this chapter, then, is *not* to suggest that overcoming the division between mental and manual labor is the singular key to anti-racist politics, or that "race" ultimately is reducible to an articulation of that division. I presume here a notion of racialization as its own specific socio-historical-psychological process in modernity, one in which certain visible "stigmata" came to be articulated as signs of some hidden, essential difference, developing "historic repertoires and cultural and signifying systems that stigmatize and depreciate one form of humanity for the purposes of another's health, development, safety, profit, or pleasure" (Singh 2004: 223). Today, these repertoires increasingly divide the world up into "those who are protected and those who are precarious," relegated to early death (Hong 2015: 22-23). The uniqueness of "race" lies, at least in part, in its peculiarly somatic-affective character (which both connects and differentiates it from sexual difference), in the anxiety and rage that supposed racial difference can elicit, especially in those identified as "white" and in contexts where other markers of power and/or stability are in crisis.[1] "The problem of race," as W.E.B. Du Bois observed, "always cuts across and hinders the settlement of other problems" (cited in Singh 2004: 75). The argument here is that it does so for the division of mental and manual labor and that, conversely, the division of mental and manual labor also increasingly cuts across and hinders the settlement of the problem of race.

Professionalizing Antiracism

Racial liberalism was made possible historically by the partial identification of racial difference with the division between mental and manual labor and by the "illusory partnership" (Robinson 2000: 192) this conception fostered, post-slavery, between progressive whites and a nascent black intelligentsia. Central to the settler colonial invention of race was an identification of "civilized" Europeans with the capacity for rationality that legitimated the placement of indigenous peoples and enslaved Africans on the margins of evolving liberal society, as a form of "unruly" nature against which such civilization had to be defended (Singh 2017). This identification remained relatively inchoate, however, insofar as 1) it was not intended to grant control functions to European manual laborers; 2) settler colonialism required the invention of secondary distinctions internal to subject populations, identifying some as "native elites" who could be "partners" in the rule of the colonized masses (Fanon 2004), or charging some chattel slaves with the management of other slaves and/ or the performance of skilled labor (Roediger/Esch 2012). In this way, the division between mental and manual labor both tendentially defined racial difference and internally divided racialized populations.

In the U.S., the question of a "partnership" between whites and blacks became particularly acute in the post-Reconstruction era. Institutions of elementary, secondary, and post-secondary education were one of the few precariously enduring remnants of radical Reconstruction. The

---

1 | I am gesturing here towards the accounts developed by Kovel 1984 and Seshadri-Crooks 2000, though I am unable in this space to develop or defend them. Experiences of class can also take on some of the affective-somatic character proper to race; in such cases, we might consider adopting the term "class-racism" which Bourdieu (1984) used in relation to his somatic conception of *habitus*.

expanding ranks of white professionals reinforced the idea of education as a viable means for improving the material and political conditions of the freed slaves. But the question of if and how such educational institutions, and their graduates, fit into evolving systems for the production and reproduction of mental laborers overlapped with the explicit abandonment of the reconstructive project of substantive racial equality. Answers to that question (those, at least, that did not involve the destruction of the whole system) tended to take two distinct but interrelated forms, as Du Bois recognized late in his career: in Booker T. Washington's model, "the Negro as an efficient worker would gain wealth and...eventually through his ownership of capital he would be able to achieve a recognized place in American culture." For the early Du Bois, on the other hand, the key was "the higher education of the Talented Tenth," the "exceptional men" of the race, "who through their knowledge of modern culture could guide the American Negro into a higher civilization" (cited by Robinson 2000: 193).

Both of these visions rested on, at best, unstable ground. Washington's investment in "industrial education" appealed to white donors, including Northern industrialists and professionals, because it promised, in the immediate term, black submission and patience as the guarantee of racial peace in the South. Indeed, the Progressives' goal of social peace generally led them to assist in expanding and codifying segregation (McGerr 2003: 183). But as a long-term vision, industrial education depended on an integrated industrialization of the South that was not to be. Even efforts at the teaching of handicrafts were resisted by whites. As Washington himself noted, "You will hear many students, especially those in the higher classes, say that they intend to practice medicine, study law, or something else, when they graduate; but the majority after all, will be found in these fields of work that lie about in the black belt of the South" (cited in Frazier 1957: 71). Many became teachers in the schools the Freedmen's Bureau had built, enclosing the educated black stratum in a segregated loop that Jim Crow would violently enforce.

Du Bois's vision of the Talented Tenth faced an analogous problem: "developing the Best of this race that they may guide the Mass away from the contamination and death of the Worst, in their own and other races," (cited by Frazier 1957: 68) foundered quickly on the refusal of Progressive elites to endorse the value of Negroes with higher education. "Du Bois had only the backing of a relatively small number of educated Negroes, especially in the North, and the vanishing remnant of northern whites who held to the idealism of the abolitionists and missionaries who had gone into the South" (ibid: 68). This problem would come to haunt Du Bois's career as scholar and activist, as donors would often turn against him (at Atlanta University, at the NAACP, in the *Encyclopedia of the Negro* project that Du Bois pitched to the Carnegie foundation, who instead funded Myrdal's *American Dilemma*), forcing him to move on to something else, radicalizing with each move.

For the later Du Bois, the commonality between his younger self and Washington lay in the fact that neither had "understood the nature of capitalistic exploitation of labor, and the necessity of a direct attack on the principle of exploitation as the beginning of labor uplift" (cited by Robinson 2000: 193). But they had also shared an implicit endorsement of mental labor as a form of political power and control. Neither seemed inclined to ask whether those who came to possess such power would be inclined to share, let alone dissolve, it, or whether they would become "a broker stratum seemingly secured from above by a ruling class that proffered them increments of privilege while ruthlessly repressing mass Black mobilization" (ibid: 191).

Put differently, neither Washington nor Du Bois appear to have clearly conceived the real source of the powers their projects sought to mobilize or how those powers would shape their ultimate outcomes. Neither industrial schools nor the Talented Tenth could deliver what they promised, though they did have important historical effects. Black mental laborers did attain a relative degree of individual economic autonomy, at least compared with tenant farmers and sharecroppers, but the power that underwrote that autonomy did not come from recognition by white progressives. Rather, because the clientele of Black doctors, lawyers, preachers, school teachers, county agents, etc. were (of necessity) also Black, those professionals proved much less at the mercy of whites than farmers permanently indebted to white landowners. Given a potential market untapped by white professionals, a degree of autonomy could be gained by monopolizing it. Something similar was the case for those graduates of industrial education who were able to acquire their own land (Forner 2017: 48). Denied recognition by white institutions, Black mental laborers served, and lived amongst, the broader Black community, modelling, intentionally or not, a relative independence. Further, the repression of Black mental laborers mitigated, to an extent, their separation from manual laborers, in which Washington and Du Bois were at least partially invested. The pressures of direct and violent racialization counteracted that separation, enforcing uncommon degrees of identification across it and providing ripe conditions for organic intellectuals. "This didn't immediately bring down the social order of the Black Belt, but the slight shift in the balance of power created small changes and gains that later organizing would build upon" (ibid: 68).

To the extent Black professionals did continue to seek "broker stratum" status, they were often reduced to a kind of hollow mimicry of the position of professional mental laborers in white society (Frazier 1957). The Talented Tenth could not lead the American Negro into a civilization that wanted no part of it and Jim Crow made clear that mental labor, without the support of some effective social power underpinning it, be it capital or a mass social movement, was largely powerless. The experience of that impotence, the mass migration of Blacks to the cities of the North and West, the continuation of segregation there, and the onset of colonial resistance and its suppressions (especially the Italian invasion of Ethiopia in 1935), moved Du Bois and others towards a more radical conception of black liberation, locating U.S. history, and their place in it, as "part of the genealogy of domination and resistance produced by the expansion of colonial (and neocolonial) capitalism" (Singh 2004: 53; Von Eschen 1997).

The onset of the Cold War, however, would leave Du Bois more marginalized than ever. For progressives – and for the apparatuses of the U.S. state over which they gained hegemony – the Cold War, and the fear of "the masses" that it deepened, led to a new reckoning with the color line. In light of the (real or perceived) socialist or communist character of anti-colonial movements, the "Negro problem" became a source of potential embarrassment, a vehicle for "Soviet propaganda" on the international stage. Responsibility for it, therefore, needed to be transferred from the state and its policies to the masses, to the same kinds of departures from civilized, middle-class norms that Progressivism had always aimed to "correct." Blacks would be, "in due time," integrated into the formal powers of the U.S. system, just as other ethnicities had been in the past. The price extracted for this form of settlement was black intellectuals' identification with that state and its global policy of defending and expanding capital accumulation.[2] The colored world was no longer to be

2 | Or, put differently, the State Department and the CIA could not discredit figures like Paul Robeson and Du Bois themselves; they needed the NAACP and the AFL to do it for them.

viewed as a power through which the racialized political economy could be radically transformed; rather, leading elements of it were to be seduced into alignment with the American way, which would now include some more genuine recognition of a broker stratum.

On these terms, white progressives sought a partnership with Black mental laborers that was something more than illusory yet would intentionally eclipse the more radical trajectory on which they had recently embarked. The terms of that partnership came to be articulated through "a new master theorem of race relations that was interpretively progressive but not socially destabilizing" (Lewis 2000: 451). By subscribing to that theorem, Black elites, as mental race laborers, would stand in for the larger populations that they would now be expected to control. In that respect, the negotiated outcomes of the Civil Rights movement at the state level would prove one of the last settlements between capital and workers negotiated by progressive elites.

The theorem for that eventual settlement found expression as early as 1944, in *An American Dilemma: The Negro Problem and Modern Democracy*, a large-scale study funded by the Carnegie Foundation and coordinated by the Swedish sociologist Gunnar Myrdal (1996; Melamed 2011: 56-63; Singh 2004: 38-41). Myrdal identified evolving racial justice with "the gradual realization of the American Creed," a teleological process through which the United States would move ever closer to fully realizing the values of liberty and equality ostensibly set down at its founding, erasing all racial differences or rendering us blind to them. It was this intrinsic national trajectory that qualified the United States for the task of "international leadership" in a decolonizing world: "the great reason for hope is that this country has a national experience of uniting racial and cultural diversities, and a national theory, if not a consistent practice, of freedom and equality for all. What America is constantly reaching for is democracy at home and abroad" (Myrdal 1996: 3). A racial settlement would qualify the United States for the role to which it aspired. "America saving itself becomes savior of the world" (ibid: 1022).

The path to this salvation was to be a program of "social engineering," overseen by the professional administrators of the state, educational apparatuses, and philanthropic institutions, a "wider dissemination of social-scientific knowledge about African American existence in the United States" that would "dispel white America's psychic isolation and opportunistic belief system" (Melamed 2011: 62). While Myrdal's study did acknowledge the divergent structural impacts of racial history, the means for addressing them centered on the beliefs, attitudes, and prejudices of white Southerners. This was because, he claimed, they already contained the cure within themselves. Poor whites were not alien to the Creed; rather, it was *intrinsic* to all (white) Americans. It was racist acts that produced a form of psychic dissonance that could be assuaged only by "the race dogma": *"The need for race prejudice is, from this point of view, a need for defense on the part of Americans against their own national Creed, against their own most cherished ideals"* (Myrdal 1996: 89, original emphasis). Whites were the principal victims of their own racism. The struggle against this psychological and moral pathology was, therefore, to be waged within individual white souls and the heroes of that struggle were to be the white progressives who undertook the programming of their enlightenment. In this way,

racial liberalism renewed white privilege by constituting the white liberal American as the most felicitous member of the U.S. nation-state on the grounds of his or her liberal antiracist disposition. Myrdal set the stage for a new, heroic form of liberal whiteness [...] To be American is to occupy the place of the universal subject – for which whiteness was once the synecdoche—with the authority to intervene into, order, and rationalize whatever such universality entailed (Melamed 2011: 59).

To be "American" thus came to be implicitly identified with being a progressive, white knowledge worker, pursuing a national interest now understood as the global hegemony of the U.S. state.

The position of Black people in this theorem was less felicitous. The progressive settlement, as white psychodrama, rendered Blacks almost entirely passive in, even marginal to, their own liberation. At best, some new Talented Tenth might play a subdued role in exemplifying the civilized potential of colored peoples, creating works that evoked sympathy in the whites to be converted. Agitation or activism were to be strictly avoided, insofar as these might provoke whites whose conversion had not yet stabilized. Identifying antiracism with U.S. imperialism rendered the terms of Black radicalism suspect, "signs of frustration and futility, or worse, ingratitude and insubordination" (Singh 2004: 43), certainly unpatriotic and probably racist.

Such ingratitude and insubordination also found an explanation in the theorem. For if the overtly racist white was pathologized, so too were those blacks outside the patriotic Talented Tenth. Since the "very defini-tion of the 'Negro race' [...] is a social and conventional, not a biological concept" (Myrdal 1996: 115), the only politico-cultural existence of that race as a distinct group was identified with its pathological reaction to white racism. *"In practically all its divergences, American Negro culture is not some-thing independent of the general American culture. It is a distorted develop-ment, or a pathological condition, of the general American culture"* (ibid: 928, original emphasis). Either the Negro was American, i.e., either she was "white," or else she was sick.

These dual pathologies of Southern white perpetrators and Black victims of racist acts became the central figures of racial liberalism, con-tinually undercutting its projected unity: the becoming-middle-class of poor and uneducated whites and the becoming-American of Black people. These figures were not equivalent, as Naomi Murakawa notes: "For white people, racism was an irrationality, a pollution to the real self. For black people, racism was an injury, a disfigurement of psychological devel-opment and therefore constitutive of the real self" (2014: 13). The white Southerner, later the "white working class," was the addressee of liberal racial discourse, summoned back to its true self; Black people were only its objects. This non-equivalence left racial liberalism ambivalent about what, ultimately, was to be done with or to Black people to bring them wholly into the American Creed.

At best, as the infamous Moynihan Report would propose in 1965, the solution might be an intensification of the progressive state's oversight of Black social reproduction: "A new kind of national goal – the establish-ment of a stable Negro family structure" (cited by Kovel 1984: 39) became the projected basis for the depathologization of Black individuals. Just as earlier Progressives had sought to make white working-class families more like white professional ones, so those intent on racial settlement would expand this project to black families. But, again, there were critical differences. The call for state oversight here was caught up in the logics of strategic rationality already expanding through the state, underpinned by a "political strategy of compelling reform by making black people seem damaged or potentially violent" (Murakawa 2014: 13). For Moynihan, infamously, a stable Negro family structure had to be imposed from outside because of the dominant maternal role in Black families, inducing improperly responsible masculine agency and a "culture of poverty." If some progressives intended this portrayal to be a strategy that would compel whites' self-interest towards deracializing state policy (defending civil rights, addressing poverty, dispensing neutral procedures of criminal justice, would ultimately produce law and order), it also laid the ground for more coercive impositions of strategic rationality to the "problem."

The tense agglomeration of factors that both *American Dilemma* and Moynihan's report assembled could only hold together so long. Passage of the Civil Rights Act in 1964 and the Voting Rights Act in 1965 both fulfilled the terms of racial liberalism's ambitions and demonstrated their failure. Not only had these achievements required precisely the agitation and resistance that racial liberalism had claimed was counterproductive but, in their wake, the importance of the links between racism, colonialism, and capitalism, between race and structures of economic exploitation, housing segregation, etc., which Black theorists had begun to trace in the 1930s and 1940s, became increasingly clear to many of those who had been part of that resistance. The new pressures of an enfranchised Black electorate, paired with the resurgence of Black nationalisms and waves of urban riots, were able to force concessions for a brief period, including those the welfare rights movement temporarily secured. But a fuller reckoning with the substantive meaning of antiracism faltered in the face of the businessmen's crusade and the internecine struggle between knowledge workers traced in the previous chapter. Racial liberalism, weighed down by its own internal contradictions, was ill prepared to face the anti-welfare counterattack, which drew on its own discourse of Black pathology, now buttressed by the supposed closure of the Civil Rights era. What would endure from the liberal settlement were its visions of political equality and pathology. The former realized, in principle, the latter remained the only explanation for continuing racial disparities that was compatible with a salvation of America engineered by white knowledge workers. The last progressive settlement established the frame for the supersession of progressivism.

Postracialism and the White Working Class

For progressives, the rising influence of anti-welfare discourse presented enormous difficulties. Having provided so many of its foundational terms, institutional and legal structures, it was unclear how they could (and, for some, if they should) resist it. Emphasis on and rewards for individualism, innovation, "merit," and human capital expressed in free competition had become so central to the labor relations of the knowledge workers who gained hegemony over the Democratic Party that it was difficult to articulate alternative principles, other than vague gestures towards empathy, that might motivate a robust defense of the welfare state amidst the increasing surplus population of a deindustrializing era. The ascension of neoliberal forms of mental labor thus became the occasion for the rise of a "postracialism" for which racial liberalism had laid the groundwork.

The translation of the latter into the former would, in a sense, require only the forgetting of history imposed by the abstract forms of rationality mental labor inherited from the Cold War: reframing social relations on the schema of rational choices made in competitive games removed them from the weight of history and its structures. Divorced from the history of racial injustice, the neoliberal reaction could, by insisting on the nonracial legal and political forms of equality that racial liberalism had legislated, make them work towards racializing effects of a deniable form. Racial liberalism could be stripped of its ambivalence by freeing it from the guilty sense of history that motivated welfare benefits and affirmative action. Racism continues to be viewed as an individual pathology, only where such pathologies have come from is no longer of interest. Better to let competition sort them out: if they are truly pathological they will fail competitiveness tests and pass away.

This "post-Civil Rights" exclusion of racial discourse from public speech rendered ongoing racist practices and racializing violence unnamable (as long, at least, as they avoid the iconography of past racisms). Private expressions of feeling are protected by the erasure of the categories by which they could be judged as racist. "Absent racial terms, intentionality no longer has to be denied. It simply can be said never to have crossed my mind" (Goldberg 2015). If you think the politics of law and order are really about race, then that's on you. Perhaps you are the racist you accuse me of being? Those who keep talking about race are the racists. Meanwhile, elect us and we will clean up the streets that we all know are crime-infested, the people who we all know are suspicious, irresponsible, lazy, drug dealing gang members, etc. Detached from its historical legacy, racism goes viral yet never comes wholly into focus. Loosed from their historical ground in racial injustices, the unequal, structured outcomes of racialization become so much evidence for the ostensible realism of privatized racisms, while the discourses of antiracism are co-opted into the service of novel defenses of white supremacy (Balibar/Wallerstein 1991).

Of course, history never wholly vanishes. It haunts. And if progressivism and Keynesianism were haunted by the social revolution (Mann 2017), postracialism (or racial neoliberalism) is haunted by urban uprisings and post-colonial revolutions, "the threat of race" (Goldberg 2008). Only, where progressivism sought to temper its fear through the economic and pedagogical functions of the state, racial neoliberalism seeks to deny the existence of the object of its fear, writing "race" out of public conceivability, extending segregation in neighborhoods and schools without legal codifying it, consigning racialized men to prisons, turning discretely away as racialized women drop off welfare rolls to who knows where, rendering their lives unprotected, subject to early death. Shorn of publicly relevant history, that haunting, and the fear it invokes, are privatized, naturalized, made to appear rational as a "choice" in the self-maximizing split second in which one glimpses a woman on the ground reaching for her cell phone or a twelve-year old boy holding a toy gun.

While the remnants of the progressive tradition proved unable to contest these transformations on principle, it did register vague, if increasing, anxieties over the carceral and workfare state it had helped to produce and legitimate.[3] Liberals remain discomfited by the increasing private-public expressions of (deniable) racism, especially as they come to be spoken from the office of the Presidency. As a response to this dilemma, central characteristics of racial liberalism have been intensified in a bid to explain the transformations it has undergone and to redeem the world that it has made. The explanation derives from a shifting pathologization of "uneducated" whites, now shorn from any faith in their Creedal unity. The redemption comes from an expansion of the professionalization of race relations under racial liberalism into a quasi-racialization of professional knowledge work itself. I take up the explanatory discourse here; the redemptive one in the next section.

Unwilling to simply accept privatized racism, yet also unwilling to move towards any full-scale reckoning with its structural character or to embrace more genuine forms of antiracist resistance, liberals today have held fast to the progressive vision of the state and of knowledge workers as

---

3 | One thinks, for example, of Bill Clinton's repeated statements of regret, during his wife's Presidential campaign, over his role as President in worsening mass incarceration. At the same time, he refused to express any regret about welfare reform, insisting that Hillary Clinton had made the legislation more "progressive."

de-racialized mediators. Yet, racial history (the history of the racial state) has institutionalized whiteness in every aspect of our political economy, in every apparatus of the state, be it mortgage assistance, social services, the neo-imperial projects of the military, criminal justice and the legal system, education, the geography of our cities and country, the heroic figures of our imagination. Progressives tend to imagine they stand outside all of this, that their commitment to procedural objectivity is at least enough to ame-liorate the worst effects until the moral arc of pedagogy arrives at justice. They can hold to this faith, in the meantime, only by projecting the inev-itably racist aggregate outcomes of state and pedagogical procedures onto the pathological desires of some other subject. Liberals thereby present themselves not as initiating or condoning racial logics but as moderating them, under immense pressure, or as transcending them, standing apart as moral witnesses in academia and other cultural apparatuses.

The pathological subject, initially conceived as the Southern white, began, in the late 1960s and 1970s, to become the white (manual) working class in general. Pivotal moments in this transition were SCLC's failed efforts to integrate northern cities, controversies over "busing" and school integration, and the political fractures over the Vietnam War. The dominant narrative around these cases became that of "hardhat" authoritarians refusing efforts to achieve racial justice while punching student protestors (Lewis 2013). Insofar as racism is viewed as a failure of sympathy caused primarily by a lack of knowledge, this narrative makes a certain internal sense: it is precisely those whites who have undergone the least formal education, had the least exposure to multicultural literature,[4] who can be expected to remain trapped in the pathology of overt racist speech and action.

Read in this manner, the supposed obduracy of the white working class in the face of progressive social engineering could become reason for dismantling the already weakening power of labor unions in center-left and social democratic parties in favor of suburban liberals, and, subse-quently, for those parties to drift rightward in an ostensible effort to attain (some of) the votes of the laborers they had helped disempower. With the

---

4 | See Melamed 2011: 115: "Because multicultural literature was presumed to be authentic, intimate, and representative, white students with minimal knowl-edge of or contact with racialized communities could nonetheless presume them-selves to have enough familiarity to legitimate their managerial-class position."

broadening of its diagnosis, the character of the pathology attributed to this subject also shifted. In a post-Civil Rights knowledge society, racism-as-pathology seems less and less explicable as a mere "pollution to the real self." Rather, for poor, "ignorant" whites, as originally (and still) for Blacks, that pathology appears to be increasingly understood as intrinsic, definitive of their "real selves." Its class consciousness fragmented, along with its unions, the white working class comes to be defined by its pathologies.

Never mind that most of the story about the "white working class" is untrue or, at best ambiguous. Data compiled by Richard Hamilton in 1971 about "civil rights attitudes" amongst whites from different classes showed no substantial difference between "manuals" and "nonmanuals." Hamilton's analysis of the 1968 presidential election also suggests interesting parallels with 2016: manual labor status – and class position in general – was "no factor at all in predicting or accounting for the [George] Wallace vote," *except* in specific regions (though in 1968 that region was the entire South) (Hamilton 1971: 460-467).[5] As Andrew Levinson concludes, from this and other data, while "liberal intellectuals think in terms of black and white and base their concern on an abstract sense of egalitarianism, the positive aspects of workers' attitudes are based on the common problems and sense of injustice they shared with working-class Blacks." It is "when the issue poses the needs of Blacks as a whole against all whites, workers often become incensed at being lumped together with the affluent and seeing their problems ignored" (Levinson 1974: 152-153).[6] Inversely, another survey of non-Southern Wallace voters showed what we might expect from the discussion at the end of chapter three: that their

---

5 | The "manual" vote for Wallace in the South also showed some remarkable ambivalences: a heavy majority favored aid from the federal government for medical expenses, while a third favored both federal intervention to guarantee "Negro job equality" and black's right to live wherever they choose: "one is not justified," Hamilton concludes," in treating the Wallace vote as a direct indication of racist predilection."

6 | "Racism" appears most overtly amongst manual laborers, Levinson also notes, when their needs are pitted against "what used to be called the 'lumpen-proletariat,' the disorganized families of the unemployed," though here his data may be reflecting the effects of the neoliberal offensive.

strongest resentments were not against Blacks but towards middle-class professionals (Ehrenreich 1989: 128).

Contemporary moral panics over the white working class are also belied by the evidence. Trump's electoral support did not come overwhelmingly from white manual laborers. Rather, the average income and wealth of Trump's supporters were higher than those for most recent Republican candidates and for all but one of his primary rivals. It appears that Clinton lost significantly more white working-class voters in the Rust Belt than Trump gained, while she also lost votes from people of color. Not quite half the working class voted (slightly above but in line with their increasingly typical response of abstaining since the Progressive reforms of elections). At best, the historical consensus will likely come down somewhere close to Mike Davis's recent analysis: the phenomenon of "Trump Democrats" was only real in "a score or so of troubled Rust Belt counties from Iowa to New York where a new wave of plant closure or relocation [...] coincided with growing immigrant and refugee populations" (Davis 2017:153). No doubt these shifts, plus the number of white manual laborers who had already shifted their votes to Republicans over the last forty years (the "Reagan Democrats"), call for some form of social and political explanation. But the implicit idea that large numbers of them were drawn to Trump by the way his xenophobic message rhymed with their intrinsic pathologies is clearly wrong. We need to insist here on what the evidence suggests: manual white laborers as a group are *not* more racist than mental laborers or capitalists, though the forms of their respective racisms may differ.

Nikhil Singh's insistence that "racism and racial animus are not fixed characteristics of an already defined group of people but a situational dimension of our common political life that is repeatedly mobilized" is helpful here (2018: 176). Mobilized in different situations, racism and racial animus will take differentiated forms, even if serving to reproduce the same differential valuation of human populations. What racial liberalism trained us in, you might say, is a tendency to recognize as racism *only* specific forms of individual, racializing judgment or speech: those articulated from a more or less dominated position, channeling frustrations into some overt, "crude" expression, often linked to resentments over the control-functions of mental laborers. By linking racism to ignorance and anti-intellectualism, progressives inoculate themselves against their own historical and structural implication in it. Meanwhile, the actually existing, multi-racial, feminized, fragmented, working class tends to dis-appear in favor of an imaginary, unified, and pathological white one.

Postracialism becomes, for progressives, a discourse addressed to the image of the white working class they have invented, an imaginary addressee that, in a neoliberal twist, resents anything that smacks of racial history. Better to let that history go or to invoke it only in the form of something we have overcome through the national unity of racial liber-alism. The naturally pathological white worker becomes the figure that validates the ever tighter embrace by liberals of neoliberal nostrums. The racist beliefs of the "white working-class" validate white liberals' failure to undertake anti-racist projects, as well as their efforts to hold onto political power, as the only group ostensibly qualified to wield it.

The Mental Labors of Whiteness

The contemporary progressive vision of racial redemption and conciliation turns on a new, diversified model of the heroic knowledge worker at the center of racial liberalism. The "professionalized" race relations (Melamed 2011:19) of the immediate post-Civil Rights era transformed, without ulti-mately undermining, the characteristics and forms of expression proper to the racial state and elite forms of white supremacy.[7] Indirect forms of racialization, like Moynihan's "culture of poverty," allowed for the main-tenance of traditional powers and privileges without any explicit appeal to skin color. Yet, the threat of increasingly radical antiracist movements and the developing conservative backlash pushed them, over time, towards the incorporation of a select(ed) minority of non-whites into the stratum of empowered mental laborers. Out of that shift came the emphasis in professional and academic circles on "multiculturalism" and "diversity," which Imani Perry has powerfully anatomized as an expression of "cor-relational" racism: apparent membership in a racial group is no longer viewed as *necessitating* the possession of unfavorable traits; though it remains a *likely* sign of them (Perry 2011: 6-7, 16-17). In other words, "racial liberalism's cultural model extended racial discipline and proce-dures beyond the color line by splintering whiteness and blackness into privileged and stigmatized forms based on normative cultural criteria"

---

7 | Or what Joel Kovel (1984: 31-33) calls the "*aversive* type of racism" (as opposed to the "*dominative*").

(Melamed 2011: 58). Race becomes an indicator of risk, offset only by other factors that perpetually signal one's worthiness and responsibility.

The criteria that offset that risk, and according to which traditional racial categories have been splintered, are, once again, those identified with (white) mental labor. If racial liberalism professionalized race relations, it might be said that racial neoliberalism *professionalized whiteness* (or "whitened" professionals):

As neoliberalism's social relations of production interpellate and order subjects within managerial and professional regimes or regimes of labor and incarceration, terms of privilege accrue to individuals and groups, such as *multicultural*, *reasonable*, *feminist*, and *law-abiding*, that make them appear fit for neoliberal subjectivity, while others are stigmatized as *monocultural*, *irrational*, *regressive*, *patriarchal*, or *criminal*, and ruled out. (ibid: 152)

In this way, a category like "Black" (or "migrant") becomes redrawn along lines more or less coincident with those that separate manual from mental labor. Rounds of credential and cultural testing can disprove the likeliness of one's skin color as sign, identifying one as a more or less proper (if still provisional) member in a meritocratic, multicultural, professional form of "whiteness." Such individual exceptions are critical to the defense of postracialism. They seem to demonstrate that race, in its traditional somatic sense, is not a determining factor in success, while reinforcing mental labor's own meritocratic legitimation.

This integration of mental labor does not challenge but rather endorses that labor's delegated power, separating credentialed people of color from racialized laborers and lumpen while apparently confirming the antiracist credentials of white knowledge workers, separating them yet further from the white working class. Neither do these shifts undermine the power of whiteness but, rather, preserve them by signifying their partial detachment from skin color. If Whiteness has functioned, since its invention, as a symbol of something like "wholeness," the absence of lack, being "fully in control of oneself and others,"[8] this now corroborates its fuller identification with the authoritative, control functions of mental labor, as one's

---

8 | See Seshadri-Crooks 2001: 98. Cp. Richard Dyer's (1997: 38-39) argument that a central marker of "whiteness" is "the attainment of a position of disinterest – abstraction, distance, separation, objectivity."

position in relation to mental labor comes to define one's relationship to "Whiteness." This renewal of white privilege allows a certain flexibility or fluidity to enter into the empirical symbols or character of whiteness, as long as its position of control is maintained. Mental labor gives to whiteness a new set of mechanisms for that control, as well as a new set of terms for legitimating it.

Still, it is important to stress the partiality, the provisionalness, and, most importantly, the *revocability* of this specific form of multicultural "whiteness." Malcolm X's pointed observation of what a white man calls a Black man with a PhD still holds true.[9] The reformation of Whiteness that allows some of those once designated as "non-white" to enter into its symbolic terrain functions, structurally, as a defense of white supremacy, no matter how "reformed." Serving to make racism deniable (and thereby serving to provide opportunities unthinkable a few decades ago to *some* persons), it also functions to defend the core racialized hierarchies that produce and reproduce both privilege and premature death. And that is why it does not simply supplant older forms of racialization, no matter how much it laments them as archaic or ignorant. The practices of racialization today flow through a kind of palimpsest of legitimating theories, facilitating rapid switches between racial scripts (Molina 2014), each of which is reinforced (and modified) by the others, each of which provides an alibi for the denial of the others.

The contradictions within and between these different forms of racialization has powerfully shaped contemporary politics in the United States, Europe, and elsewhere in recent years. For white manual laborers, as well as for whites more generally marginalized from institutional forms of control (the "lower middle class" or petite bourgeoise, for example, or mental laborers with marginal credentials), the partial fusion of racial identity and the division between mental and manual labor places them at a greater symbolic distance from Whiteness, producing, in some people, a more anxious or resentful embodiment of its traditional forms. Such anxieties are only intensified by the neoliberal fragmentation of collective forms of agency, the pervasive individualization of responsibility, the reduction of relations to market-like forms of competition, etc. The lessening of control over one's situation in labor as in life, paired with the intensification of the demand that one be in control, can generate what

---

9 | Yancy 2018 is bracing evidence of that, if any is needed.

Jennifer Silva (2013: 17-18, 99-108) has called a form of "hardness" against oneself and others, a sense that individuals *must* be responsible for their own outcomes, paired with a suspicion (reinforced by the right-wing assault on the welfare state) that racialized others receive illicit forms of aid from the state and its policies.

Even the ideological articulations of racist theories are marked by the division between mental and manual labor, insofar as they express, as Balibar (Balibar/Wallerstein 1991: 21) argues, "a 'will to know,' a violent *desire for* immediate *knowledge* of social relations." The racist theories that speak to this desire precisely differentiate themselves from "other socio-logical theories [like racial liberalism], developed within the framework of a division between 'intellectual' and 'manual' activities (broadly con-ceived)." Racist theories, in other words, "are forms of imaginary tran-scendence of the gulf separating intellectuality from the masses" (ibid). While Balibar offers this as a general characteristic of *all* racist theories, I lean towards viewing it as a character of such theories in the progressives' century, and, especially, since the onset of "official antiracism," since, that is, the bifurcation of racism wherein the privileged, "aversive" form could conceive of itself as an anti-racist theory marking the superiority of educated professionals. It is at that moment that abstract, principled denouncements of racism and racist theories themselves enter into a dan-gerous, mutually reinforcing, reciprocity around the separation of mental labor. The forms that racism takes are today co- (or over-)determined by fundamental, if misrecognized and distorted, defenses and critiques of the borrowed powers and privileges of mental labor, articulating that critique as a perverse and cruel struggle over the proper character of Whiteness.

Splinters of Race and Class

Missing from many contemporary debates about politics and racism are those whom racist theories works to exclude, dehumanize, and sentence to a likely early death. While mirroring the historical character of racial liberalism, today such omissions of people of color are particularly ironic insofar as the manual working class in the United States and other wealthy countries, increasingly (un- or precariously) employed in service or repro-ductive labor, is increasingly racialized and feminized. This trend has con-tributed to the supposed disappearance of "the working class," insofar as "the groups who now fill these positions have been conceived of politically, economically, and historically primarily in terms of their identity (biopolitical status)—as blacks, women, poor whites ('white trash'), or immigrants (poor immigrants, of color)—rather than as workers" (Arnold 2008). In a further irony, this shift in the conception of the proletariat has been paralleled and complicated by a simultaneous "dilution" of race, through the assumption of a "raceless" or "post-racial" era, into "class configurations" (Goldberg 2002: 233). In the milieu of hyper-individualization, "race as class is fractured from its high modernist totalizations into micro-class formations" (ibid: 262). As the working class "vanishes," the ostensible identity of non-white races fractures along the lines traced by the ideological division of mental and manual labor.

What was salvaged from the project of racial liberalism was the thing that had, generally, mattered most to liberals: the elevation of a small set of brokers or leaders from non-white groups. Conceiving of the Civil Rights Era as settled history rendered it impermissible to question that "the African American community deserved representation in a pluralistic and meritocratic body politic, but such power should be exercised by the 'best and brightest' of the black community as defined by the 'best and brightest' of the white community" (Ferguson 2013: 9). Critically, this reconfiguration of racialization fragmented traditional forms of community in anti-racist politics, built on a shared experience of racialized oppression. Excluded from the main currents of power in American life, Black knowledge workers shared the experiences of, and, for the most part, did not exercise control over, the populations they were confined to serving. Thus, when E. Franklin Frazier (1957) undertook his famous critique of the "black bourgeoisie," one of his central arguments was that they suffered from the delusion of "status without substance." They imagined themselves a normal middle-class only by maintaining an illusory withdrawal from society. But it was also this "precariousness of the black elite and relative lack of access to capital" that encouraged significant fractions of it to become deeply engaged in "broader campaigns for social justice" (Von Eschen 1997: 54). Orphaned by capital, vulnerable to premature death, the only source of power on which Black intellectuals could draw was that of the mass anti-racist movement.

With the "whitening" of professionals, today the "Black" elite *can* exercise real functions of delegated capitalist control. "There have always been class differences amongst African Americans," as Keeanga-Yamahtta Taylor notes, "but this is the first time those class differences have been expressed in the form of a minority of Blacks wielding significant political power and authority over the majority of Black lives" (2016: 80). That minority has proven unable or unwilling to fundamentally protect, let alone improve, the conditions of poor and working-class blacks, while often, as with Obama, legitimizing the discourse of pathology and the "culture of poverty." In a sense, they too appear trapped by the ongoing legacy of racial liberalism: the same racializing logic that has finally incorporated them into positions of power also legitimates anti-welfare and mass incarceration projects by identifying "race" with an increasingly unredeemable form of social pathology. The assimilation by ascension of a small number of "de-racialized" knowledge workers, whose inverse side is the consignment of surplus or superexploited, racialized populations to intensifying regimes of surveillance, discipline, incarceration, defines the increasingly unsustainable position of what is left of "progressivism" in neoliberal times. The counterinsurgent war neoliberal knowledge workers undertake is increasingly directed against this racialized "enemy" at home, and the new multicultural professional elite is expected (and trained) to participate, lest their revocable Whiteness be revoked.

As suggested at the beginning of this chapter, the intertwined history of racialization and the separation of mental from manual labor, as well as its peculiar denouement in the partial racialization of that separation, should not be read as suggestions that the division between mental and manual labor is ontologically or politically "prior" to race, that overcoming that division would be enough to undermine racism. The increasing racialization of the proletariat and the increasing professionalization of "whiteness" are newly hegemonic processes in recent decades but they build on the long, intertwined histories of class, race, and control. Progressives who advise us to better understand what the white working class wants and to accommodate ourselves to it only help to keep that history buried.

The "management" of surplus populations and the processes of racialization, for example, have always been inextricably linked. From the Indian wars to the policing of slave populations, from the enforced economic and political marginalization of "freed" peoples to the systems of militarized "policing" of former and present colonies, both the identification and the management of "surplus populations," as well as the legitimacy of their reproduction, are shaped by the invention and re-invention of race. Those populations can neither be properly understood nor practically mobilized without a direct confrontation with the procedures of racialization. Likewise, the link between management, control, and "Whiteness" can be traced back to the "burdens" of colonial and plantation administration. Thus, "if we are to ever forge a sustainable solidarity between the ethnically diverse proletariat in the imperialist core (as well as with those beyond)," as Satnam Virdee (2017) puts it, "it is more than likely we will have to go through race, rather than around it."

At the same time, potentials for solidarity today may well be heightened by these dual trajectories of race and class, if also complicated by the ambiguous status of de-credentialized "whites" in these new structures. Any opposition to the ostensibly neutral powers and privileges of mental labor must also be, centrally and essentially, anti-racist struggle. The specific forms of excessive violence that underpin the production of surplus and low-wage, manual labor populations, cannot be overcome by an appeal to the neutral abstractions of class forms in *Capital*, nor to the postracialism of today's professionals. Rather, as Melissa Harris-Perry (2011) suggests, they represent something like a "blackening of America" in which the "social, economic, and political conditions that have long defined African-American life have descended onto the broader population." Efforts to nullify this violence, in its specificity, and to replace it with collective forms of agency *can* translate across differently racialized communities – this was the lesson of the Chicago Panthers' original "Rainbow Coalition" – but they cannot be effectively deracinated. In the era of Trumpism and its promise to re-supply "the wages of whiteness in the absence of wages" (Narayan 2017), the struggle of racialized outsiders must be at the center of any leftist politics.

Chapter 6: Machines of Mental Labor

> If the computer is a tool, then decision theory is its master. (Bell 1973: 33)

The left's political disorientation today, the product of an entrenched identification with the social position of mental labor, ramifies well beyond progressive practices of and responses to "postracial" racialization. The material instantiation of the knowledge economy in computer and network technologies and the ever more abstract models (or technologies) of global finance, where self-valorizing capital seems to flow directly from the ingenuity and audacity of quants and investment bankers, produce newly seductive and troubling effects. For those inclined to view the world as shaped by autonomous ideas and the future as the outcome of a battle over them, these dual technologies appear to signal, respectively, the promise and the peril of the mind's powers.

The historical development of these two technologies are deeply interlinked. Computers and networks make global finance in the form we know it possible, while finance capital has taken over from the state a significant portion of the role of funding and directing further developments in hardware and software. And, as noted in Chapter 4, computer and network technologies emerged from the same hothouse of military-funded weapons and strategic research that produced strategic rationality. They were set to work, by the 1960s, on the growing problem of counter-insurgency, laying the groundwork for the modern internet through the production of a networked system of data collection, compilation, and distribution that could connect decision makers in Washington to bombers over the Ho Chi Minh trail (Edwards 1997; Levine 2018). Over the same decades, the pressures of increasingly mobile capital flows on the Bretton Woods convertibility of the dollar into gold and on Depression-era regulatory schemas for banking and finance drove a round of state-led innovations in the design and regulation of increasingly global financial markets, drawing foreign capital into U.S. circuits of debt and exchange, while reshaping other nations' political economies on the model of the U.S. (Albo/Gindin/Panitch 2010; Panitch/Gindin 2014).[1]

The core argument of this chapter is that both of these innovations should be understood as material-ideological instantiations of the command and control functions of neoliberal mental labor in contemporary times. Each becomes a vehicle by which such functions are at once empowered to degrees largely unimaginable in the Progressive era *and* masked or occluded, made to appear as neutral or natural. In relation to this development, the left's responses have been marked by contradiction, as shaped by its ongoing efforts to differentiate the autonomous, "progressive" form of mental labor from the neoliberal one. Its disorientation can be glimpsed if we return to the scene sketched in Chapter 1: the "movements of the squares" that occurred in the long (and still unfolding) aftermath of the 2007/2008 financial crisis.

Central to the crisis itself, of course, was the ever more Byzantine infrastructure of financial markets, models, and state regulations, that underwrote the spread of opaque asset forms, from derivatives to mortgage-backed securities, and enabled not only speculative profits but also, as their inverse side, the "universalization of financial inclusion" (Soederberg 2014). The response of the left to the crisis was marked by the continuing influence of the "Keynes-Veblen-Proudhon tradition" (Sotiropoulos, et al. 2013), which understands finance as a fictitious, parasitical, and distorting influence on "the real economy." The profits of investment bankers were broadly viewed as unproductive grafts onto productive capital. Investment banking itself became a figure of mental labor gone wrong, spinning out and selling increasingly complex financial vehicles abstracted from actual goods, restructuring corporations in the service of "shareholders' value," rentiers ever-yet-to-be-euthanized. The financial crisis was, briefly, celebrated as the fated demise of these labors. Many proclaimed Neoliberalism dead, until it rose again, Lazarus-like, propped up on unprecedented

---

1 | I am not suggesting that the U.S. state played the *only* role here, either relative to other nation-states or to private capital, but it did play a uniquely powerful one. At the same time, as Morton and Bieler (2018) emphasize, the agency of "the U.S. state" is not that of an autonomous subject but the ongoing crystallization of balances of forces.

swathes of sovereign debt and record corporate profits, depressed work-force participation rates and falling wages (Brynjolfsson/McAfee 2011).

Two years later, the Arab Spring, followed by 15-M, Occupy, and others, elicited an inverted frenzy of praise from the left for "Facebook democracy," a "networked public," and the participatory *ethos* of social media. The utopic figure of contemporary leftism – the universalized mental laborer, at once manager and laborer, intrinsically autonomous, needing only to be liberated from a (finance) capital consigned to the role of external rentier – became fused with its apparent material base in automated, information- and knowledge-driven forms of computerized production and processing. Visions of the hacker depict one amongst several alternative images of a heroic mental power, organizing resistance in cyberspace, employing a nascently collective knowledge, embodying a utopia that is already (virtually) here. These claims too were ultimately dampened in the wake of renewed military regimes, a widening migration crisis, and the quick collapse of networked movements.

A central part of what I will argue in this chapter is that these responses represent dual misreadings of contemporary political economy, shaped by an implicit presumption of mental labor's political autonomy and effectiveness in the wake of the neoliberal reconfiguration of mental labor's core characteristics and values. The political crisis of the present is, for many liberals, implicitly construed as a struggle between opposed forms of mental labor. But in a politics reduced to the internecine conflict between fractions of mental laborers, only capital can win. No doubt, this rendering is somewhat schematic, but it also captures something central, I wager, to contemporary efforts at constructing politics on the model of mental labor. There is no way forward for the left conceived on these terms, precisely because the still-abstract vision of a mental labor, no matter how creative and "revolutionary," underestimates the material force of the social relations that capital embodies and of the "dead (mental) labor" embodied in these technological forms of fixed capital. To trace, albeit briefly, the intertwined political-ideological characteristics of computers and finance is to bring home, by bringing up-to-date, the impasses that follow from a politics in the shadow of the utopia of empowered minds.

Algorithms, Self-Regulation, and Mental Labor

The wholly automated car factory, the self-driving car, the terrorist caught before they can even commit an act of terror, the artificial intelligence that will redeem, supplant, or destroy us: the dream-image of the computer today pictures ideas that have become intrinsically effective, that once "written down," or, rather, installed as software, can run on and on, providing answers to questions we didn't yet know that we had, finding apparent order in systems so complex that we cannot understand them unaided. This dream-image has likewise tended, metaphorically, to become an image of ourselves and our potential that David Golumbia (2009: 7) calls "computationalism": "the view that not just human minds are computers but that *mind itself* must be a computer – that our notion of intellect is, at bottom, identical with abstract computation." This dream-image of the computer can be grasped, at least for our purposes here, as the figured potential of two combined elements: the strategic rationality sketched in Chapter 4 and the "negative feedback" or self-correction that was a central component of "cybernetics." These two elements combine in the figure of "algorithmic computation," of a closed world that is simultaneously expansive, tending to bring everything inside.

At its core, the basic character of an algorithm is that of an *"effective procedure,"* "a set of rules that tells the player precisely how to behave from one moment to the next." The autonomy of such a procedure requires "a language in which we can express, without any ambiguity whatever, what a player is to do from one moment to the next" (Weizenbaum 1976: 46-47), and which thereby secures a "guaranteed completion" (Golumbia 2009: 40). An algorithm embodies the expectation of reaching some specific desired result: "from the beginning, then, algorithms have encoded a particular kind of abstraction: the *abstraction of the desire for an answer*" (Finn 2017: 24). They are not static or contemplative ideas ensconced in stone or scribbled on paper; rather, they make something happen; they "must always be implemented to be used" (ibid: 47).

The computerized algorithm came into existence as a means for carrying out the calculations of strategic rationality more quickly and/or more effectively. It realizes and effects the productive abstraction to which game theory aspired. Grounded in rigorous simplification and quantification (of motives, outcomes, etc.), "mathematical calculation can be made to stand for propositions that are themselves not mathematical, but must still conform to mathematical rules" (Golumbia 2009: 14). The computer is a "player" that is identical with the "game," that can *only* follow the "rules," at least for the time during which it runs that specific software. Under a host of suggestive anagrams (ENIAC, MANIAC, EDVAC [Dyson 2012; Edwards 1996]), the earliest computers were developed to substitute for the human, almost always female, "computers," whose capacities, even when numbered in the hundreds, were outstretched by the calculations required for missile firing tables or predicting the behavior of an atomic implosion weapon. But they were quickly swept up, in theory even more than in practice, into the efforts to design a better command and control system, a decision-making process that could incorporate the vast amount of data that small sets of rules solicited and respond more quickly, more objectively, to events than a human being or, at least, a human being alone, could.

In this context, the idea of self-regulation that achieved concentrated development in "cybernetics" (Wiener 1948; Edwards 1996; Franklin 2015) became critical. Self-regulating systems were premised on the idea of "'negative feedback,' or circular self-corrective cycles, in which information about the effects of an adjustment to a dynamic system is continuously returned to that system as input and controls further adjustment" (cited by Edwards 1996: 181). By way of this notion, the rule-bound calculations of strategists and computers could be conceived of as on-going, adaptive processes, occurring over time, across multiple "plays."[2] An initially simple algorithm could become increasingly complex– while maintaining its character as mathematical calculation – as it played out multiple adaptations of its rules in relation to a changing stream of data. A computer was not simply a calculator; it was a responsive, evolving, self-regulating information-processor. And what it was programmed to seek information for, above all, were the tasks of prediction and control.

The initial problem that Weiner had set out to solve – that of theorizing humans "as component parts of weapons systems" (Edwards 1996: 180) – facilitated a vast expansion of machine metaphors. Cybernetics defined itself as the "entire field of control and communication

---

2 | As Franklin notes, von Neumann abandoned game theory and spent the last years of his life working on "automata," which "replac[ed] the concept of the player with that of a cybernetic machine capable of self-regulation through communication and feedback even when unforeseen inputs arise" (2015: 62).

theory, whether in the machine or in the animal" (Wiener 1949: 19). *Every* organism, system, individual, and society, became thinkable as a self-regulating machine that processed "information" (negative entropy) in order to respond productively to its environment and each such machine, once put in play (alone or networked with other information-processors), could run on its own, through potentially endless cycles of self-regulating adaptation (Turner 2006; Franklin 2015). The only management required for established systems (which, for Hayek and others, would come to include "the market") would be maintaining "the stability of certain key variables" (Franklin 2015: 72). This idea underwrote ongoing aspirations in the military for wholly automated systems of command and control from SAGE to Star Wars. It also underpinned the ideology of computationalism: if all things, including human beings, are information-processing machines, then humans can be understood as, at base, computers and computers can, potentially, do everything that humans do.

The increasing computational power and social applications of computers, in their metaphoric overlap with human cognition, has produced marked and contradictory effects on the ideological conception and political practice of mental labor. To an extent, the materialization of algorithmic programming in computers can appear to supersede the division between mental and manual labor altogether. For in the computer is achieved, at least in principle, the reduction of mental labor to material differences:

What appear to be 'immaterial' products of labor are the result of pattern production that can be accomplished by machines (whether they be composed of wood, iron, and paper cards, and powered by heat engines, or of plastic, silicon, and copper and powered by electric currents). These machines are fully physical. (Caffentzis 2013: 199)

And the computational labors they undertake are as material (and manual) as any other. What had appeared as the unique contribution of human thought to production processes could be programmed into the material patterning functions of a machine, revealing "the deep computational structure" of the labor process as a whole (ibid: 196). Further, if everything and everyone is an information-processing machine, the very grounds for distinguishing mental from manual labor might seem to collapse. "The mystique of skill is penetrated by Turing machine analysis, and a fundamental continuity between labor – mental and manual – is verified" (ibid: 168).

But this material continuity is not the same as a political-ideological one. In practice, the computer enables the subjection of many forms of once-mental labor to the same scientific management and superfluity as manual forms, reasserting, in changed form, a fundamental separation premised on control: there are those who design the rules of the game and those who merely play. That ambiguity defines the ideological polarities latent in cybernetics: if you focus on "self-regulation," its message can appear to be a kind of utopic horizontalism in which mutual adaptations between organisms are the basis for a dynamically evolving harmony. The algorithmic labor process and *polis* then appeared as potentially horizontalist, participatory enterprises. If, on the other hand, you focus on the acts of programming, the design of the algorithms required for producing such self-regulation (at least in machines) and the potential for the control of *re*-programming (in humans as well) by changing elements of algorithms or "key variables" in the environment, then they appear, politically, as an enormous centralization of power and control, a "visible production of what Adam Smith called the 'invisible hand'" equivalent to *"the politics of the 'end of politics'"* (Tiqqun 2001: 7). In the relations of production, they appear as an alienating automation of Taylorism, "in which workers' knowledge is first routinized, then codified and transferred from its variable (human) component to its fixed, machinic form" (Dyer-Witheford 2015: 178). To a certain extent, versions of cybernetics could differ from one another on their emphasis here, as well as in the extent of their efforts to democratize programming capacities.[3] But in the militarized research and corporate development of cybernetics in the U.S., central command and control functions predominated, to an extent that Weiner himself would come to regret. At the same time, the ontological and epistemological centrality of information can tend towards visions of materiality or corporeality as being secondary (Hayles 1999). If humans are informa-

---

3 | See, for example, Pickering 2010 and Medina 2011. Tiqqun 2001 develops a critique that extends to *all* versions. The extent to which computers can (or must) be a part of any socialist planning project is an important one. The point of what follows is that, whatever else one can say, any transition towards socialism must involve a fundamental break with the functions and forms of programming (and, perhaps also, user interfaces) they run today.

tion-processing machines, this means, generally, that our consciousness are *code*: they might one day be uploaded into a computer (a fantasy that remains present in much science-fiction).

Tellingly, combinations of dematerialized and horizontalist visions were most pervasive amongst the techno-pioneers (and programmers) of the personalization of computers and the early internet. "We are creating a world," as John Perry Barlow wrote, "that all may enter without privilege or prejudice[...] Your legal concepts of property, expression, identity, movement, and context do not apply to us. They are all based on matter, and there is no matter here. Our identities have no bodies" (cited by Turner 2006: 13). This "Declaration of the Independence of Cyberspace," written while attending the World Economic Forum in 1996, claims to escape the powers assembled in Switzerland by some miraculous, yet potentially universal, act of incorporeal transcendence. But such claims could also articulate an aspiration to *control* those powers, as for the executive editor of *Wired*, Kevin Kelly, who, two years later, argued that "the principles governing the world of the soft – the world of intangibles, of media, of software, and of services – will soon command the world of the hard – the world of reality, of atoms, of objects, of steel and oil, and the hard work done by the sweat of brows" (cited by Turner 2006: 15).

In such visions, computers and information technologies more generally become material props for etherealized versions of the political utopia of empowered minds: "because we are essentially information, we can do away with the body" (Hayles 1999: 12). Not only might everyone become a mental laborer, but mental laborers themselves might become disembodied postracial spirits, delinked from bodily stigmata and hard power. How then can they govern the world? Here the metaphoric valences of algorithms as "effective procedures" do important work: "software is axiomatic. As a first principle, it fastens in place a certain logic of cause and effect, a causal pleasure that erases execution and reduces programming to an act of writing" (Chun 2011: 97). Software simply "runs" and, in that running, information operates as a seamless form of control. The gap between conception and execution seems to vanish. Materialized in information-processing machines, the human mind wrests free of its body, yet becomes more, not less, materially effective.

Powers of the Machinic Mind

Is mental labor, under such a conception, the new object of command and control or the subject of its implementation? The programmer or the programmed? Does the computer reduce mental labor to the physical patterns of machines or make ideas themselves directly agential? The answer, in one sense, is both, but for different persons. As Ursula Huws (2014: 73-74) argues, "Each innovation simultaneously requires a new cohort of creative 'knowledge workers' who, in the very process of developing new innovations, bring about, albeit indirectly, the routinization of the work of others." Some forms of mental labor have been changed, especially those in the lower ranks of its internal hierarchies. But this change is not so much the "proletarianization" *of* knowledge workers as it is the political and ideological "manualization" of their labor. As computers demonstrate, ideas can also be executed without being conceived.

The self-regulatory character of much contemporary labor – the growing ranks of call-center workers who must improvise on the margins of their scripts, while managing their own emotions, the Toyotist calls for auto workers to contribute their own ideas for improving production or cooks to design a better sandwich, and the "playbor" we perform in our "leisure" time, offering up ever more information to social networks and advertisers – complicate any traditional notion of what "manual labor" is. But the question is not whether workers use their minds or their communicative and affective capacities in these forms of labor; rather, it is whether the conception and control of the labor process as such are separated from its execution. As Mandel noted:

[t]he radical technicization and rationalization of the administration of enterprises and companies represents a dialectical unity of two opposite processes – the growing *delegation* of the power to decide questions of detail on the one hand, and the growing *concentration* of the power to decide questions crucial for the expansion of capital accumulation (1975: 243).

This unity facilitates the routinization of many forms of once-mental labor, while reversing the meaning of workers' "self-regulation." Previously, workers' conceptions of how to shape their own labor processes were centered on reducing the stresses they imposed, opening up pockets of free time within them, allowing for discussion and resistance. Soldiering was, as Taylor knew, the expression of *workers'* knowledge. Now, such ideas are directed towards the speeding up of production and ensuring that algorithms runs smoothly (given their limited capacities to deal with contingencies of the actual world). Workers' ideas are solicited (demanded) by management, which assesses them according to its own goals. Counter-conceptions are transformed into yet another individual responsibility, selectively expropriated for the furthering of accumulation.

The combination of cybernetics and capitalism, in other words, co-opts (manual) workers' knowledge into a routinized process in which control functions have been increasingly centralized by higher echelons of professional design and programming and the materialization of those designs in the algorithmic and surveillance procedures of computational and communications technology. As long as production remains premised on the private ownership of the means of production, fixed capital, and the command and control functions it materializes, will remain a largely external force. "Call centre work offers us the most disturbing scenario possible for the famous 'general intellect' described by Marx in the *Grundrisse:* one in which it is extracted by management, embedded in machines, and imposed through software" (Brophy 2017: 221). Algorithms function not as autonomous collective labor but as a set of instructions written into the very operation of an external fixed capital, the face, the interface, they show to us and the way we interact with them.

The central ideological figuration of the division between mental and manual labor today thus runs along the division between algorithms and data. Networked computers enable flows of information unprecedented in human history, but they do so through the mediation of "black box" algorithms (Pasquale 2015) that structure how that information is processed, how pieces of data are related to other pieces, to whom information is available, and how the outputs shape and control the activities and opportunities of different persons. As users, we (can) see and respond to the data or information (at least those parts of it to which we have or find access) but we are never allowed to see the algorithms. And, since data itself is increasingly the outcome of processes mediated by algorithms, we "see" the data without understanding how it was constructed and what it excludes.[4] "[S]ituated in an overall context characterized by a division

---

4 | For a discussion of how algorithms function in deciding what information is actually delivered to us on social networks and how this can constrain their

between mental and manual labor," information technology "is also functionally determined by that division" and functions to reproduce it.[5]

The specific forms that division takes here – hidden, automated systems of control amidst an apparently leveled network of interactions – ramifies in turn across the social field: production, particularly of information technology, seems to be distributed across networked global production chains, yet "the resulting network formations are highly hierarchical," governed by "flagship" corporations' control over technological development (Lüthje, et al. 2013: 36). Labor appears to become flexible, creative, self-driven, and self-regulated, yet the same process that offers outsize rewards for certain investment bankers, consultants, and artists, consigns many more to insecure, low-wage work or the growing surplus labor army. These tensions, this dialectical unity, are not signs of the nearing disintegration of cybernetics, the liberation of a now autonomous collective mental process, but its very exercise as a means of ever more refined control. "A society threatened by permanent decomposition can be all the more mastered when an information network, an autonomous 'nervous system' is in place allowing it to be piloted" (Tiqqun 2001:15). The underside of networked Post-Fordism is a neo-Taylorism of algorithmic insistence.

In the face of this intensifying system, celebrations of "Facebook democracy" and the like appear increasingly suspect. Visions of the internet as a rhizomatic "distributed network," without central hubs or radial nodes, the site of "radically distributed communications between autonomous entities" (Galloway 2004:141-142; 121)[6] confront the distributional struc-

---

potential as vehicles for the organization of social movements, see Tufecki, 2017: Chapter 6.

5 | The quote is from Poulantzas 1978: 31, though what he is describing there is the position of "the school."

6 | Galloway, it should be said, also recognizes the existence of "adistributed, bureaucratic institutions" that set universal standards for technologies, networks, interfaces, etc. The radical distribution of control requires a prior or coincident focusing of control "into rigidly defined hierarchies [...] The generative contradiction that lies at the heart of protocol is that *in order to be politically progressive, protocol must be partially reactionary.*" And who populates these institutions? A "self-selected oligarchy" consisting largely of "highly educated, altruistic, liberal-minded professionals from modernized societies around the globe," "a small

ture of the internet as a *hierarchy* of nodes, where a few sites or pages have a massive number of links and views, while the vast majority have few or none (Dean 2009: 27-30; Hindman 2009: 38-57; Barabási 2014). "Hierarchies and hubs emerge out of growth and preferential attachment" (Dean 2009: 30), reinforced by the PageRank algorithm designed by Google, which heavily weights the number of links (and the number of links to linking pages) in search results. In this way, the internet reproduces and reinforces the hierarchies of mental labor, materializing that hierarchy in the auto-execution of seemingly neutral algorithms. Likewise, anarchist invocations of "the dark web" must confront its origins as a product of the military apparatuses of the U.S. state (which continues to fund it): where better to hide activities of "the dark state" (Levine 2018: 219-269)?

These points underline the limits of leftist genres of information politics. Even the most complex and cogent of such approaches, like McKenzie Wark's, tend to construe their political goals as one of returning mental labor to its proper autonomy within the expanded parameters of networked life and its decentralized flows, Thus, Wark's account of contemporary political struggle centers on an antagonism between the "hacker class," champions of free information, and the "vectoralist class," which transforms that information into intellectual property. The hackers' struggle is defined by the ontological potential of information: only it, unlike land or capital, "may be free from the commodity form altogether" (Wark 2004: §253). The hacker becomes a kind of handmaiden to this natural potential. She "comes into being through the pure liberty of knowledge in and of itself" (ibid: §055).[7]

Wark's argument for an alliance between hackers and other "producers," across the mental/manual divide, turns on a yet more tenuous extension of this natural-ontological condition. Information's latent freedom from commodification links it to broader interests: "The producing classes as a whole can only reconcile their interests by freeing nature from the grip of property, which is what actually divides them" (ibid: §148). Information's reproducibility, its ontological distance from

---

entrenched group of techno-elite peers" who operate according to familiar models of a quasi-horizontalist "openness" (Galloway 2004: 122).

7 | Wark's account of the hacker ethic draws on Levy 1984. On the history of that ethic, see Turner 2006: 134: "this ethic emerged at a time when the sharing of information allowed everyone to profit." That time did not last long.

any logic of scarcity, provides the basis for a common resistance but only insofar as class relations are understood as an *external* imposition of forms of private property onto productive (self-regulative) activity. In order to maintain the idea of information as naturally "free," that is, Wark must adopt the "general intellect" conception of collective labor as (always) already autonomous and expropriated, rent-like, from outside. Hacking, then, operates in (virtual) freedom from social relations of production and the material institutions (computational technology, fiber optic cables, source code, software, algorithms, etc.) that embody the power relations within them. Thus, it is not so surprising that the hacker adheres to mer-itocratic values ("the allocation of resources based on talent rather than wealth"). The mistake is thinking that such values can be attributed to "the producing classes as a whole" (ibid: §065). [8]

Here, it might be useful to recall an earlier formulation of the char-acter of information technology by Shoshana Zuboff: "The devices that automate by translating information into action *also* register data about these automated activities, thus generating new streams of information" (1988: 8, emphasis added). Rather than information being virtually free, its expanding generation is intrinsically connected to the productive (and, by extension, reproductive and destructive) acts which generate it, to the goals towards which the machinery and its programs have been built and paid for, and to the social relations of power that determine the meaning and implications of those acts. Control over the process is also control over the kind or form of information it generates and over who has access to it.

David Golumbia makes a similar point concerning the central role of computerized spreadsheets in the management of corporations:

While the information in the manager-level spreadsheet might, in general, be kept hidden from subordinates, it is in some ways more real than the persons employed by the company. It frequently contains information of vital importance to the employees, for example productivity rates, employee costs, costs vs. revenue generation, and so on, and yet is in general considered part of "management infor-

---

8 | Notably, for Wark (2004: §036, 060) it is *only* hackers who "create...new kinds of relation, with unforeseen properties, which question the property form itself" and who discover "the knowledge latent in the experience of everyday working life, which can be abstracted from its commodified form and expressed in its virtu-ality".

mation" to which only manager-level employees are entitled access [...] It is when spreadsheets become the focus of discussion that it becomes clear who is part of the management and ownership of a corporation and who works for it. (2009: 158-159)

Precisely because information is shaped by the labor processes that generate it, the algorithms that control and surveil those processes, liberation does not turn on merely "freeing" it. Rather, that information itself reinforces (and enforces) the power relations it informs us about: "The spreadsheet encourages everyone in management to think of the parts of a company as 'resources' that can be understood as 'assets' or 'liabilities'; each human being is more liability than asset, regardless of rhetoric about 'human assets' or 'human resources'" (ibid: 159).[9]

The question is not one of whether information is free but of whether the conception of and control over the processes of production, reproduction, and information generation are in the hands of the direct producers as a whole, not just mental laborers. Otherwise, celebrations of information's desire to be "free" will continue to be overwhelmed by the functions of capital, a tendency the careers of many hackers epitomizes.[10] Otherwise, the vision of information as an intrinsic good will indirectly justify ever-increasing acts of surveilling control, public and private. Cybernetics "claims that *the control of a system is obtained by establishing an optimum degree of communication between parties to it.*" But this objective "calls above all for the continuous extortion of information – a process of the *separation* of beings from their qualities, of the production of differences"

---

9 | Golumbia (2009: 169) makes a similar point about "Customer Relationship Management" [CRM] software, which "helps to implement a hard-and-fast division between the sovereign intelligence that runs organizations and the various intelligences that work for them. A small coterie of management typically has access to the setting of parameters in CRM software, while more employees use the software or help to maintain it. As such, CRM software (and its affiliates) has contributed to the Hobbesian picture of a corporation run by a small, even oligarchical, group of princely leaders and a large, undifferentiated group of workers."

10 | Cf. Steiner 2012: 7: "It's no coincidence that the most upwardly mobile people in society right now are those who can manipulate code to create algorithms that can sprint through oceans of data, recognize millions of faces, and perform tasks that just a few years ago seemed unthinkable."

(Tiqqun 2001: 10, original emphasis). Some of us design algorithms; some of us become data. Those are the inverse sides of a cybernetic frame that extends the imperatives of prediction, control, and accumulation to the whole of society. Not only our labor, but also our health, music and television consumption, shopping, political opinions, our children and our care of them, our thermostats and light bulbs, conversations, e-mails, and web-surfing become information that someone else collects, uses, and profits from.[11]

Finance and the Power of Risk

Golumbia (2009: 182) makes another critical point for thinking through the political impacts of mental labor's materialization in information technologies: "not merely individual human beings but also institutions are empowered by computerization." Granted, the rise of personal computers and the internet has empowered individuals to an extent, but that empowerment is dwarfed by the powers that computers have simultaneously granted to state apparatuses and corporations that govern the production of information technology and the processing of information. Utopic potentials for participatory politics and aesthetics have to be balanced against the sheer bulking force of an infrastructure that compiles individual acts into massive pools of aggregate data, that approaches networked "freedom" as the occasion for surveillance, data mining, and social steering.

This point is of particular salience in relation to finance capital, which, after the military apparatus of the state, was one of the first fields to invest heavily in, and revolutionize its own procedures by, computer and communication technologies. "Finance capital both gambles on investment in new technologies and adopts them to enlarge the scope, speed, and complexity of its operations" (Dyer-Witheford 2015: 94). Hacked data, algorithms for pricing assets, and their transmission to traders on the floor, became an early source of advantage in arbitrage trading that led to today's "high-frequency trading," carried out entirely by computers, and com-

---

11 | The centralization of control via computer and communications technology also facilitates the contemporary organization of transnational corporations, where design and control elements are located in the North, while production sites, call centers, routinized aspects of software writing, etc. are distributed to lower wage sites.

prising as much as 60 percent of all trades (Steiner 2012: 49-74; Bridle 2018: 104-109; Dyer-Witheford 2015: 177-179). The production and pricing of investment vehicles (MBSs, CDOs, and so on), as well as the assessment and pricing of applicants' credit-worthiness for mortgages, credit-cards, and student loans, are also increasingly automated, subjecting each of us to the judgment of algorithms. In a world where one corporation can spend $300 million "to build a private fibre link between the Chicago Mercantile Exchange and Carteret, New Jersey, home of the NASDAQ exchange," in order to shave four milliseconds of the communication time between the two sites (each millisecond translating into as much as $100 million a year profit in high-frequency trades [Bridle 2018: 107]), it is difficult to credit the empowerment my own iMac and "high-speed" internet offer.

That the financial crisis did not, as widely forecast in its immediate aftermath, bring down the political economy inscribed in such algorithms is, in large part, a function of the sheer amount of investment in that infrastructure (and in the assets it values and trades), the economic foundation of capital's power. It would not, at all costs, be allowed to collapse, as the state bailouts made clear. Likewise, resistance to that power, in the moment of its crisis, was undercut by the widespread view on the left that all of that investment, and the mental labor that gives it form, was somehow extraneous to or parasitic on the "real economy." This view fundamentally mistook the central role of finance in contemporary capitalism, not only in the functioning of the economy but in the state-facilitated imposition of competitive logics onto the social order as a whole. In fact, the "failure" of finance, and of neoliberal political economy in general, that the crisis represents, actually became the condition for its widening success, further submitting both individuals and states to those competitive logics. Across its now four-decade long reign, neoliberal governance has mastered the steering of manifestations of capitalism's contradictions such that they become productive from the standpoint of capital: their costs borne principally by workers and the impact of those costs structured in ways that further submit workers to the goal of accumulation and its future contradictions. It is not accidental, in other words, that financial and corporate profits rebounded quickly after the crisis while unemployment lingered and wages remain suppressed. For finance is the means of this steering.

The peculiar characteristics of finance capital, put briefly, are not a function of a parasitic relation to capitalist production but of its embodiment of capital itself *as a (self-valorizing) commodity*. When one buys a financial security or when one takes on debt, one is buying a portion of capital "priced on the basis of the income it is expected to yield in the future" (Sotiropoulos, et al. 2013: 150). The availability of finance is necessary, of course, for the reproduction of capital (since it provides a mechanism for distributing capital to where it can be most profitably invested) but it also functions as the site for reckoning with the complex, uncertain future of privatized production and competitiveness, which neoliberalism is always attempting to master, or at least hedge.[12] This is another way of understanding the intermeshing of finance and strategic rationality: what both seek are rule-bound information processes that develop guidelines for actions in the present moment based on quantifiable models of future outcomes.

The dramatic increase in the global trading of stock options, derivatives, and other investment vehicles that began in the 1970s (driven by multiple factors, including the freeing of currency movements and the crisis of overproduction that pushed capital to search for new avenues to profit) presented new problems for this governance. There were few, if any, precedents on which the future yields of such vehicles could be based. Efforts to hedge uncertainty regarding increasingly complex, global flows of capital needed to be based on some manner of pricing capital *as a commodity*, the elements and flows of which now seemed to eclipse the limits of human comprehension. What filled the void was the incorporation of certain "beliefs" about the market and its elements into "algorithms, procedures, routines, and material devices" that provided specific, ostensibly accurate pricing models (MacKenzie 2006: 19).

The Black-Scholes-Merton model first developed a model for pricing stock options[13] based on the notion of "replicate portfolios." "A three-

---

12 | From the standpoint of neoclassical economics, such a projection of future income is ostensibly not problematic since markets are assumed to be efficient and market information is assumed to be transparent and evenly distributed amongst market agents. Yet, at the same time, these assumptions produce their own contradiction, insofar as they imply that the expected winning on any particular investment will be zero and, so, that the only investment goal should be maximum diversification. This discrepancy tends to be explained away by psychological or behavioral factors (Sotiropoulos, et al. 2013: 144, 146-147).

13 | A purchased right, but not the obligation, to buy or sell an underlying asset at a specific future time.

month forward purchase of foreign exchange," for example, "is equivalent to borrowing for three months in the domestic currency, buying the foreign currency in the spot market, and investing this amount for three-months in a foreign-currency denominated asset" (Sotiropoulos, et al. 2013: 172). If the future pay-offs of the latter portfolio can be calculated (based, of course, on its own series of assumptions about future trends and possibilities), then the price of the option should, in theory, be equivalent. When this model was first developed, however, the going prices for options significantly diverged from the model itself. Traders' embrace of the model generated a wave of computerized arbitrage practices that effectively drove option prices into line with the model's predictions. In the process, the inherently abstract presuppositions of the model – costless market transactions and the possibility of unlimited short-selling – became, tendentially, real, as the volume of options trading skyrocketed. "The practice that the Black-Scholes-Merton model sustained helped to create a reality in which the model was indeed 'substantially confirmed'" (MacKenzie 2006: 166).

Maintaining (and expanding) the relevance of such pricing models required "unfettered and 'unregulated' financial transactions [...] because otherwise there would be no replicate portfolios" (Sotiropoulos, et al. 2013: 172-173). The rising importance of derivatives thus reciprocally develops with the neoliberal abandonment of market restrictions on finance. But, as Dimitris Sotiropoulos, John Milios, and Spyros Lapatsioras argue, the driving impetus behind these processes was not some form of speculative greed, taking flight in an ever more distant, parasitic relation to the "real economy." Rather, derivatives came to play two fundamental and central functions for contemporary, globalized capitalism: 1) providing a commensuration (and, so, commodification) of risks, underpinned by "ideas, images, and estimations of future events in the context of capitalist ideology" (ibid: 161); 2) imposing the calculated costs of such risks on all market agents who take on debt or need access to financing (corporations, states, and individuals), and thereby imposing practical adherence to the norms of that ideology, i.e., compelling actions that serve to reproduce and expand exploitation and the accumulation of capital. Finance, in other words, is not an excessive appendage to the capitalist economy, but "a technology of power, which facilitates and organizes the reproduction of capitalist power relations" (ibid: 179). The uncertainty of the future becomes a means for leveraging the governance of capitalist social relations.

Central to these claims is the idea that "capitalist reality is not trans-parent" (ibid: 148). Pricing models can produce the reality they calculate precisely because the pricing of future value streams must always be based on a set of assumptions that may or may not prove true. The most critical assumptions, however, are those that will serve to reproduce the fundamental social relations of capitalist production. Market "fundamen-tals" are ideological representations "of the dynamics of capital that is nec-essary for the reproduction of capitalist exploitation" (ibid: 160). Capital that spins out more of itself depends on (while fetishizing) the exploitation of labor power: what one is buying when one buys a financial security (or what one is becoming subjected to when one agrees to one takes on secu-ritized debt) is *exploitation* "as a 'thing,' as a *sui generis* commodity, as a financial security" (ibid: 150). Thus, the "accuracy" of the pricing model to some given objective reality is not as important as the disciplining function the model, and trading based upon it, performs. "Markets may misjudge the 'efficiency' of an economic agent, they may overlook funda-mental information in their pricing, but *the interpretive criteria they follow disciplines agents to the norms of the logic of capital regardless of the pricing accuracy*" (ibid: 160, original emphasis).

This is why costs accrued or risks taken by market agents can appear, on one level, to be quantitatively equivalent, yet will be priced by market models in very different ways: "what is worse for an exporting capitalist enterprise (questioning its capacity to produce profits): a workers' strike or an exchange rate appreciation that leads to the same profit loss? What is worse for the capitalist state: public deficits and debt surging due to tax reductions for capital and the rich, or due to the financing of social benefits?" (ibid: 174). That we know the answers immediately reflects the pervasiveness of the norms that financial models of risk discipline us into: "an organic ideological interpretation of capitalist reality" in which, of course, the "risk profile of a wage earner depends on his or her docility in the face of the reality of labor relations" (ibid: 168). The hyper-liquidity of finance capital and the automation of trading by algorithms attuned to those norms allows for rapid and flexible responsiveness to evolving "risk profiles," testing and reinforcing compliance to specific norms and policies. Financial markets, thus, are a peculiar and pervasive institution-alization of the ambitions of strategic rationality, imposing a set of calcu-lations upon each of us by which we are "necessarily constrained to [...] resort to appropriate *risk-management* attitudes and strategic action [...] In this sense, not only does risk calculation (along with the resultant pricing of the various types of security) imply 'power' over the future (the aspect of hedging) but also, and above all, it implies control over the present" (ibid: 168-169).

The more uncertain the future appears, the more fine-grained the control capital seeks over the present becomes. While the risk relative to mortgage interest, insurance rates, or traditional stock investments could be calculated based on personalized data – probabilities based on the payment histories of wage earners or quarterly corporate profits – new modes of risk computation, like financial derivatives, calculate risks attached to qualities, aspects, or elements that are abstracted from any substantive individuality or personality. Ever more complex algorithms impose ever more complex systems of ordering on an ever more uncertain world. The "war on terror" replaces the fixed antagonism of the Cold War with an unknown adversary who could be anyone boarding a plane, crossing a border, or attending a wedding in some "failed" state. "Black swan" financial crises, unprecedented ecological catastrophes, logistical chains traced out across the globe and subject to disturbances across numerous locations, and the ongoing political crisis itself, where "the people" are perceived as a future threat to "democracy," all contribute to dramatic changes in the figure (and figuration) of "risk."

In place of probabilistic inferences based on consistent causal chains and personalities, "intuitive" leaps are required to preempt future exceptions, identifying what might happen before it has even begun or what someone might do before an idea has entered their head. The procedure for such leaps turns on more intensive algorithmic acts of separation and computation: "The emphasis is on the breaking down of data into component elements that can be recombined and written into the algorithmic rules, such that one might 'find out relations that might exist'" (Amoore 2013: 43). Preemption turns not on establishing the identity of a subject but on the calculation, across fields of extracted data, of correlations between elements that might signal a future intent:

[i]f past travel to Pakistan and duration of stay over three months, in association with flight paid by a third party, then risk flag, detain; if paid ticket in cash and this meal choice, in association with this flight route, then this risk score and secondary searches; if two tickets paid on one credit card and seated not together, then these questions at the border (ibid: 59).

This is the form of strategic rationality that intends to win a game before the playing has even started, in anticipation of a competition that might never have started. The equation of justice with wealth maximization here authorizes "a mode of calculation as though it had juridical authority" (ibid: 44). Who will be detained or deported, what corners will be patrolled by police, who will be subject to stops and searches, becomes the function of algorithms, bestowing even greater powers upon the mental labor that programs them, allowing "private consulting, risk management, and software and biometrics engineering to flourish as expert knowledges, to act as though they were sovereign, as proxy forms of sovereignty" (ibid: 6).

Thus, if, as Amadea (2016: xx) argues, the operationalization of strategic rationality "invents a particular subjectivity," it is, in our computational world, one unevenly distributed in terms of its power and its costs. In fact, it would be better to say that it invents (at least) two subjectivities, separated by a widening disjunction that cuts along the political-ideological line of mental and manual labor. On the one hand, there is the subjectivity of the increasing precarious working class (now composed of service and "manualized" information processors, alongside industrial producers), which less identifies with strategic rationality than submits to its effects, "coming to terms with the idea that short-term flexibility and flux are the natural order of things," a view that, amongst the adult children of industrial workers in in Jennifer Silva's ethnographic study, goes almost unquestioned. Accepting the "self-regulating" character of the market, they have a harder time "managing betrayal in institutions such as education, the state, or the law, where they expect to find people who will help them" but do not (Silva 2013: 95-96). Fighting off such felt betrayal, itself partially the product of neoliberal state transformations, often turns on the therapeutic rejection of *any* dependence as the felt price of adulthood, facilitating an isolating embrace of neoliberal individualism, despite the fact that, within that system, they will never be judged good risks.

The subjectivity of investment bankers,[14] on the other hand, is grounded in a "culture of smartness," premised on their recruitment

---

14 | And, in analogous ways, hackers, high-level software programmers, consultants, risk managers, etc. I am not aware of similar ethnographic studies of such mental laborers, but there is surely reason to think that similar characteristics extend well beyond investment bankers to all those whose work involves "programming" the capitalist infrastructure on which the world runs.

from Ivy League schools, represented "by a specific appearance and bodily technique that signals that impressiveness" through characteristics like "being impeccably and smartly dressed, dashing appearance, mental and physical quickness, aggressiveness, and vigor" that "reference the default upper-classness, maleness, whiteness, and heteronormativity of ideal investment bankers" (Ho 2009: 41). For such paragons of neoliberal mental labor, flexibility is not a natural fate submitted to but a combat ethic "chosen" by those already inculcated into it (and cushioned by large signing bonuses, severance packages, etc.). "It is investment bankers' experience as employees (which in turn reshapes the market models they learn and proclaim) that instills a specific disciplinary model of employee liquidity, insecurity, and workplace relations [and] motivates them to export this model to the rest of US business" through the imperatives of "shareholder value" and liquidity creation (ibid: 214). They do not submit to markets, *they make them,* and they make them in their own image, confident in their own "smartness," "superior skills," and the rightness of the disciplinary model they impose upon others (ibid: 247-248). In the gulf between these two subjectivities, seemingly united by their common acceptance of the neoliberal creed of individualism and flexibility, lies perhaps the starkest figuration of the political and ideological division between mental and manual labor today.

Stack and State

If the materialization of mental labor in the fixed capital of our "knowledge economy" produces new figures of mental and manual labor, does it also produce one of *the state?* This is the question posed by Benjamin Bratton's recent analysis of "the Stack" as "an accidental megastructure," the "aggregation of platforms" into a "planetary-scale computing system." At the center of that analysis is the claim that this aggregate system has reached "a scale of technology that comes to absorb functions of the state and the work of governance" (2015: 7).

On one level, that claim echoes Louise Amoore's (2013) regarding the extension of sovereignty or juridical authority to algorithmic calculations and the consultants and engineers who market them to the state. But, in Bratton's account, the Stack represents a much more pervasive and automatic form of governance, which generates layers of "energy, infrastructure, legal identity and standing, objective and comprehensive maps, credible currencies, and flag-brand loyalties" parallel to those of the nation-state. Citizens of some country remain so, but they also have alternative "*User*" credentials, like Google IDs, that are "more useful and effective for daily life.

For these, the terms of participation are not mandatory, and because of this, their social contracts are more extractive than constitutional. The *Cloud Polis* draws revenue from the cognitive capital of its *Users*, who trade attention and micro-economic compliance in exchange for global infrastructural services... (Bratton 2015: 295)

Overlapping, yet occupying different scales, holding different relations to territory, and employing different formal mechanisms, Stack and state "become dramatically less distinct from one another, interlacing and folding up in new ways, producing emergent institutional forms not reducible to the direct combination of the two" (ibid: 121).

The Stack thus articulates a new figure of sovereignty: "Platforms govern in and as algorithmic decision-making machines," yielding "*the machine as the State*" (ibid: 341; 8). For Bratton, however, this is not a dystopic, Skynet fantasy. The machinic State is not a dictatorial authority. Its modes of governance do not predetermine specific outcomes but, rather, set criteria for agency: the technical protocols of communication and operations, "a *rigorous standardization of the scale, duration, and morphology of their essential components*," the assignment of User identities and the compilation of data attached to them, the simplifying interfaces shaping our relation to data and algorithms, and so on. These protocols "decide what an interface will or won't do for which *User* and when" and, yet, at the same time, "allow for more diverse and unpredictable combinations within a given domain" (ibid: 42-44, 47-49, 233, 341-342, original emphases).

The "machinic" character of this new state frees it from the subjective, goal-oriented character Bratton attributes to the traditional state. If "the essence of algorithmic governance" is the automation of "the decision over the exception" (ibid: 341), this, in addition to the Stack's sheer complexity, suggests, for Bratton, a kind of intrinsic flexibility to the modes of governance at play. The traditional "up-versus-down heuristic" of governor vs. governed "will prove to be a far [too] limited model for scaling the complex geopolitical design questions at hand in the future" (ibid: 453).

Rather, this complexity, and the "integral accidents" that follow from it, appear as a resource for ongoing transformation. The automaticity of the process provides occasion for improvisation: if "the deciding of outcomes is something that happens in the course of the interaction itself," then this "could be a result of the *User*'s disciplining the algorithm of automation as much as it is the algorithm delimiting the *User* behavior by what it shows, hides, allows, or prohibits" (ibid: 342). Software "is not only how to govern but [...] it itself must be governed" (ibid: 453). With this emphasis, Bratton shifts the trajectory of analysis away from the liberation or enslavement of individuals, "pro-Stack" or "anti-Stack," to those of the (re)design of this machinic state: the Stack we want, "the Stack-to-come."

It is with these gestures, I want to suggest, that Bratton's fascinating discussion passes over into another utopia of empowered minds, an envisioned struggle of software engineers over the anarchic potentials of Stack complexity, defined by a "focus on composing and elevating sites of governance from the immediate, suturing interfacial material between subjects, in the stitches and the traces and the folds of interaction between bodies and things at a distance, congealing into different networks demanding very different kinds of platform sovereignty" (ibid: 363). In such moments, Bratton neglects Amoore's insight (which is sometimes, as the quote above about the "Cloud polis" suggests, his own) that the site of "sovereignty" in the Stack is not so much *the software* as those who design and program it, and the capacity to do so is not anonymously distributed but underwritten by the powers of capital and state. To think otherwise is to imagine autonomous powers of mental labor able to enter into and transform the vast infrastructure that embodies the power of capital, a *"world of apparatuses so blended with the capitalist project that it has become a political project"* (Tiqqun 2001: 5, original emphasis).

There are two interrelated sources of Bratton's error here, I think, which can cast at least some light on the contemporary functions of mental labor. Both relate to Bratton's tendency to understand complexity as the confusion of powers, the loss of fixed coordinates of "up" and "down." In light of the histories traced here, James Bridle's argument that "the complexity of contemporary technologies is itself a driver of inequality" seems more convincing.

It concentrates power into the hands of an ever smaller number of people who grasp and control these technologies, while failing to acknowledge the fundamental problem with computational knowledge: its reliance on a Promethean extraction of information from the world in order to smelt the one true solution, the answer to rule them all. (Bridle 2018: 132)

The failure of that "smelting" – the same failure of strategic rationality I sketched in chapter four – may be less a reason to take over and redesign these algorithmic processes, than a sign of the need to establish a certain distance from, and skepticism towards, them.

In the first place, Bratton overstates the formal differences between the sovereignty of the Stack, as he describes it, and that of the traditional capitalist state. He generally speaks (always in passing) of the latter as if it were a kind of subject, oriented by clearly intended outcomes, capable of subjective "decisions." It is in relation to this conception that the complexity of the Stack supposedly undermines the authority of traditional powers. However, as Poulantzas argues, states are not subjects, their "sovereign" decisions are not determined by some pre-given unity or goal. Rather, the state itself is an institutionalized set of material processes in which the contradictions between fractions of the dominant class are worked through, "a structural mechanism whereby an apparatus filters the information given, and the measures taken, by other apparatuses," arriving at a "unity" that represents a temporary configuration of "a multiplicity of diversified micro-policies" (Poulantzas 1978: 134-135). The state is a strategic field but this means, inversely, that it is not an anarchic site open to endless "re-programming." It manifests a strong form of "path dependence" (Jessop 2002), wherein the outcomes of previous struggles shape the terrain of current ones. As a "hierarchic-bureaucratized" structure, any given state-form favors certain strategies and cements the hegemony of a specific class or fraction, as determined by the balance of forces. Complexity, then, is not an intrinsic threat to the state's coherence or to the dominance of specific powers; rather, it is the means by which that power is embodied and actualized.

Thus, if the Stack was a state, we would need to extend the logics of class conflict and path-dependence to it. Drawing on prior discussions, these might be traced to its design protocols and algorithms as embodiments of the delegated control functions of mental labor. If the Stack is composed of a set of accidental convergences and integral accidents, each component of it is, nevertheless, designed or engineered largely in accordance with the strategic imperatives of the capital and state apparatuses that funded and approved their development and implementation. Amongst the apparently anarchic liberations of hacker-space, there are hegemonic forces, locating themselves in "decision-making centers [...] made impermeable to all but monopoly interests, becoming centers for switching the rails of state policy or for bottling up measures taken 'else-where' in the State" (Poulantzas 1978: 137). In fact, a "machinic state" would appear to be more impervious to the struggles of those excluded from the privileges of mental labor than one constrained by its representative character. What need does the Stack have of legitimacy?

In the second place, Bratton's suggestion that, in the Stack, algorithms govern takes too much for granted the idea that, as closed world systems, they actually can do so. An algorithm, as Ian Bogost (2015) and Ed Finn (2017) have recently insisted, *is never what it claims to be*, nor is any computational system ever "merely algorithmic" (Bogost 2015). Just as the abstract procedures of strategic rationality cannot capture the qualitative complexities of real world decisions and processes, so their computational expressions cannot deliver what they promise without an endless series of non-algorithmic patches, fixes, and fudges. Underneath the "façade of computational perfection" is a "mess of interconnected systems, policy frameworks, people, assumptions, infrastructures, and interfaces" (Finn 2017: 49). Netflix's vaunted recommendation algorithm, for example, is premised on the work of "human taggers" who, with the help of a "thirty-six-page guide to measuring about 1,000 quanta" assign films and television shows a set of genre tags (ibid: 92). The Google search algorithm must be constantly "corrected" by human intervention, so that it does not so prominently display racist or pornographic content. And, as sketched above, the "objective," algorithmic calculations of "risk" are, in fact, shaped by specific applications of the evolving ideology of capital accumulation.

The "automaticity" of algorithmic governance is less a potential site for subversive re-programming than an ideological mask for the continuing service, intentional or not, of all-too-human mental labor to the reproduction of capitalist society. The "black box" hides algorithms, certainly, but also the fact that computation is never merely algorithmic, that the seamless, pure world of automatic computation is itself a kind of fetish, masking ongoing human labor, guided by the imperatives of capital. "[D]ata is created, not simply aggregated, and often by means of laborious, manual processes rather than anonymous vacuum-devices" (Bogost 2015). In that sense, the Stack is not a state but an expanded articulation of the political and ideological relations of production to society as a whole, a form of semi-automatic *outsourcing* of state-functions that makes them appear as natural, seamless market-like functions unsusceptible to question or challenge. In this light, Bratton's aspirational re-programming looks something like a computational form of "parliamentary cretinism."

Bratton is likely correct that the Stack is so pervasive that there is little sense in being for or against it *as such*, only in asking what we can do with, how we can relate to it. But any move toward a productive mobilization of the resources of the Stack would also have to conceive of what form struggles external to it could take, by what processes qualitative aspects of the world (including human needs, or what Marx called "wealth") could be integrated with it or, rather, how the Stack could be subordinated to them,[15] and, most fundamentally, how the separation of control and execution could be refigured in ways that no longer entail the relentless routinization of forms of labor submitted to algorithmic guidance. Precisely because the Stack *is not* a state, it may also be that revolutionary transformation involves maintaining a certain distance from it and all the surveillance and control functions it exercises. "The revolutionary process may appropriate technologies or develop new ones, but it may also free people from technological dependencies" (Dyer-Witheford 2013: 196). Certainly, it should free us from the fetish of algorithms, of a seamless, pure mental labor, turning us all into data, subject to endless, abstract re-combinations and risk-scoring.

---

15 | I share, in other words, Bridle's (2018: 128-129) concern that "[w]e are inserting opaque and poorly understood computation at the very bottom of Maslow's hierarchy of needs – respiration, food, sleep, and homeostasis – at the precise point, that is, where we are most vulnerable."

Chapter 7: No One Has Yet Determined What a Mind Can Do

> To seek to overcome 'expert idiocy' is to strive towards an understanding of the totality of society as a whole.
> (MANDEL 1975: 265)

There are few things as dispiriting (at least within political theory) as reaching the final chapter of a book, or section of an essay, in which a compelling critique of key aspects of contemporary social order, domination, or exploitation has been articulated, only to discover there some vague call for a different manner of thinking, imagining, perceiving, or writing. Often, this call is punctuated by references to work of fiction, contemporary or classical, taken to suggest this new form. There is a 50% or better chance that Bartelby the Scrivener will be cited.

The dispiriting thing here is not really the new models of conception or perception *as such*. Often (though, admittedly, not always) these are cogent and suggestive, offering intimations of what forms of life, experience, decision-making, or modes of valuation might look like in a world not (or less) defined by regimes of competition, commodification, and bureaucratization. Rather, what saps the spirit is the peculiar disconnect between the analytic sections of such a text, mapping out material practices, structures of violence and control in the complex procedures of a political economy, and the sudden implied message that if we, as intellectuals, only started thinking, imagining, perceiving, or writing differently that would itself transform those practices and logics.

There is rarely, if ever, a clear articulation of how or why such a result would follow. The inference at work seems to be that, if there are perceptual or conceptual logics at play in the social world, then inventing new logics will, over time, change that world. It is against such a magical notion of the "power of ideas" (and of empowered minds) that this book has been written. Absent an attachment to any form of counter-power or capacity, such proposals tend to become arguments for the ongoing development of disciplinary knowledges, a valorization of the position of the academic akin to that which Stephen Schryer (2011: 51) traces in the literary and academic worlds of the post-war U.S.: appropriating the Progressive emphasis "on technical expertise and its argument that the professional is the caretaker of public morality" but divorcing it from "the idea that disciplinary knowledge can or should be used to reform society actively in accordance with that morality." As caretakers of alternative modes of thought, feeling, and perception, intellectuals' distance from actual transformations becomes a symbol of the purity of critique.

One could argue, of course, that political theorists play a kind of preservative role, keeping new modes of thought alive (as "messages in bottles") until they can be received in some kind of better world by a social agent ready to receive them. But if the character of such ideas is detached from any presently conceivable mass practice, from any social position other than those of contemporary intellectuals, then they must themselves be marked by the separation between mental and manual labor, embodying a freedom that is not so much free as dematerialized, ignoring the social relations and infrastructures of control that ultimately shape their meaning and decide upon their enactments.

The same can be said, picking up the discussion from the first chapter, of some more directly and intentionally activist forms of thinking, those that claim to find an orientation for action in the abstract conception of a communicative, productive infrastructure already installed in our thoughts and feelings. No doubt, these forms of thought represent an advance over the previous type, pressing theory towards action, engagement, resistance. They often articulate instructive analyses of specific aspects of the contemporary world, specific dilemmas of transformative agency. But still one wonders what, precisely, we are to do with claims that what the "multitude" wants is "to create sustainable relations of access and use for all" (Hardt/Negri 2017: xiv)? Or that "what is needed for contesting the austerity plans is a *different idea of life*, which consists for example of sharing rather than economizing, conversing rather than not saying a word, fighting rather than suffering" (The Invisible Committee 2015: 52)?

In relation to such benign abstractions, the assertion that contemporary revolts are "the political struggle of a knowledge class whose work is exploited and lives are expropriated by communicative capitalism" (Dean 2014: 1) has the merit of concretely situating those to whom such abstractions might appeal. But in light of Dean's own observation that the members of this "class" are characterized by an "intense attachment to individuality, difference and uniqueness – attachments that would hinder solidarity" (ibid: 9), what potentials can we find here for a solidarity that would cross the division between "knowledge class" and those who execute their conceptions? Is the organization of knowledge workers itself a desirable goal? Is the liberation of information by hackers really what all of us need?

Compare those claims with Didier Eribon's observation about the politics of the working-class milieu in which he grew up:

In working class environments, a leftist politics meant first and foremost a very pragmatic rejection of the experience of one's own daily life. It was a form of protest, and not a political project inspired by a global perspective [...] My family divided the world into two camps, those who were 'for the workers' and those who were 'against the workers,' or, in slightly different words, those who 'defended the workers' and those who 'did nothing for the workers.' How many times did I hear sentences that encapsulated this political attitude and the choices that resulted from it! On one side was 'us' and those who were 'with us'; on the other side was 'them.' Nowadays who fulfills the role played by 'the Party'? To whom can the exploited and powerless people turn in order to feel that they are supported or that their point of view is expressed? (2013: 45-46)

Huey Newton argued in a similar vein concerning what separated the practice of the Black Panther Party from the state's welfare programs: "We were doing what the poverty program claimed to be doing but never had— giving help and counsel to poor people about the things that crucially affected their lives" (1973: 121). On one level, these two perspectives are not intrinsically opposed – Newton also observes that "All of these programs were aimed at one goal: complete control of the institutions in the community" (ibid: 177) – but his and Eribon's insistence on beginning with the experience and needs of daily life returns us to the questions posed by figures like Sennett and Cobb (1972) and James (1993) concerning the relationship between those immediate experiences and global political perspectives. If "the Party" did not solve those problems, it could, for a time, depend on a certain political perspective already contained in the consciousness of working class identity. Today, with that class perspective atomized, and with the separation of mental from manual labor having become the most immediate experience of it remaining, the problem is only redoubled, and the weakness of any politics premised on that separation amplified. Rather than new modes of thinking, we need to identify sites where the overcoming of that separation could begin and models for practices that might initiate it.

Power and Theory

In the bulk of this book, I have focused on historical dynamics in which knowledge workers derive their power and social authority from capital (often mediated by the state) while performing its functions: advancing accumulation and articulating political and ideological "fixes" for the pressing contradictions or dilemmas that such accumulation faces. The tendential identification of mental labor with capital's functional aspect follows from: 1) the fact that, capital, as ownership and control of the means of production (and, increasingly, the infrastructures of communication and the reproduction of labor power), always wields enormous social capacity and authority, while workers' capacities turn on the difficult development of counter-institutions and the identification of key sites at which flows of value can be interrupted; 2) the social position of knowledge workers itself derives from workers' exclusion from the means of production, such that, outside of some explicitly and politically developed link between themselves and a mobilized working class with durable counter-powers, their conceptions will be effective only insofar as they draw on and reinforce the power of capital. This is the lesson of progressivism: it is not that progressive reforms ultimately failed because they were only "reformist"; rather, any efforts at reform or revolution sustained only by a mental labor whose default position is its separation from the dominated masses will "succeed" only to the extent that substantial fractions of capital align behind it. It is not that "power corrupts," as if the issue was one of moral resistance to temptation; rather, power (capital) structures the range of possibilities. Compelling workers to sell their labor to some capitalist, lest they face starvation, it likewise compels knowledge workers to take on its functions in production and social reproduction, should they wish to draw a salary, have access to the latest technologies, and so on. No doubt, there always exist margins in which a lucky few can persist in isolation or hidden resistance. But an effective, transformative movement is only possible on the basis of the power of a broad social movement. If knowledge directs, it directs and articulates a social power that it cannot independently generate.

The form of that direction, the logic of the knowledge in question, is also of central importance in determining whether alternative powers will press towards transformation of or accommodation with existing social relations. Ideals of technical efficiency, quantitative rationalization, strategic self-maximization, or even an abstract ideal of "the public good" – all of which turn on a separation between the position of knowing and that of the actions or agents to be guided by it – legitimate and reinforce trajectories that are ultimately capitalist, even where they motivate, for a time, collective action on the part of the dominated.

Something along these lines was Charles Bettelheim's (1976, 1978) insight into the trajectory of the Russian Revolution. The seizure of the means of production by a state that had itself been seized opened the possibility for a radical transformation of Russian society. Yet, the logic of hard choices driven by the civil war, the failure of revolutions in Western Europe, and the dilemma of incorporating a majority peasant population into a socialist transition, shaped policies that retained the core political and ideological relations of capitalist production. Workers were driven to ever greater efficiency and productivity:

There is no question of allowing the Soviet workers to exercise collective control over the utilization of the means of production, over the way current production is used, or over the activity of the party and its members. The factories are run by managers whose relation with 'their' workers are relations of command, and who are responsible only to their superiors. (Bettelheim 1976: 44)

Politically, "the process whereby the state machinery was acquiring independence triumphed over the resolutions of the party congresses, over the decisions of the party's leading bodies, and over Lenin's appeals" (ibid: 329). Mental labor remained separated from manual in both "economy" and "politics," only with the Party bureaucracy playing both leading roles.

For Bettelheim, the ideological expression of those separations coalesced under the Stalinist doctrines of the primacy of the productive forces, the "full conformity" of productive relations with them, and the disappearance of exploitation, such that the accelerated growth of the productive forces could appear as an unconflicted path towards communism. These theses "contributed to blocking any organized action by the Soviet proletariat to transform the productive relations," leaving "the objective basis for the existence of classes" (ibid: 25), the separation of conception and execution, mental and manual labor, town and country, and worker and peasant, unaltered.

The conclusion that Bettelheim drew from this analysis was that the central political goal of revolutionary struggle was the "smashing" of existing social relations - indexed by the division between mental and manual labor and the subordination of the masses to the state – and the creation of new ones, characterized by "control by the producers over their conditions of production and existence" (Sweezy/Bettelheim 1971: 66). Precisely because of the sedimented force of these ideological and political relations, their role in constituting subjects, this was not a goal that could be achieved through spontaneous and immediate action of the exploited. Rather, he suggested, it would be the "result of *protracted class struggle* waged under the dictatorship of the proletariat," guided by "the most advanced form of Marxist-Leninist thought" (ibid: 66), and requiring "that the party of the proletariat *remain in fact* the servant of the laboring masses, that it be capable of drawing the lessons from all their revolutionary initiatives, and that it commit itself to these initiatives and to assist in their development" (ibid: 73).

In this form, the dilemma (or dialectic) of the supersession of the separation of mental from manual labor receives direct expression: it depends on a form of agency that, at once, presupposes that separation (as a given historical condition) and tendentially moves towards its overcoming. The supersession of the privileges of mental labor requires an alignment of certain mental laborers with the power of the masses that resist and resent those privileges, an exercise of mental labor directed towards something other than, indeed opposed to, its own reproduction as a seemingly autonomous power.

Gramsci (1971: 334) made a similar argument fifty years earlier:

A human mass does not 'distinguish' itself, does not become independent in its own right without, in the widest sense, organizing itself; and there is no organisation without intellectuals, that is without organisers and leaders, in other words, without the theoretical aspect of the theory-practice nexus being distinguished concretely by the existence of a group of people 'specialised' in conceptual and philosophical elaboration of ideas.

If this claim appears to be voiced in a more transhistorical frame than Bettelheim's, elsewhere Gramsci himself invokes the question raised by such a voicing: "is it the intention that there should always be rulers and ruled, or is the objective to create the conditions in which this division is no longer necessary?" (ibid: 144). Interestingly, he does not directly answer the question. If the general tenor of Gramsci's theory might seem to imply the latter answer (Coutinho 2012: 59), what he actually suggests is that the question itself serves primarily as a means "to avoid the fundamental problem" (Gramsci 1971: 145). The issue is not the future but the *present* status of intellectuals, the role that they can (or must) play in the struggle against exploitation and domination.

That role, Gramsci is clear, cannot simply wish away the historical separation of mental and manual labor, the differential training provided for the physiological and psychological stance of the intellectual. Yet, it must be directed towards a developing "unity" or "contact" with those who are led. If leadership is not to be a form of domination, it must relate "organically" to the problems posed by experiences and struggles of those it leads: "work[ing] out and mak[ing] coherent the principles and the problems raised by the masses in their practical activity." It is a matter of "starting with a philosophy which already enjoys, or could enjoy, a certain diffusion, because it is connected to and implicit in practical life, and elaborating it so that it becomes a renewed common sense possessing the coherence and the sinew of individual philosophies" (ibid: 330).

What Gramsci proposes, in other words, is a form of theory grounded on and guiding an alternative source of power to that of capital: "the energies and initiative" of a working-class movement (Thomas 2009: 438). In a sense, this proposal parallels strategic rationality to the extent that it explicitly expands and strengthens the (potential) hegemony of the power in relation to which thought centers itself, avoiding thereby the vagaries of a notion like the "public good" or "national interest," which will be filled in by whatever power can control its articulation. Yet, at the same time, Gramsci's proposal aspires to *concretize* its premises in relation to an evolving, and initially contradictory, practice, "coinciding and identifying itself with the decisive elements of the same practice" in order to "accelerate the historical process taking place, rendering practice more homogeneous, coherent, efficient in all its elements, strengthening it to the maximum" (Gramsci 1971: 364-365).

Rather than abstract principles of self-maximizing individuality, in other words, the philosophy of praxis "comprehends its own conditions of possibility as the very practices that it seeks to comprehend and transform" (Thomas 2009: 382). But this means that the theorist cannot remain divorced from those practices; rather, she must enter into them.

The mode of being of the new intellectual can no longer consist in eloquence, exterior and momentary mover of affections and passions, but in joining in actively in practical life, as constructor, organizer, 'permanently active persuader' because not pure orator – and nevertheless superior to the abstract mathematical spirit (Gramsci 1971: 10; I follow Thomas's [2009: 417] translation).

The intellectual aligned with the working class is, therefore, a "humanistic" intellectual: the study of history, political concepts and struggles, epistemological grounds of science and knowledge, cultural and anthropological forms, and so on, allow an evolving grasp on social relations and history that an "abstract mathematical spirit," like that of strategic rationality, cannot develop. But this is also a "neo-humanism" (Thomas 2009: 425), one not committed to maintaining the autonomy of thought but to the rendering coherent of material practices. The "concrete action of man" in historical reality is the basis of thought (ibid: 426). The intellectual must no longer be a "specialist" but a "leader (specialist + politician)" (Gramsci 1971: 10).

Following Peter Thomas's remarkable *The Gramscian Moment* (2009), I would argue that Gramsci's remains the most developed account of how mental labor could (begin to) reform itself towards the tendential removal of its separations. And yet, in the context of the contemporary political crisis, it also points to further dilemmas. For the context in which Gramsci developed it was one in which the political mobilization of workers' around elements of Marxist theory was already a real and compelling force. That mobilization may have been distorted by mechanistic and economistic strains of theory and it may have been decimated (in part, because of those distortions) by the mobilized forces of the fascist offensive, to which capital granted its power, but it nevertheless appeared as a viable basis for an ongoing movement, especially if strengthened to its maximum by philosophers of praxis. In this context, Gramsci could write with a certain confidence, even within his prison cell, that "[m]ass adhesion or non-adhesion to an ideology is the real critical test of the rationality and historicity of modes of thinking" (Gramsci 1971: 341).

What substitute for such confidence can we adhere to today, in the face of the networked ephemerality of recent social movements of the left? Thomas's book ends on an anticipatory note, arguing that Gramsci's

insights into the forms of possible proletariat hegemony retain today their fertility for further theoretical and practical investigation, awaiting the energies and initiatives of a reviving working-class movement which alone will be able to confirm and, if necessary, to transform them in practice (2009: 438).

But, we might wonder, what else can be done besides "awaiting"? The unfolding political crisis would seem to summon some other form of response, while complicating any formulation of one, given the deep suspicion of and resentment towards mental labor and the peculiarity of a political crisis without a political class formation to orient leftist struggles. In what remains of this chapter and book, I offer two provisional reflections on the sorts of "theoretical and practical investigations" we might undertake.

The Renewal of Workers' Inquiry

The fundamental limitation of those theories of the "empowered mind," both liberal and radical, considered in Chapter 1 is that they presuppose a capacity within capitalism (realized or nascent; on the part of capital or of workers) to directly supersede the division between mental and manual labor, either 1) at the economic level, through the universalization of "knowledge work" or "immaterial labor," or; 2) at the political level, through a transformative agency attributed to knowledge workers, in the name of a collective commons of the general intellect. In both cases, the implicit conception of that supersession is grounded in a supposedly universalizing character of knowledge work today: ever more workers taking up individualized, flexible responsibility or drawing upon and adding to the resources of communication and affective interaction and production. What is missed, in other words, is the intrinsic shaping of contemporary forms of mental labor (and the habits, expectations, perspectives, of those trained for it) by the control functions of capital, the split between conception and execution.

Identifying the centrality of "organization" or "leadership" to mental labor, as Bettelheim and Gramsci do, opens up an alternative perspective, not by suggesting that organization as such must be abandoned but by recognizing that the organization of the exploited and dominated, the rendering coherent of their own practices of resistance, is substantively distinct from the forms of control that subsume their productive and reproductive activities to the imperative of capital accumulation. Resistance requires a *fundamental interruption* of those control forms, well prior to any prospective fusion of mental and manual labor. Workers' autonomy begins in a negation of the existing labor process. It is not, in other words, that workers do not have independent capacities for development, that they have not participated to one extent or another in the "general intellectuality" of the age of public education, mass media, etc. Rather, those capacities and that participation can only take form through more or less explicit opposition to capital, through the construction of alternative, or counter-hegemonic practices and institutions. "[I]n no case," as Silvia Federici (2011: 70) puts it, "is 'commoning' a given, an automatic development immanent in the work itself."

Consider, for example, Enda Brophy's (2017) discussion of resistance by call center workers in a communicative workplace. Despite drawing upon the Autonomist tradition and its notions of general intellect and immaterial labor, she articulates that resistance as developing through a communicative process distinct from and counter to the communicative practices that characterize their work itself. As an increasingly top-down, scripted, and surveilled model of interaction, she argues, call center work is "geared towards the production of what we could call *abstract communication*, or communication that is instrumental, homogeneous, measurable, and thereby divorced from the concrete knowledge, abilities, or experience of those who enact it" (ibid: 6). The fixed capital that plays a role in producing such abstract communication is not embodied in the workers or their minds but in the technological infrastructure (the computer, the phone, their algorithmic interaction and assessment) that enables and controls their work.

Their practices of resistance, on the other hand, "are the vernacular of a gathering counter-perspective from below, one that is developing within and against the process of language put to work in call centres" (ibid: 77).

But even the claim of "within" seems uncertain here: the examples Brophy (ibid: 66-70, 110-111) offers that might be construed as occurring *within* the process of language put to work are generally forms of either "slacking" or of refusing to take part in abstract communication at certain moments in the name of "personal standards of professionalism and human decency." While these are forms of limited resistance within the labor process, it seems doubtful that they can be construed as drawing on a "directly productive" (Lazzarato 1996: 143) character of "subjectivity as fixed capital" (Read 2003: 132). Rather, there is a counter-perspective at play, one that "extends horizontally among workers" (Brophy 2017: 7) but is *opposed* to, not materialized in, the control-functions written into technological fixed capital. And, as resistance develops into more collective forms, its externality to the existing labor process becomes more manifest. As the German activist group, Call Center Collective, describes "counter-mobilization and horizontal communication," it is "communication *without management and telephones*" (cited by Brophy 2017: 46; emphasis added). This is not resistance based on an already constituted "general intellect." It is an experiment towards the production of one.

I do not mean to deny the political relevance of, for example, the downshifting of the character of jobs (both in content and precarity) available to many college graduates, nor of the frustrated expectations those shifts produce. These can be important mobilizing forces (just as the resentment of mental labor's control can also be). But it is worth considering just how different these experience of frustrated expectations and capacities are from those which craftspeople underwent in the early period of large industry. Like the artisans of the early and mid-19th century, today's once or would be knowledge workers do not embody the *supersession* of the division between mental and manual labor. They suffer (unevenly) from its imposition on labor processes, their loss of control over them. Yet, they also undergo such "proletarianization" in fundamentally transformed circumstances.

Artisanal resistance to proletarianization was at the leading edge of transformations to relations of production that were just beginning. The knowledge and control they sought to separate from workers were solely those concerning their own labor processes. Artisans' resistance may, at times, have been an effort to preserve their own waning privileges, but it could also lay "the ideological foundations for the movements of their grandchildren, the factory proletariat" (Davis 2018: 25). The resistance of lower grades of mental laborers (or of lower echelons of agents ostensibly trained for such labor) today, however, occupies a quite different historical and structural position. To the extent it is, or is perceived as, an effort to preserve or reinvent existing powers and privileges, those are identified with systemic and pervasive forms of control extended over the workplace, the state, and the broader social practices of reproduction. A movement that merely seeks to get those powers back (if also to improve distributive equality) is not a workers' struggle but, ultimately and perhaps unwittingly, a struggle against workers. Such a struggle therefore requires a fundamental break with the standard practices of knowledge work, an intentional effort to understand and further the practices of those already submitted to its control.

The recent wave of teachers' strikes might be understood, provisionally, as one form of such a struggle. Standardized curricula and tests, as well as various quantitative forms of teacher assessment linked to them, have increasingly undermined teachers' autonomy and control over the pedagogical process, routinizing its character. Especially in low-income urban and hinterland areas, teachers are often viewed by the state apparatus as more or less interchangeable functionaries in the warehousing of surplus labor power (as the short-term provisioning practices of programs like Teach for America suggests). Pay, which was never high, has stagnated in tandem with the loss of control. Still, the remaining ambiguities of the pedagogical process – as both the reproduction of labor power *and* the development of the autonomous capacities of persons – has provided a potential starting point for resistance, especially where such development has not been conceived of as an abstract public good but has inspired a strengthening of ties and reciprocal understanding between teachers and the communities they serve. The widespread support for the initial strikes in Chicago, for example, suggests the potential for overcoming the separation between schools and communities (Uetricht 2014) in a potentially more radical way than temporary occupations by the cognitariat. Still, the model for more general forms of such struggles remains unclear: The renewed practices of workers' inquiry that Brophy (2017) and others (Woodcock 2016; Viewpoint 2013; the Notes from Below website) have recently traced seem like a possible site for beginning to develop the coherence and the generalization of these struggles. Increasing attention to surplus populations (the reciprocal effect of the drive towards relative surplus value), including urban "slums" (Davis 2006) and "hinterlands"

(Neel 2018), migrants and migrant workers, and racialized communities' resistance to the carceral state, also seem to be sites where engaged intellectual inquiries could provide avenues for the collective production and developing coherence of new institutional projects and class compositions *explictly opposed to* the control functions of mental labor. More experiments are needed.

Populism as Common Sense Politics

Interruptions of the functions proper to capitalist labor processes intersect, of necessity, with the political sphere. As Michael Lebowitz (2003: 96) argues, challenges to the power of capital, as owner of the means of production and the products of labor, must always go beyond "confrontation between *specific* capitalist and *specific* wage-laborers." The 19th century struggle over the length of the working day in England, for example, involved a specifically political struggle and "the use of the state" for its success (ibid: 97). For Marx, "this very necessity of *general political action*" derived from capital's monopolization of control over the means of production: "in its merely economic action capital is the stronger side" (cited by ibid: 97). Against such strength, workers had to bring to bear "continuous pressure from without" and a "general, socially coercive force," that is, "*general laws*, enforced by the power of the state.

In enforcing such laws, the working class do no fortify governmental power. On the contrary, they transform that power, now used against them, into their own agency. They effect by a general act what they would vainly attempt by a multitude of isolated individual efforts. (Cited by ibid: 98)

Marx's claim that the state became "their own agency" is striking, insofar as, at the time, English workers did not even have the right to vote. But that optimistic assertion of the transformation of the power of the state (which he himself would amend after the example of the Paris Commune), does not belie Marx's broader point: the power materialized in the state, though it too ultimately derives from capital, can (and perhaps must) be leveraged, through political action as general as the state purports to be, as a (partially) external site for the transformation the character of productive relations.

Today, however, the translation of specific forms of resistance into a general, political form, faces starker difficulties. The state's embodiment of popular ignorance persists, if softened by somewhat more inclusive representative forms (undermined in the U.S. by gerrymandering, the electoral college, etc.). But, more fundamentally, what we appear to lack are forms of common identity at the "economic-corporative level," which could provide a basis for a transcendence of the "merely" economic level towards the generality of hegemonic struggles (see Gramsci 1971: 181). The atomization of workers and the destruction of "counter-hegemonic appa-ratuses" (like unions, workers' papers, communist parties, etc.) that the knowledge economy imposed has left a kind of vacuum in the spot from which "politics" was to establish the relation between common sense and "the upper level of philosophy," undermining the role that "organic" intel-lectuality was to play in that translation (ibid). We are in a political crisis lacking a clear set of class formations or social antagonisms to organize around, which is why racist and misogynistic theories have been so suc-cessful at filling that vacuum for some.

To the extent that there *has* been a general political form of response to this crisis, it has been a populist one. The potential of that form has been the subject of much debate. For progressives, of course, populism, in both its rightist and leftist forms, appears as a fundamental threat to the stable democratic procedures and institutions of elite-managed democracy. But the response to populist formations from the left has been discordant. For some, the liberal dismissal of populism is, in fact, the only content of the concept: if populism once existed (in the 19th century People's Party or mid-20th century Latin America), today it has simply become an epithet, the inheritance of cold-war nostrums according to which all movements to the left or right of liberalism are consigned to that night in which all cows are totalitarian (Dussel 2007, D'Eramo 2013). From this perspec-tive, any popular politics of the left must refuse the concept of populism. For "radical democrats," inspired by the work of Laclau (2007), populism opens the potential for new popular identities, arranged under empty sig-nifiers beyond the traditions of left and right. Here, populism becomes something like the ontological core of politics as such, leaving it unclear how to evaluate any specific movement. Each new populist upsurge thus evokes a confusing crossfire of enthusiasm, hedged support and stern denouncement.[1]

In this context, a definitive statement like that offered by Jodi Dean - "there is no such thing as a left populism" (Dean 2017: S43) – is bracing and, in some ways, salutary. At the same time, I want to suggest, it articulates the inverse side of her focus the struggle of the "knowledge-class," expressed here as a tendency to reject political conceptions and practices not grounded *a priori* on a consistently articulable theoretical position. If we, instead, pose the question of whether a left populism exists (and what it is) in light of Gramsci's focus on the contradictory character of common sense and the intellectual project of rendering it coherent, we may arrive at another perspective.

To make sense of Dean's claim, we need to understand what she means by populism as such. In the now standard liberal definition, it is defined by a vision of the political field composed of a beleaguered, pure "people" rising up against a corrupt elite that has usurped the rights of popular sovereignty. To an extent, Dean agrees with this conception (as do I). In her book, *The Communist Horizon* (2012: 98), she identifies populism with "the imagined totality of the people," with a vision of a "smooth (naturalized) flow from actual people to the collective power of the sovereign people." Unlike the liberal view, however, Dean insists that what populism's projected unity of "the people" masks is precisely the class antagonisms at the heart of capitalist society. Still, recognizing the decline of explicitly class-based discourses, she argues that such antagonisms today are *also* expressed through a discourse of "the people," but one conceptualized not as a totality but as "the part-of-no-part," an "interruption of a given order by those who have no part," yet which identifies itself as, in some sense, a community (the "people of communism"). This "people as the rest of us [...] the people as a dividing and divisive force" (ibid: 80) introduces a constitutive gap into political agency and it is this gap, for Dean, that ensures the open, transformative character of a politics that can never be reduced to an achieved representation. "No matter how popular the sovereign, the people and government are not present at the same time. Where the people are present, there is chaos, disruption. Where the government is present, then the people are not" (ibid: 97).

---

1 | For a more detailed discussion of populism and its forms, on which this brief discussion draws, see Bray 2015, forthcoming.

Dean's account, therefore, is directed towards the interruption of any identification of populism and leftism. "The people of communism" are, precisely, that interruption. Yet, if this distinction is relatively clear at a theoretical level, it is less clear how useful it can be as a prism through which to understand existing movements, parties, or processes. If both "populism" and "communism" turn on an antagonistic division between "the people" and some "elite," if the people of communism is a "collectivity" (though *not* a "whole" or a "unity" [ibid: 102]), how can the two be rigorously distinguished in the confusion of any actual struggle involving large numbers of people, employing the concepts they find at hand? Indeed, how could any collectivity be kept *entirely* distinct from some form of identification with a prior whole, even if in the mode of supplanting or fracturing it? Inversely, how whole has *any* such "whole" ever actually been?

To the extent that the nation-state remains the hegemonic form of institutionalized political power today, even if that hegemony is in partial crisis, no "popular politics" could occur without a degree of identification between "the people" and what Poulantzas (1978) calls a *people-nation*, even if such identification involves a simultaneous fracturing. If "the "people," as "part," represents a collectivity, then that collectivity will retain, to some degree, a national orientation, unless we are to envision a political movement comprised only of subjects wholly cleansed from the influence of the institutions that (re)produce hegemony.[2] On the other hand, no state, nor the people-nation it claims to represent, has ever actually been whole: as a temporarily crystallized balance of forces, any representation of it as whole is always undergoing some form of fracturing through the tensions between those forces. So how are we to distinguish,

---

2 | I have in mind here the "distinctively dialectical discourse of race and nation" that Nikhil Singh uncovers in Black politics in the US during the 20th century, which refused the "integrationist/separatist opposition" and articulated the term "nation" in a manner that simultaneously drew together geographically dispersed blacks around a shared racial exclusion in a bid for popular sovereignty *and* linked that bid with commensurate ones by colonized subjects around the world (Singh 2004). While Singh, like Dean, is concerned principally with the conceptual vocabularies of "intellectual activists," his historical emphasis opens his account to the evolving and shifting play of concepts in that dialectic, as experimental responses to the "double bind" in which black intellectual activists found themselves.

a priori, between populism and its leftist alternative if the contradiction between "totality" and "division" defines the unsteady play of concepts over time internal to such movements, threatening to be both less and more than any specific participant intends? Such a distinction could only emerge over the course of struggle. If the violence of right-wing struggles (as of racism and xenophobia in general) articulates the impossible effort to stabilize an enduring balance of forces, why should the left's not be to engage with and open them up?

Dean's recent article helps clarify the level at which she is addressing such a question: her focus is on "populism" as a discursive or strategic position *of movement or party leaders*. As she notes in a Facebook response to questions about her essay, the issue for her "involves the political stakes of organizing under the name and idea of populism," which she identifies with Laclau and his adherents in parties like Podemos. It is from this angle that "the attempted parallel with right populism smuggles in a more fundamental aversion to revolutionary and communist politics" (Dean 2017: S43). And it is for this reason, also, that she consistently holds a party like Syriza at a certain distance from "populism," because some of its leadership has a historical relationship to the communist tradition (Dean 2017: S43).

While I agree with Dean's insistence that Laclau's theory of populism is strategically useless, it is important to emphasize that his theory also misunderstands the phenomena it is ostensibly conceptualizing. Laclau, after all, did not take himself to be merely offering strategic advice (it is actually unclear if he took himself to be offering such advice at all) but to be accounting for what populism is and has been. The core problem with his position is not its strategic weakness but its molding of populism to the "post-Marxist" ontologization of political identity production that Laclau had developed earlier (Bray 2015). Leaders and parties that think Laclau's conceptions chart a coherent path to transformative politics are likely doomed, for all the reasons Dean lists (avoiding anti-capitalism, issues of class, etc.). But the structure of her argument would seem to imply that right-populists organize under the name of populism and are the only ones who can, in a sense, do so legitimately. Yet, they don't generally call themselves populists either. Almost no one does. Which would suggest that populism is not primarily something that leaders avow (unless, of course, they are Laclauians).

Here we should return to the liberal description of populism while giving it a different emphasis: whether a movement is populist is much less a matter of its leaders' views on capitalism and class, than of the general conceptual framework in which political mobilization makes sense to its mass constituency. The resurgence of political movements articulating their goals as the reassertion of popular sovereignty against some elite "private government" should be seen, in other words, as articulating a core element of contemporary *common sense*, fostered by contemporary socio-politico-historical conditions (including the atomization of class and the centralization of control). Thus, analyzing and responding to it only as a position held by professional theorists and political leaders may be problematic or even counterproductive. Rather than rejecting "left populism" out of hand, rather than purifying ourselves a priori from its temptations, we need to recognize its ambiguous, contradictory existence and work to render it coherent, in Gramsci's sense: able to understand its own historical conditions and, thereby, work through its own internal contradictions, "increas[ing] not only logical consistency, but also the capacity to act" (Thomas 2009: 370). This trajectory would rejoin Dean's position in some key respects but by a different route, with different implications.

To see at least certain leftist forms of populism as capable of being induced towards such coherence also involves recognizing the extent to which Laclauian (and liberal) conceptions of it have occluded populist movements' reciprocal demands for both popular sovereignty *and* the "economic independence" that renders it possible (Bray 2015). No doubt the shifting historical meanings of "independence" (from producerism to tax reductions) have twisted the meaning of that reciprocity but that does not remove all critical valence or potential from the attack on "private government." No doubt populist movements often occlude class in the way Dean describes but that is because they tend to emerge in periods, like our own, where traditional class identities (like the industrial working class) are on the wane. Populism today generates a kind of collective, antagonistic political subject, "prior to" the development of economic-corporative ones and yet, in the content of those antagonisms, it tends to foster a nascent form of class perception, *grounded especially in an antagonism to the control functions of mental labor as embodied by the state*. Rather than seeing left wing populism as an attempt to parallel right wing movements, and draw supporters away from them, we should see right wing populism as an effort to mobilize and neutralize potentially left-wing energies, symptoms of class conflict expressed through the available language of representative democracy, articulated in and against the state, intersecting with and amplified by the control functions of contemporary media technology and the historical intertwining of resentment against the privileges of mental labor and changing forms of racialization.

So, while I agree with Dean that theorizing and organizing today should be centered on something like "the universal interest in equality" and that those theorizing and organizing on the left should reject Laclau's position as guide, I also think we should not extend those points into some rejection of "left populism" tout court. In The Farmers' Alliance, The Black Panther Party, MAS, Podemos, Syriza, the Sanders campaign, and so on, there have always been forms of left populism bringing peoples together, across contradictions and tensions, to struggle for a share in that from which they are excluded (and to reckon, in larger or smaller, more or less contradictory, ways with the changes that would need to occur for such a share to become possible). If we see the mere "bringing together," the "discursive construction of an identity" as the fore-given *telos* of such movements, then Dean is absolutely right. But if we see them (or some of them) as the common sense expression today of a general struggle against "capital as a whole," against those who exercise its control-functions, as a set of knowledge-practices, over people's means and forms of life, then our perspective shifts. In this light, the problem of theory today would be less that of awakening the popular masses than of addressing the blindness of knowledge workers to the political implications of their own structural position in the social division of labor. Here too our task should be to "accelerate the historical process taking place, rendering practice more homogeneous, coherent, efficient in all its elements, strengthening it to the maximum" (Gramsci 1971: 364-365). In relation to populism, this task might be aided if we undertook to conceive of it beginning from the model of the Black Panther Party, rather than Trumpism or even Podemos.

Powers of the Mind

To yoke together extended forms of "workers' inquiry" and leftist populisms may seem strange, at first glance. But it may appear less so, if we see each as a site for engagement with existing struggles – no matter how partial or contradictory – against the specific economic and political articulations of the division between mental and manual labor, against the capitalist functions of control that simultaneously reshape and delegitimate the perspectives, experiences, and conceptions of those consigned to manual labor and political ignorance. If neither is complete in itself, if they cannot be easily or seamlessly combined into some immediately identifiable common project, this only indicates that we are in the nascent stages of a long process of class formation and political struggle that has yet to arrive at a coherent mass form. The proposal of this book is that a central aspect of that process must be a coming to terms with the separation of mental from manual labor and the elements of its history that I have endeavored to trace here. That history, its sedimented effects, cannot be spontaneously overcome, nor has capitalism already superseded them.

From the perspective of mental laborers – of the person who has written and the people who are likely to read this book – one central lesson is that we should be suspicious of our own ongoing efforts to imagine new modes of thinking, experiencing, writing, to spin new conceptions out of old, and to imagine that they will alone be adequate or effective responses to the economic and political crises of our time. "'Professional' philosophers [...] can indeed contribute to changing *senso comune* – but only on condition that they recognize the extent to which *senso comune* already shapes their own philosophical practice" (Thomas 2009: 430). In that sense, we need less to imagine "new" ideas than to imagine new ways of building up counter-hegemonic institutions, as the material basis for new collective modes of thinking, experiencing, and writing, for a partisan knowledge developed in co-practice and co-conception with the dominated and exploited, without the imprimatur of absolute certainty or the promise that no harm will come to anyone. The possibility of such a knowledge demands that we reckon with the limits of what can be known (and controlled) at the same time as it calls us to move towards the maximum degree of coherence. It requires us to think more carefully, more historically, more in tune with the practices of those already resisting and the forms of resistance that are yet possible, at the same time as it requires us to recognize that thought alone will change nothing. A belief in the power of ideas, no matter how well intended, will likely legitimate the powers that reproduce domination and exploitation. The supposed autonomy of thought is a fate we must escape. To become empowered, minds must choose a side.

Bibliography

Albo, Greg/Gindin, Sam/Panitch, Leo (2010): In and Out of Crisis: The Global Financial Meltdown and Left Alternatives, Oakland: PM Press.

Amadae, S.M. (2003): Rationalizing Capitalist Democracy: The Cold War Origins of Rational Choice Liberalism, Chicago: University of Chicago Press.

Amadae, S.M. (2015): Prisoners of Reason: Game Theory and Neoliberal Political Economy, Cambridge: Cambridge University Press.

Amoore, Louise (2013): The Politics of Possibility: Risk and Security beyond Probability, Durham, NC: Duke University Press.

Antunes, Ricardo (2013): The Meaning of Work: Essays on the Affirmation and Negation of Work, Leiden: Brill.

Arnold, Kathleen R. (2009): America's New Working Class: Race, Gender, and Ethnicity in a Biopolitical Age, University Park: Penn State Press.

Balibar, Etienne (1983): "Sur le concept marxiste de la 'division du travail manuel et du travail inellectuel' et la lute des classes." In: Belkhir, Jean (ed.), L'Intellectuel: L'Intelligentsia et les Manuels, Paris: edition Anthropos.

Balibar, Etienne (1994): Masses, Classes, Ideas: Studies on Politics and Philosophy before and after Marx, New York: Routledge.

Balibar, Etienne (2012): "Civic Universalism and Its Internal Exclusions: The Issue of Anthropological Difference." In: boundary 2 Spring.

Balibar, Etienne (2014): Equaliberty: Political Essays, Durham, NC: Duke University Press.

Balibar, Etienne (2015): Citizenship, Cambridge: Polity.

Balibar Etienne (2017 [1995]): The Philosophy of Marx, Updated, New Edition, London: Verso.

Balibar, Etienne/Wallerstein, Immanuel (2011 [1991]): Race, Nation, Class: Ambiguous Identities, London: Verso.

Barabási, Albert-László (2014 [2002]): Linked: How Everything Is Connected to Everything Else and What It Means for Business, Science, and Everyday Life, New York: Basic.

Barkin, Joshua (2013): Corporate Sovereignty: Law and Government under Capitalism, Minneapolis: University of Minnesota Press.

Belkhir, Jean, ed. (1983): L'Intellectuel: L'Intelligentsia et les Manuels, Paris: edition Anthropos.

Bell, Daniel (1976 [1973]): The Coming of Post-Industrial Society: A Venture in Social Forecasting, New York: Basic.

Bettelheim, Charles (1976): Class Struggle in the USSR: First Period: 1917-1923, New York: Monthly Review.

Bettelhein, Charles (1978): Class Struggle in the USSR: Second Period: 1923-1930, New York: Monthly Review.

Bhattacharya, Tithi (2017): "How Not to Skip Class: Social Reproduction of Labor and the Global Working Class." In: Bhattacharya, Tithi (ed.), Social Reproduction Theory: Remapping Class, Recentering Oppression, London: Pluto, pp. 68-93.

Bieler, Andreas/Morton, Adam David (2018): Global Capitalism, Global War, Global Crisis, Cambridge: Cambridge University Press.

Bogost, Ian (2015): "The Cathedral of Computation." In: The Atlantic January 15: https://www.theatlantic.com/technology/archive/2015/01/the-cathedral-of-computation/384300/.

Boltanski, Luc/Chiapello, Ève (2018 [2005]): The New Spirit of Capitalism, New Updated Edition, London: Verso.

Bourdieu, Pierre (1984): Distinction: A Social Critique of the Judgment of Taste, Cambridge, MA: Harvard University Press.

Bourdieu, Pierre (2000): The Weight of the World: Social Suffering in Contemporary Society, Stanford: Stanford University Press.

Boutang, Yann Moulier (2011): Cognitive Capitalism, Cambridge: Polity.

Bouteldja, Houria (2017): Whites, Jews, and Us: Toward a Politics of Revolutionary Love, South Pasadena: semiotext(e).

Bratton, Benjamin (2015): The Stack: On Software and Sovereignty, Cambridge, MA: MIT Press.

Braverman, Harry (1998 [1974]): Labor and Monopoly Capital: The Degradation of Work in the Twentieth Century, New York: Monthly Review.

Bray, Michael (2015): "Rearticulating Contemporary Populism: Class, State, and Neoliberal Society." In: Historical Materialism 23.3, pp. 27-64.

Bray, Michael (forthcoming): The People in Crisis: A Historical Materialist Theory of Contemporary Populisms, Leiden: Brill.

Bridle, James (2018): New Dark Age: Technology and the End of the Future, London: Verso.

Briggs, Laura (2017): How All Politics Became Reproductive Politics: From Welfare Reform to Foreclosure to Trump, Oakland: University of California Press.

Brophy, Enda (2017): Language Put to Work: The Making of the Global Call Centre Workforce, London: Palgrave Macmillan.

Brown, Wendy (2015): Undoing the Demos: Neoliberalism's Stealth Revolution, Brooklyn: Zone Books.

Brynjolfsson, Erik/McAfee, Andrew (2011): Race Against the Machine: How the Digital Revolution is Accelerating Innovation, Driving Productivity, and Irreversibly Transforming Employment and the Economy, Lexington, MA: Digital Frontiers Press.

Burris, Beverly H. (1993): Technocracy at Work, Albany: SUNY.

Caffentzis, George (2013): In Letters of Blood and Fire: Work, Machines, and the Crisis of Capitalism, Brooklyn: PM.

Cahill, Damien/Konings, Martijn (2017): Neoliberalism, Cambridge: Polity.

Carlaw, Kenneth/Oxley, Les/Walker, Paul/Thorns, David/Nuh, Michael (2012): "Beyond the Hype: Intellectual Property and the Knowledge Society/Knowledge Economy." In: Livingstone, D.W./Guile, David (eds.), The Knowledge Economy and Lifelong Learning, Rotterdam: Sense, pp. 7-42.

Chernomas, Robert/Hudson, Ian (2017): The Profit Doctrine: Economists of the Neoliberal Era, London: Pluto.

Chun, Wendy (2011): Programmed Visions: Software and Memory, Cambridge, MA: MIT Press.

Coutinho, Carlos Nelson (2012): Gramsci's Political Thought, Leiden: Brill.

Croly, Herbert (2006a [1909]): "The American Democracy and Its National Principle." In: Eisenach, Eldon J. (ed.), The Social and Political Thought of Progressivism, Indianapolis: Hackett, pp. 19-24.

Croly, Herbert (2006b [1914]): "Labor Unions." In: Eisenach, Eldon J. (ed.), The Social and Political Thought of Progressivism, Indianapolis: Hackett, pp. 168-175.

Dalla Costa, Mariarosa (2015): Family, Welfare, and the State, Brooklyn: Common Notions.

Dardot, Pierre/Laval, Christian (2013): The New Way of the World: On Neoliberal Society, London: Verso.

Davies, Will (2017 [2015]): The Limits of Neoliberalism: Authority, Sovereignty and the Logic of Competition, Revised Edition, London: Sage.

Davis, Mike (2002): Planet of Slums, London: Verso.

Davis, Mike (2017): "The Great God Trump and the White Working Class." In Catalyst 1.1, pp. 151-172.

David, Mike (2018): Old Gods, New Enigmas: Marx's Lost Theory, London: Verso.

Dean, Jodi (2009): Democracy and Other Neoliberal Fantasies: Capitalism and Left Politics, Durham, NC: Duke University Press.

Dean, Jodi (2012): The Communist Horizon, London: Verso.

Dean, Jodi (2014): "Communicative Capitalism and Class Struggle." In: Spheres 1, pp. 1-16.

Dean, Jodi (2016): Crowds and Party, London: Verso.

Dean Jodi, (2017): "Not Him, Us (and we aren't populists)." In: Theory & Event 20.1 Supplement, pp. S30-S44.

D'Eramo, Marco (2013): "Populism and the New Oligarchy." In: New Left Review II.82, pp. 5–28.

de Ste. Croix, G.E.M. (1981): The Class Struggle in the Ancient Greek World from the Archaic Age to the Arab Conquests. Ithaca: Cornell University Press.

Drucker, Peter (1993): Post-Capitalist Society, New York: HarperCollins.

Dussel, Enrique 2007, "Cinco Tesis Sobre el 'Populismo.'" http://enrique dussel.com/txt/ Populismo.5%20tesis.pdf.

Dyer, Richard (1997): White, New York: Routledge.

Dyer-Witheford, Nick (2015): Cyber-Proletariat: Global Labour in the Digital Vortex, London: Pluto.

Dyson, George (2012): Turing's Cathedral: The Origins of the Digital Universe, New York: Vintage.

The Economist, Rulers of the world: read Karl Marx! May 3, 2018: (https://www.economist.com/news/books-and-arts/21741531-his-bicentena ry-marxs-diagnosis-capitalisms-flaws-surprisingly-relevant-rulers).

Edwards, Paul (1996): The Closed World: Computers and the Politics of Discourse in Cold War America, Cambridge, MA: MIT Press.

Ehrenreich, Barbara (1989): Fear of Falling: The Inner Life of the Middle Class, New York: HarperCollins.

Ely, Richard (2006 [1903]), "The Evolution of Industrial Society." In: Eisenach, Eldon J. (ed.), The Social and Political Thought of Progressivism, Indianapolis: Hackett, pp. 50-58.

Eribon, Didier (2013): Returning to Reims, Los Angeles: semiotext(e).

Erikson, Paul/Klein, Judy L./Daston, Lorraine/Lemov, Rebecca/Sturm, Thomas/Gordin, Michael D. (2013): How Reason Almost Lost Its Mind: The Strange Career of Cold War Rationality, Chicago: University of Chicago Press.

Fanon, Frantz (2004): The Wretched of the Earth, New York: Grove Press.

Federici, Silvia (2011): "On Affective Labor." In: Peters, Michael A./Bulut, Ergin (eds.), Cognitive Capitalism, Education and Digital Labor, New York: Peter Lang.

Ferguson, Karen (2013): Top Down: The Ford Foundation, Black Power, and the Reinvention of Racial Liberalism, Philadelphia: University of Pennsylvania Press.

Finn, Ed (2017): What Algorithms Want: Imagination in the Age of Computing, Cambridge, MA: MIT Press.

Flannery, Kent/Marcus, Joyce (2012): The Creation of Inequality: How Our Prehistoric Ancestors Set the Stage for Monarchy, Slavery, and Empire, Cambridge, MA: Harvard University Press.

Florida, Richard (2012 [2002]): The Rise of the Creative Class, Revisited, New York: Basic.

Floyd, Kevin (2016): "Automatic Subjects: Gendered Labour and Abstract Life." In Historical Materialism 24.2, pp. 61-86.

Forner, Karlyn (2017): Why the Vote Wasn't Enough for Selma, Chapel Hill: Duke University Press.

Franklin, Seb (2015): Control: Digitality as Cultural Logic, Cambridge, MA: MIT Press.

Fraser, Steve (2015): The Age of Acquiescence: The Life and Death of American Resistance to Organized Wealth and Power, New York: Little, Brown & Co.

Frazier, E. Franklin (1957): The Black Bourgeoisie, New York: Free Press.

Freeman, Joshua A. (2018): Behemoth: A History of the Factory and the Making of the Modern World, New York: Norton.

Fuchs, Christian (2010): "Labor in Informational Capitalism and the Internet." In: The Information Society 26, pp. 179-196.

Galloway, Alexander (2004): Protocol: How Control Exists after Decentralization, Cambridge, MA: MIT Press.

Geismer, Lily (2015): Don't Blame Us: Suburban Liberals and the Transformation of the Democratic Party, Princeton, NJ: Princeton University Press.

Goldberg, David Theo (2002): The Racial State, Oxford: Blackwell.

Goldberg, David Theo (2008): The Threat of Race: Reflection on Racial Neoliberalism, Oxford: Wiley-Blackwell.

Goldberg, David Theo (2015): Are we all postracial yet? Cambridge: Polity.

Golumbia, David (2009): The Cultural Logic of Computation, Cambridge, MA: Harvard University Press.

Gramsci, Antonio (1971): Selections from the Prison Notebooks, New York: International.

Gramsci, Antonio (1995): Further Selections from the Prison Notebooks, London: Lawrence & Wishart.

Grisinger, Joanna (2016), "A Century of Reason: Experts and Citizens in the Administrative State." In: Skowronek, Stephen/Engel, Stephen M./ Ackerman, Bruce (eds.), The Progressives' Century, New Haven: Yale University Press, pp. 360-381.

Haber, Samuel (1964): Efficiency and Uplift: Scientific Management in the Progressive Era, 1890-1920, Chicago: University of Chicago Press.

Hader, Asad (2018): Mistaken Identity: Race and Class in the Age of Trump, London: Verso.

Hamilton, Richard (1971): Class and Politics in the United States, New York: John Wiley & Sons.

Harcourt, Bernard E. (2018): The Counterrevolution: How Our Government Went to War Against Its Own Citizens, New York: Basic.

Hardt, Michael/Negri, Antonio (2000): Empire, Cambridge, MA: Harvard University Press.

Hardt, Michael/Negri, Antonio (2004): Multitude: War and Democracy in the Age of Empire, New York: Penguin.

Hardt, Michael/Negri, Antonio (2009): Commonwealth, Cambridge, MA: Belknap Press.

Hardt, Michael/Negri, Antonio (2012): Declaration, New York: Argo-Navis.

Hardt, Michael/Negri, Antonio (2017): Assembly, Oxford: Oxford University Press.

Harris-Perry, Melissa (2011): "Are We All Black American Now?" In: The Nation April 18, https://www.thenation.com/article/are-we-all-black-americans-now/.

Hayek, F.A. (2014): The Collected Works of F.A. Hayek, Volume 15: The Market and Other Orders, Chicago: University of Chicago Press.

Hayes, Chris (2012): Twilight of the Elites: America After Meritocracy, New York: Crown.

Hayles, N. Katherine (1999): How We Became Posthuman: Virtual Bodies in Cybernetics, Literature, and Informatics, Chicago: University of Chicago Press.

Hindman, Matthew (2009): The Myth of Digital Democracy, Princeton, NJ: Princeton University Press.

Ho, Karen (2009): Liquidated: An Ethnography of Wall Street, Durham, NC: Duke University Press.

Hong, Grace Kyungwon (2015): Death beyond Disavowal: The Impossible Politics of Difference, Minneapolis: University of Minnesota Press.

Huws, Ursula (2014): Labor in the Global Digital Economy: The Cybertariat Comes of Age, New York: Monthly Review.

Illouz, Eva (2008): Saving the Modern Soul: Therapy, Emotions, and the Culture of Self-Help, Oakland: University of California Press.

The Invisible Committee (2009): The Coming Insurrection, South Pasadena: semiotext(e).

James, C.L.R. (1993): American Civilization, Oxford: Blackwell.

Jappe, Anselm (2013): "Sohn-Rethel and the Origin of 'Real Abstraction': A Critique of Production or a Critique of Circulation?" In: Historical Materialism 21.1, pp. 3-14.

Jessop, Bob (2002): The Future of the Capitalist State, Cambridge: Polity.

Jessop, Bob (2012): "A Cultural Political Economy of Competitiveness – And Its Implications for Higher Education." In: Livingstone, D.W./ Guile, David (eds.), The Knowledge Economy and Lifelong Learning, Rotterdam: Sense, pp. 57-83.

Kenney, Martin/Florida, Richard (1993): Beyond Mass Production: The Japanese System and Its Transfer to the U.S., Oxford: Oxford University Press.

Khurana, Rakesh (2007): From Higher Aims to Hired Hands: The Social Transformation of American Business Schools and the Unfulfilled Promise of Management as a Profession, Princeton, NJ: Princeton University Press.

Kloppenberg, James T. (2016): "Barack Obama and the Traditions of Progressive Reform." In: Skowronek, Stephen/Engel, Stephen M./

Ackerman, Bruce (eds.), The Progressives' Century, New Haven: Yale University Press, pp. 431-452.

Kolko, Gabriel (1963): The Triumph of Conservatism: A Reinterpretation of American History, 1900-1916, New York: The Free Press.

Kornbluh, Mark L. (1999): Why America Stopped Voting: The Decline of Participatory Democracy and the Emergence of Modern American Politics, New York: NYU Press.

Kovel, Joel (1984 [1970]): White Racism: A Psychohistory, New York: Columbia University Press.

Laclau, Ernesto (2007): On Populist Reason, London: Verso.

Laplanche. J./Pontalis, J.-B. (1973): The Language of Psychoanalysis, New York: Norton .

Lazzarato, Maurizio (1996), "Immaterial Labor." In: Hardt, Michael/Virno, Paolo (eds.), Radical Thought in Italy: A Potential Politics, Minneapolis: University of Minnesota Press, pp. 133–147.

Larson, Magali Sarftti (2017 [1977]): The Rise of Professionalism: Monopolies of Competence and Sheltered Markets, London: Routledge.

Layton, Jr., Edwin T. (1971): The Revolt of the Engineers: Social Responsibility and the American Engineering Profession, Cleveland: Case Western Reserve University.

Lebowitz, Michael (2003 [1992]): Beyond Capital: Marx's Political Economy of the Working Class: New York: Palgrave MacMillan.

Lee, Richard A., Jr. (2004): The Force of Reason and the Logic of Force, New York: Palgrave MacMillan.

Levine, Yasha (2018): Surveillance Valley: The Secret Military History of the Internet, New York: PublicAffairs.

Levinson, Andrew (1974): The Working Class Majority, New York: Penguin.

Lewis, David Levering (2000): W. E. B. Du Bois, 1919-1963: The Fight for Equality and the American Century, New York: Henry Holt & Co.

Lewis, Penny (2013) Hardhats, Hippies, and Hawks: The Vietnam Antiwar Movement as Myth and Memory, Ithaca: Cornell University Press.

Lüthje, Boy/Hürtgen, Stefanie/Pawlicki, Peter/Sproll, Martina (2013): From Silicon Valley to Shenzhen: Global Production and Work in the IT Industry, Lanham, MD: Rowman & Littlefield.

MacKenzie, Donald (2006): An Engine, Not a Camera: How Financial Models Shape Markets, Cambridge, MA: MIT Press.

Mahler, Jonathan (2018): "How One Conservative Think Tank Is Stocking Trump's Government." In: New York Times Magazine June 20: https://

www.nytimes.com/2018/06/20/magazine/trump-government-heri
tage-foundation-think-tank.html.

Malm, Andreas (2016): Fossil Capital: The Rise of Steam Power and the
Roots of Global Warming, London: Verso.

Mandel, Ernst (1975): Late Capitalism, London: New Left Books.

Mann, Geoff (2017): In the Long Run We Are All Dead: Keynesianism,
Political Economy, and Revolution, London: Verso.

Marx, Karl (1973): Grundrisse, London: Penguin.

Marx, Karl (1976): Capital, Volume 1, London: Penguin.

Marx, Karl (1981): Capital, Volume 3, London: Penguin.

Marx, Karl/Engels, Friedrich (1976a): The German Ideology, Part I. In:
Tucker, Richard (ed.), The Marx-Engels Reader, New York: Norton, pp.
146-200.

Marx, Karl/Engels, Friedrich (1976b): Manifesto of the Communist Party.
In: Tucker, Richard (ed.), The Marx-Engels Reader, New York: Norton,
pp. 469-500.

Mason, Paul (2013 [2012]): Why It's (Still) Kicking Off Everywhere: The
New Global Revolutions, London: Verso.

Mason, Paul (2015): Postcapitalism: A Guide to Our Future, New York:
Farrar, Strauss & Giroux.

McGerr, Michael (2003): A Fierce Discontent: The Rise and Fall of the
Progressive Movement in America, 1870-1920, Oxford: Oxford University Press.

McGerr, Michael (2016): "Progressivism, Liberalism, and the Rich." In:
Skowronek, Stephen/Engel, Stephen M./Ackerman, Bruce (eds.), The
Progressives' Century, New Haven: Yale University Press, pp. 243-263.

Melamed, Jodi (2011): Represent and Destroy: Rationalizing Violence in
the New Eacial Capitalism, Minneapolis: University of Minnesota
Press.

Mettler, Suzanne (2011): The Submerged State: How Invisible Government Policies Undermine American Democracy, Chicago: University
of Chicago Press.

MacLean, Nancy (2017): Democracy in Chains: The Deep History of the
Radical Right's Stealth Plan for America, New York: Viking.

Milkman, Ruth/Luce, Stephanie/Lewis, Penny (2013): Changing the Subject: A Bottom-Up Account of Occupy Wall Street in New York City,
New York: The Murphy Institute.

Mirowski, Philip (2002): Machine Dreams: Economics Becomes a Cyborg Science, Cambridge: Cambridge University Press.

Mirowski, Philip (2013): Never Let a Serious Crisis Go to Waste: How Neoliberalism Survived the Financial Meltdown, London: Verso.

Mirowski, Philip/Plewhe, Dieter, eds. (2009): The Road from Mont Pelerin: The Making of the Neoliberal Thought Collective, Cambridge, MA: Harvard University Press.

Molina, Natalia (2014): How Race Is Made in America: Immigration, Citizenship, and the Historical Power of Racial Scripts, Oakland: University of California Press.

Moody, Kim (2017): On New Terrain: How Capital is Reshaping the Battleground of Class War, Chicago: Haymarket.

Murakawa, Naomi (2014): The First Civil Right: How Liberals Built Prison America, Oxford: Oxford University Press.

Myrdal, Gunnar (1996 [1944]): An American Dilemma: The Negro Problem and Modern Democracy, 2 volumes, New Brunswick: Transaction.

Narayan, John (2017): "The wages of whiteness in the absence of wages: racial capitalism, reactionary intercommunalism and the rise of Trumpism." In: Third World Quarterly 38.11, pp. 2482-2500.

Negri, Antonio (1991): Marx Beyond Marx: Lessons on the Grundrisse, Brooklyn: Autonomedia.

Nelson, Daniel (1995): Managers and Workers: Origins of the Twentieth-Century Factory System in the United States, 1880-1920, 2nd ed., Madison: University of Wisconsin Press.

Newton, Huey (2009 [1973]): Revolutionary Suicide, New York: Penguin.

Nye, David E. (2013): America's Assembly Line, Cambridge, MA: MIT Press.

Pai, Hsiao-Hung (2016): Angry White People: Coming Face-to-Face with the British Far Right, London: Zed.

Panitch, Leo/Gindin, Sam (2012): The Making of Global Capitalism: The Political Economy Of American Empire, London: Verso.

Pasquale, Frank (2015): The Black Box Society: The Secret Algorithms That Control Money and Information, Cambridge, MA: Harvard University Press.

Peck, Jamie (2013): Constructions of Neoliberal Reason, Oxford: Oxford University Press.

Perry, Imani (2011) More Beautiful and More Terrible: The Embrace and Transcendence of Racial Inequality in the United States, New York: NYU Press.

Phillips-Fein, Kim (2009): Invisible Hands: The Businessmen's Crusade Against the New Deal, New York: Norton.

Phillips-Fein, Kim (2017): Fear City: New York's Fiscal Crisis and the Rise of Austerity Politics, New York: Metropolitan Books.

Pollack, Norman (1990): The Humane Economy: Populism, Capitalism, and Democracy, New Brunswick: Rutgers University Press.

Postel, Charles (2009): The Populist Vision, Oxford: Oxford University Press.

Postone, Moishe (1993): Time, Labor, and Social Domination: A Reinterpretation of Marx's Critical Thoery, Cambridge: Cambridge University Press.

Poulantzas, Nicos (1975): Classes in Contemporary Capitalism, London: Verso.

Poulantzas, Nicos (1978): State, Power, Socialism, London: Verso.

Quart, Alissa (2018): Squeezed: Why Our Families Can't Afford America, New York: Ecco.

Rana, Aziz (2016): "Progressivism and the Disenchanted Constitution." In: Skowronek, Stephen/Engel, Stephen M./Ackerman, Bruce (eds.), The Progressives' Century, New Haven: Yale University Press, pp. 41-64.

Read, Jason (2003): The Micro-Politics of Capital: Marx and the Prehistory of the Present, Albany: SUNY.

Read, Jason (2005): "The Present as Pre-History: Adorno and Balibar on the Transformation of Labor." In: International Studies in Philosophy 37.2, pp. 95-112.

Rinehart, James/Huxley, Christopher/Robertson, David (1997): Just Another Car Factory? Lean Production and Its Discontents, Ithaca: ILR.

Robinson, Cedric J. (2000 [1983]): Black Marxism: The Making of the Black Radical Tradition, Chapel Hill: University of North Carolina Press.

Rodgers, Daniel T. (1998): Atlantic Crossings: Social Politics in a Progressive Age, Cambridge, MA: Belknap.

Roediger, David R./Esch, Elizabeth D. (2012): The Production of Difference: Race and the Management of Labor in U.S. History, Oxford: Oxford University Press.

Schryer, Stephen (2011): Fantasies of the New Class: Ideologies of Professionalism in Post–World War II American Fiction, New York: Columbia University Press.

Sennett, Richard/Cobb, Jonathan (1972): The Hidden Injuries of Class, New York: Norton.

Seshadri-Crooks, Kalpana (2000): Desiring Whiteness: A Lacanian Analysis of Race, New York: Routledge.

Shenhav, Yehouda (1999): Manufacturing Rationality: The Engineering Foundations of the Managerial Revolution, Oxford: Oxford University Press.

Silva, Jennifer M. (2013): Coming Up Short: Working-Class Adulthood in an Age of Uncertainty, Oxford: Oxford University Press.

Singer, André (2014): "Rebellion in Brazil: Social and Political Complexion of the June Events." In: New Left Review II.85.1, pp. 19-37.

Singh, Nikhil (2004): Black Is a Country: Race and the Unfinished Struggle for Democracy, Cambridge, MA: Harvard University Press.

Singh, Nikhil (2017): Race and America's Long War, Oakland: University of California Press.

Sklar, Martin J. (1988): The Corporate Reconstruction of American Capitalism, 1890-1916: The Market, the Law, and Politics, Cambridge: Cambridge University Press.

Skowronek, Stephen (1982): Building a New American State: The Expansion of National Administrative Capacities, 1877-1920, Cambridge: Cambridge University Press.

Skowronek, Stephen/Engel, Stephen M. (2016): "Introduction – The Progressives' Century." In: Skowronek, Stephen/Engel, Stephen M./Ackerman, Bruce (eds.), The Progressives' Century, New Haven: Yale University Press, pp. 1-15.

Smith, Tony (2013): "The 'General Intellect' in the Grundrisse and Beyond." In: Historical Materialism 21.4, pp. 235-255.

Soederberg, Susan (2014): Debtfare States and the Poverty Industry: Money, Discipline and the Surplus Population, New York:: Routledge.

Sohn-Rethel, Alfred (1978): Intellectual and Manual Labour: A Critique of Epistemology, London: MacMillan.

Soss, Joe/Fording, Richard C./Schram, Sanford F. (2011): Disciplining the Poor: Neoliberal Paternalism and the Persistent Power of Race, Chicago: University of Chicago Press.

Sotelo Valencia, Adrián (2018): The Future of Work: Super-Exploitation and Social Precariousness in the 21st Century, Chicago: Haymarket.

Sotiropoulos, Dimitris P./Milios, John/Lapatsioras, Spyros (2013): A Political Economy of Contemporary Capitalism and its Crisis: Demystifying Finance, New York: Routledge.

Steiner, Christopher (2012): Automate This: How Algorithms Took Over Our Markets, Our Jobs, and the World, New York: Portfolio.

Stengers, Isabelle (2018): Another Science is Possible: A Manifesto for Slow Science, London: Polity.

Suskind, Ron (2004): "Faith, Certainty and the Presidency of George W. Bush." In: The New York Times Magazine October 7: https://www.nytimes.com/2004/10/17/magazine/faith-certainty-and-the-presidency-of-george-w-bush.html.

Sweezy, Paul M./Bettelheim, Charles (1971): On the Transition to Socialism, New York: Monthly Review.

Taylor, Federick Winslow (1998 [1911]): The Principles of Scientific Management, Mineola: Dover.

Taylor, Keeanga-Yamahtta (2016): From #BlackLivesMatter to Black Liberation, Chicago: Haymarket.

Teles, Steven M. (2016): "How the Progressives Became the Tea Party's Mortal Enemy: Networks, Movements, and the Political Currency of Ideas." In: Skowronek, Stephen/Engel, Stephen M./Ackerman, Bruce (eds.), The Progressives' Century, New Haven: Yale University Press, pp. 453-477.

Temin, Peter (2017): The Vanishing Middle Class: Prejudice and Power in the New Economy, Cambridge, MA: MIT Press.

Thaler, Richard H./Sunstein Cass R. (2008): Nudge: Improving Decisions About Health, Wealth, and Happiness, New Haven: Yale University Press.

Thomas, Peter D. (2009): The Gramscian Moment: Philosophy, Hegemony and Marxism, Leiden: Brill.

Thompson, E.P. (1966 [1963]), The Making of the English Working Class, New York: Vintage.

Tiqqun (2001): "The Cybernetic Hypothesis." In Tiqqun 2: http://cybernet.jotit.com.

Tufecki, Zeynep (2017): Twitter and Tear Gas: The Power and Fragility of Networked Protest, New Haven: Yale University Press.

Turner, Fred (2006): From Counterculture to Cyberculture: Stewart Brand, the Whole Earth Network, and the Rise of Digital Utopianism, Chicago: University of Chicago Press.

Uetricht, Micah (2014): Strike for America: Chicago Teachers against Austerity, London: Verso.

Umney, Charles (2018): Class Matters: Inequality and Exploitation in 21st Century Britain, London: Pluto.

Vanneman, Reeve/Cannon, Lynne Weber (1987): The American Perception of Class, Philadelphia: Temple University Press.

Veblen, Thorstein (1921): The Engineers and the Price System, New York: B.W. Huebsch, Inc.

Vercellone, Carlo (2007): "From Formal Subsumption to General Intellect: Elements for a Marxist Reading of the Thesis of Cognitive Capitalism." In: Historical Materialism 15, pp. 13-36.

Vercellone, Carlo (2009): "Cognitive Capitalism and Models for the Regulation of Wages." In: Edu-Factory Collective (eds.), Towards a Global Autonomous University, Brooklyn: Autonomedia.

Viewpoint Magazine (2013): Workers' Inquiry, https://www.viewpointmag.com/2013/09 /30/issue-3-workers-inquiry/

Virdee, Satnam (2017): "Race, Class and Roediger's Open Marxism" (http://salvage.zone/online-exclusive/race-class-and-roedigers-open-marxism/).

Von Eschen, Penny (1997): Race against Empire: Black Americans and Anticolonialism, 1937–1957, Ithaca: Cornell University Press.

Von Neumann, John/Morgenstern, Oskar (2004 [1944]): Theory of Games and Economic Behavior, Princteon, NJ: Princeton University Press.

Voss, Kim (1994): The Making of American Exceptionalism: The Knights of Labor and Class Formation in the Nineteenth Century, Ithaca: Cornell University Press.

Wark, McKenzie (2004): A Hacker Manifesto, Cambride, MA: Harvard University Press.

Waterhouse, Benjamin C. (2014): Lobbying America: The Politics of Business from Nixon to NAFTA, Princeton, NJ: Princton University Press.

Weizenbaum, Joseph (1976): Computer Power and Human Reason: From Judgment to Calculation, San Francisco: W.H. Freeman & Co.

Wiebe, Robert H. (1967): The Search for Order, 1877-1920, New York: Hill & Wang.

Wiener, Norbert (1949): Cybernetics; Or, Control and Communication in the Animal and Machine, New York: Wiley.

Windham, Lane (2017): Knocking on Labor's Door: Union Organizing in the 1970s and the Roots of a New Economic Divide, Chapel Hill: University of North Carolina Press.

Woland/Blaumchen (2014): "From Sweden to Turkey: The Uneven Dynamics of the Era of Riots." In: SIC International Journal of Communication 2, pp. 7-13.

Wood, Ellen Meiksins (1981): "The Separation of the Economic and the Political in Capitalism." In: New Left Review I.127, pp. 66-95.

Woodcock, Jamie (2017): Working the Phones: Control and Resistance in Call Centers, London: Pluto Press.

World Bank (1994): Higher Education: The Lessons of Experience, Washington, D.C.: World Bank.

World Bank (2002): Constructing Knowledge Societies: New Challenges for Tertiary Education, Washington, D.C.: World Bank.

Wright, Steve (2017 [2012]): Storming Heaven: Class Composition and Struggle in Autonomist Marxism, London: Pluto Press.

Yancy, George (2018): Backlash: What Happens When We Talk Honestly about Racism in America, Lanham, MD: Rowman & Littlefield.

Zuboff, Suzanne (1988): In The Age Of The Smart Machine: The Future Of Work And Power, New York: Basic.

Index